THE HEALING OF PERSONS

BOOKS BY PAUL TOURNIER

The Whole Person in a Broken World

Guilt and Grace

A Doctor's Casebook in the Light of the Bible

The Meaning of Persons

The Healing of Persons

PAUL TOURNIER

Translated by Edwin Hudson

With a Foreword by Dr. Georges Bickel,
Professor in the Faculty of Medicine, Geneva

1817

Harper & Row, Publishers, San Francisco
Cambridge, Hagerstown, New York, Philadelphia
London, Mexico City, São Paulo, Sydney

Translated from the French *Médecine de la Personne*, Delachaux & Niestlé, Neuchâtel and Paris

First Harper & Row paperback edition published in 1983.

LC   83-10769
ISBN   0-06-068351-1

83   84   85   86   87   10   9   8   7   6   5   4   3   2   1

To Dr. FRANK N. D. BUCHMAN,
whose teaching has had
a profound influence
on my personal life
and has obliged me
to reflect upon the true
meaning of my vocation,
I dedicate this book.

Contents

II. MEDICINE AND THE PERSON

Foreword

When Dr. Tournier told me how disturbed he had been, in the course of ten years' medical practice, by the insufficiency of classical and official medicine as regards certain chronic diseases, and how he had gradually become convinced that in many cases what mattered was the eradication of the psychological causes of the condition rather than the correction of its passing corporeal manifestations, I could not but encourage him wholeheartedly to devote himself to the task of moral salvage to which he felt called.

Among those who come daily to ask for the help of our art, there is indeed a multitude of unfortunates for whom the most carefully prescribed medicines and diets are only a palliative, the insufficiency of which we are the first to sense, because we are convinced that the disease whose symptoms we observe is only the exteriorization of an infinitely deeper malady, the true nature of which the patient does not always permit us to analyze. Thus we feel, as our examination proceeds, that the disease is situated neither at the level of the organs whose failure we observe nor at the level of the nerves whose functional imbalance we are trying to correct, but that the organic disturbances about which the patient is consulting us are the end product of a more intimate disorder which in general will not yield to our objective exploration and will be uncovered only by a completely honest and trusting examination of conscience.

Some patients, of course, sense this failure on the part of modern medicine to comprehend the intimate cause of their ills, and they complain of it. According to their attitude of mind or the advice of those around them, they turn then to psychoanalysis or to Christian Science, which often brings them momentary relief, but which will not procure for them the definitive liberation that alone can lead to the individual and total solution of what Dr. Tournier rightly calls "personal problems," problems that are raised for all sincerely thinking persons among us.

With fine courage and fervor, Dr. Tournier makes a frontal attack on these personal problems. His excellent book provides striking examples of this on every page. I have myself met most of the cases he describes, or similar ones. I know the courage required to tackle them, the perseverance needed to study them, and the endless devotion for which their solution calls.

All who read this book, both doctors and patients, must congratulate the author for having put his encouraging experiences within the reach of everyone. Of course his book does not cover the whole ground of medicine, but it deals with an aspect of it which is too often neglected. It is profoundly human, and likely to disturb the consciences of all, and I am sure that many sufferers will find in it, in the prayerful meditation which it enjoins, the beginning of their cure.

GEORGES BICKEL

Author's Preface to the American Edition

I have received a large number of most interesting letters from the United States since the publication there of several of my books. I have been greatly moved by all this serious and sincere evidence of a community of ideas and of spirit. I feel therefore that I owe it to my American readers to provide a few words of frank explanation as this, the first book I wrote, appears.

I am very much indebted to the publishers, Harper & Row, who were the first to introduce me to the United States. But they have brought out first several of my more recent books, whereas this one was published in Switzerland as long ago as 1940. As a result, my American readers are, so to speak, discovering me in reverse.

This is not without its disadvantages. We all change considerably in the course of twenty-five years. My readers will doubtless notice many differences between what I have written in recent years and what I had written long before in this book. They will find in it much that will seem oversimplified. It is true that as one gains experience one becomes more aware of the complexity of many problems which one has in the past approached from a somewhat naïve standpoint. One does not talk of them in the same way; one does not see them in such clear-cut terms of black and white.

Nevertheless, I am glad that this work is appearing in the United States just as I first wrote it, without laborious emendations, which would have spoiled its spontaneity; for it is still the book I value most, the book of my youth, a first cry torn from my heart by my first experiences. When one discovers a truth, one tends to express it in terms that are too absolute. Later on, one speaks of it with more moderation, but at the risk of losing its essence.

The truth which had struck me at that time was that all men are struggling, more or less consciously, and more or less secretly, with personal problems which have a considerable influence on their health—conflicts, rebellions, negative attitudes, moral failings, and spiritual anxieties. I was concerned, that is to say, with the effect of what goes on in the mind on what goes on in the body, with special reference to the genesis of disease and the processes of healing.

This interaction is much better understood today, thanks especially to the work done in the United States on psychosomatic medicine. I wrote this book at a time when these researches were still little known in Europe, so that my American colleagues may be surprised that I make no mention of them. They may also feel that the influence of the mind on the body is so well known now that it is no longer necessary to dwell upon it.

However, I think I can say that what we in Europe understand by the term *médecine de la personne* goes rather beyond psychosomatic medicine, while still being in full accord with it. Psychosomatic medicine is a strictly objective discipline, subject only to the methods of the natural sciences, whereas the medicine of the person takes account, in addition, of facts which are accessible only to the moral sciences. Thus it implies a double view of man—that of the physical, chemical, and psychical phenomena which determine him and which belong to the realm of the natural sciences, and that of his behavior as a *person*, as a spiritual being, free and responsible, involving factors which can be approached only by other methods, which belong to the field of morality rather than to that of technology.

In the light of this, the mission of the doctor can also be seen to be twofold: He must first make use of every available technical resource with a view to the curing of the disease, whether it be surgery or drugs, physiotherapy, advice on hygiene, or psychotherapy. But his art remains incomplete if he does not also make some effort to help the patient to solve the problems in his life.

Is this possible? Is it, indeed, the doctor's job? I think it is. But it is clear that in this second function the doctor does not act so much as a scientist, but rather as a man, through his heart and his faith more than through his intellectual knowledge, through the love he bears his patient, by his personal commitment to him, by their personal contact, by the radiation of his own personality.

The best clinical practitioners have always spontaneously exercised this beneficent moral influence over their patients; but at a time when medicine is making such great technical progress, we are in danger of forgetting its importance. If ever the patient comes to feel that he has become merely a "case" to his doctor, and no longer a "person," then medicine will have become to that extent less human.

But how are we to help our patients resolve their personal problems? How are we to develop our personal influence over them? Science and technique can be taught. Moral authority, however, comes not by scientific training, but from our own spiritual maturity, and from the experience of our own lives, from the answers we have found to our own personal problems through the grace of God.

Thus my first few years' experience in the practice of the medicine of the person, the account of which is set down in this book, was in large measure the fruit of the spiritual evolution which I had undergone as a result of my contact with the movement known as the Oxford Group. I was already a Christian before this, but my contact with the Group had helped me to apply my faith to my practical, personal, family, and professional life. Anyone who knows the movement will have no difficulty in recognizing its imprint in this book.

It is probably because of this particular origin that the English translation is only now appearing, since an English publisher informed me, some years ago, that he was prepared to publish it on condition that I withdrew the dedication to Dr. Frank N. D. Buchman, the founder of the movement. I refused, of course; one does not deny one's friends, especially those who have been God's instruments in one's life. Nevertheless, by then I had already severed my connection with the movement, which had changed its name and its character, having become Moral Rearmament, and having adopted mainly political and ideological aims in which I was unable to follow it.

But I have retained all my gratitude to Dr. Buchman and his early collaborators. In particular, I have continued the practice of written meditation which they taught me, that attentive listening to what God is saying to us "in our ear" as Calvin said, in order to conduct our personal lives in accordance with his purpose. This attitude of being open to divine inspiration and of practical obedience belongs, of course, to the whole Christian tradition. Illuminated by the Bible, it is within the reach of every man, and consequently of every doctor desirious of experiencing it in his personal life and in his work.

This means that unlike psychosomatic medicine, the medicine of the person is not a specialty. It does not require so much a scientific psychological training, which many doctors cannot . acquire, as a certain inner maturity in the doctor himself, the result of laying himself open to the action of grace. That is why Dr. Paul Plattner wrote that the medicine of the person concerns first of all the person of the doctor himself. It is therefore a matter of a spirit which can animate any doctor, a deeper relationship which he establishes with each one of his patients, insofar as he becomes himself more fully a person, and insofar as his patients become also more fully persons through coming into contact with him.

It is much simpler and much more universal than psychosomatic medicine. For instance, under the influence of the psychosomatic school a beginning has been made in Europe—though more tentatively than in America—in the introduction of psychotherapists into hospital surgical departments. Professor Jean Gosset, of Paris, who has been a pioneer in this, has nevertheless admitted the difficulty of this collaboration between surgeon and psychologist.[1]

This is precisely because the psychologist is a specialist, armed with techniques appropriate to his specialty, with his own technical language, to which the surgeon remains more or less a stranger. And so the patient passes from one specialist to another, without there being any reciprocal understanding between them to enable them

[1]*Semaine des hôpitaux de Paris,* June 8, 1961.

to sort out together the true extent of the neurotic and of the organic components of the patient's disorder, and to envisage the person of the patient in its fundamental unity.

Let me not be misunderstood: I am aware of the great step forward represented by this appeal for the collaboration of the psychologists, and also of the importance of the observations which their techniques make possible. But if, in addition, the surgeon himself takes an interest in his patient as a person, in the problems of his personal life, of his relationships with his family, his friends, society, and the world, there is then established between the patient and the surgeon to whom he is entrusting his life a vitally important personal relationship for which sending the patient to a psychological specialist can be no substitute.

This was well expressed by Professor Jacques Dor in his inaugural lecture in the Chair of Surgery at the University of Marseilles, entitled "Surgery of the Person." He thus proclaimed that surgery is not only a technical discipline, but also an encounter between human beings, a mutual relationship and understanding between two persons in the full sense of the term—namely the physical, psychical, and spiritual unity of man.

This, of course, is true over the entire field of medicine. Many sick people today are grateful for the excellent technical care they receive in hospital or in the consulting room, but still feel the need for a more personal relationship with their doctor to rescue them from the spiritual isolation into which sickness plunges them. Such a really human contact can in many cases contribute to their cure. Many doctors too are grateful for the knowledge and the techniques that scientific progress brings them, but long to add to them a truly human experience which will give a new dimension to their vocation.

That is no doubt why this book remains, of all I have written, the most widely read in Europe, why it is the one which has had the biggest impact in the world of medicine, among both doctors and nurses, as well as patients, and has contributed, alongside many other recent works, to the development of the movement for a medicine of the person. I hope that my American colleagues will join, in increasing numbers, in our common effort, taking this view of the researches which are already so well developed in their own country. For every doctor has his own conception of the human person and of how medicine should be applied to the healing of the person. In the light of our varying experiences and convictions, a dialogue must be begun so that we may attain to a clearer idea of the conditions and the function of the personal factor in medicine.

P. T.

Geneva, 1964

Author's Preface to the Third Edition

I recently treated a young woman who had undergone a very well-conducted course of psychoanalysis lasting a number of years.

She was a Christian, and had even been an active propagator of her faith. She suffered, however, from psychological difficulties, and she had at last been forced to recognize that she was using her faith to hide from herself the fact that she had a number of unsolved problems in her life and in her heart.

Having courageously decided to throw an honest light on the dark complexity of her mind, she went to the analyst. It was a further act of courage to persevere with the course of treatment, which revealed many of the secret springs of her behavior.

But the human mind is so complex that one could go on indefinitely analyzing it, and the doctor himself advised his patient to look to a man who shared her faith for the help she needed in the process of reconstruction.

And so one day I saw that young woman come to me and ask me only to be the silent witness of her confession, the confession of a wrongdoing which, throughout the duration of the analysis, had weighed on her life without her being delivered from it. And I saw her rise, radiant.

I mention this case because it seems to me to illustrate the truth that men's problems are at one and the same time infinitely complex and exceedingly simple—complex from the technical point of view, and simple from the spiritual point of view; and also because I have heard, to my great surprise, that several readers of this book have thought it possible to conclude from it that I denied the complexity of men's physical and psychological problems. As if all that was necessary to resolve them was a religious act, thus rendering superfluous the patient and laborious efforts of the doctors! Nothing is further removed from my mind and my experience.

The more I have to deal with human distress, the more I study men's lives with a passionate desire to understand and help them, the more I seek to throw light on the reciprocal reactions of body, mind, and spirit, the more do I understand the difficulty of practicing medicine sincerely.

So I should like to take the opportunity presented by this third edition of my book, to go over each page and illustrate it with further cases which would open up new perspectives in the complicated labyrinth of men's lives, and to replace many overhasty assertions with more carefully differentiated conclusions. I should like, also, to admit the justice of the objections that some theologians have raised on various points, so as to conform more exactly with the teaching of the church.

But I realize at the same time that such a task would be endless; it would never be completed.

I confine myself therefore quite simply to admitting the fact here. This book has no pretensions to being a systematic exposition of medicine, psychology, or of theology. It is a collection of experiences and thoughts that have arisen out of everyday practice. They could be added to and corrected *ad infinitum* from the experiences and thoughts of each of my colleagues.

But however difficult medical practice is, however complicated the web of factors governing every life we try to heal or relieve, we cannot deny that there are times when the leaden sky is torn open, when a quite simple spiritual experience, which is neverthless never easy to bring about, introduces into the situation an element so revolutionary that all the multifarious complexities we have been studying are swept aside.

Moreover, the unexpected welcome given to this book by large numbers of doctors and others, both the sick and the healthy, demonstrates that in spite of all the technical advances made by medicine, the deep mystery of man and disease troubles all thinking people, and especially those who are trying to heal the sick. It shows that it is quite true that in the secret places of men's hearts there are wounds to which they remain unreconciled and whose remedy they eagerly seek.

I have therefore decided, through lack of time, to republish these pages without making any great changes. I have corrected a few details and shortened the technical part of the chapter on temperaments. If my book encourages sick people to talk more confidently to their physician about the secret wounds festering in their hearts, they will find his help more effective. And their experiences will fill better than I could the gaps in its pages.

There is, however, one more question which many readers have addressed to me and which I cannot omit to mention here: "Does it last? What has happened in the long run to the patients of whom you write?"

There are some of whom I have heard nothing more. There are many, too, whom I have seen again, or who have written to me. There are a few who have pointed out to me certain errors of detail in the accounts given of their lives. There are some whose good health has been maintained, and others whose physical, psychological, or spiritual state has undergone setbacks. Several, of whom I had heard nothing for a long time, have informed me that the spiritual flame lit at a decisive moment in their lives had never stopped burning, in spite of fresh trials, and had led them through many a difficulty to new victories. Several have admitted to me that on reading these accounts they have come to themselves, realizing that their faith had weakened and that they had slipped into fresh acts of disobedience. I have had the joy of seeing some of them experiencing anew the power of grace, more deeply and more richly.

So, in answer to the question "Does it last?" I can only say that the spiritual life is no different from everything else in this world: No step forward is maintained unless it is followed by further steps.

He who does not go forward, goes back. Physical, psychical, and spiritual health is not a haven in which we can take refuge in a sort of final security, but a daily battle in which our very destiny is constantly at stake.

P. T.

PART

1

PERSONAL PROBLEMS

CHAPTER

1

Medicine and Life

I recently saw again one of my first patients, whom I shall call Thérèse.

Shortly after my final medical examinations I was house doctor in the surgical department of a children's hospital.

A girl there was suffering from Pott's disease. She had spent more than a year stretched on a board. Two cold abscesses had spread along the sheaths of the psoas muscles and formed fistulas in both groins. As had been feared, superinfection had taken place, and her condition threatened to become progressively worse.

I threw all my energies into the struggle to snatch that young life from the jaws of death. I had become a doctor in order to help my fellow men, and now at last, after years of study, I could begin to practice my profession. Thérèse gave me one of the first opportunities I had had to devote myself with zeal and fervor to my task. Several times a day we performed irrigations with Dakin's solution. At the same time we treated the tuberculosis using the Sahli technique. Several months later we had the joy of seeing our efforts crowned with success. Thérèse was saved, and her general condition rapidly improved.

NOTE: The Glossary beginning on page 289 explains medical terms appearing occasionally in the text.

Since then I had often thought of her, and wondered what had become of her.

And now, fifteen years afterward, she had come to my surgery, accompanied by her mother. "She is worn out," the latter said to me. "They overwork her at the office. I should like you to give her a certificate so that she can get a few days' leave."

As I examined Thérèse, I talked to her. Experience had taught me, I told her, that overwork was not always the sole cause of overtiredness. Often secret troubles were an important factor.

Thereupon Thérèse burst into tears.

I learned that she had made a rash and unhappy marriage, that she had suffered a great deal, and that her husband was now in prison in a foreign country.

Thérèse seemed to want to prolong the interview and to confide in me further, but her mother cut her short, declaring that none of this had anything to do with the purpose of the visit.

When Thérèse and her mother had gone, I sat thinking. I saw again in my mind's eye those months in the hospital; my youthful enthusiasm as a new doctor, proud of his power over death. And then I saw the life led now by that poor despairing woman, who was going to try to find in a dismal holiday an illusory relief from her tears.

The doctor sets out to try to save men's lives. But if he does not succeed at the same time in showing them how to overcome the difficulties they will meet afterward, his task remains incomplete. Such a doctor is like a mother who abandons the child she has just brought into the world, leaving him helpless to face life.

There is indeed nothing more wonderful to a doctor than to save a life. But what happens to it afterward? And how many people, for lack of having received something more than healing from their doctor, proceed to spoil the life just given back to them? And how many are there who once again compromise their health by their manner of life?

For our mode of life is the most important factor that determines our health.

When a patient comes to consult us, he tells us the ills he is suffering from, and asks for a remedy. But he is not so ready to tell us of all the things that need to be put right in his way of life, about his vices, the passions that dominate him, the conflicts, rebellions, doubts, and fears that beset him. He knows very well that all this is sapping his powers of resistance, spoiling his pleasure in life, and undermining his health. But he has fought for so long in vain against himself and against circumstances! What he wants from medicine is relief from the consequences of all his faults, and not to be told that he should undertake an impossible reformation of his life.

Most illnesses do not, as is generally thought, come like a bolt out of the blue. The ground is prepared for years, through faulty diet, intemperance, overwork, and moral conflicts, slowly eroding the subject's vitality. And when at last the illness suddenly shows itself, it would be a most superficial medicine which treated it without going back to its remote causes, to all that I shall here call "personal problems." I use this rather vague phrase intentionally: The whole of the rest of my book is meant to make its meaning clear.

There are personal problems in every life. There are secret tragedies in every heart.

"Man does not die," a doctor has remarked. "He kills himself."

If we talk so little about the problems which trouble us most, it is usually because we have lost hope of ever finding a solution to them.

This book is devoted to the study of the very complex relationships which always exist between our personal problems and our health.

God has a purpose for our life, as for the world. And if the world is sick today because it is disobeying God's laws, men too are sick because they do not live in accordance with God's purpose. So the highest role of the doctor is to help men to discern what is God's purpose for their lives and to conform therewith.

Every act of physical, psychological, or moral disobedience of God's purpose is an act of wrong living, and has its inevitable consequences. Moreover, it does not compromise only the health of the person who commits it, but also that of other persons, and that of his descendants.

"Treat the patient, not the disease." Such is the precept our masters teach us, and which we are reminded of every day by medical practice. Take two patients suffering from the same disease: One makes a rapid recovery, while the other is handicapped by some secret worry which has destroyed his will to live.

But to treat the patient and not the disease means penetrating into these personal problems, which our patients often hide from us in order to keep them hidden from themselves.

A man—let us call him Ernest—came to consult me because of functional digestive troubles. He had recently had jaundice, but tests of liver function revealed nothing special. I corrected his diet and interrogated him about his "morale." He declared himself to be very happy at home. But his mother and his wife did not get on well together. Our conversation about his family conflict soon led to an exchange of views about our conception of life. This was, for Ernest, the start of a spiritual evolution which forged a bond of friendship between us. And later he told me that when he came to consult me he knew very well that his digestive troubles had some connection with an affair of the heart which he had not had the courage to confess to me. Although fond of his wife, he had not been able to resist an amorous attraction to another woman, which, without ever having been consummated, had nevertheless had a profoundly disturbing effect upon him. It was only later, following his inner transformation, that he found the strength to unburden himself to a friend, and then to his wife, and to free himself from the dangerous attachment.

It often thus happens that our patients are aware of the deep moral causes of the ills they tell us of, and are even perhaps burning with the desire to confess them to us, but cannot overcome their inner resistance, and eagerly grasp at the physiological explanation which we offer them.

To treat the patient rather than the disease means helping our patients to resolve their problems. And this solution is often to be found, as was the case with Ernest, only on the spiritual level.

Esther was a patient who for years showed the typical symptoms of asthma. She had a constitutional predisposition to the disease: Her father was diabetic. But the determining cause of her asthma was the terror that as a child she had always had of her father. She recalls that often she had only to hear his key in the front door for an attack to come on. She tried several courses of conventional treatment, but without success.

Later she spent some time abroad, staying with a man of saintly character, who had a profound influence upon her. Her asthma improved, without disappearing altogether. Several years later she met a friend whose faith she envied. She asked her what was the secret of her faith, and in reply her friend suggested that she should ask God in prayer what it was that was weighing on her life. When she came thus into God's presence her thoughts turned at once to her father. She remembered wrongs she had done him, for which she had never asked his forgiveness. The idea of writing him a letter and apologizing started a terrific battle within her, but victory was won at last, and the letter was sent. She felt immediate deliverance from the fear he inspired in her, and her asthma was cured.

Menstrual troubles are often the physiological expression of moral anxiety, and I shall have occasion to give several examples in this book. A girl, whom we shall call Lucienne, came to consult me for amenorrhea. Sickly and thin, she had not menstruated for nearly a year. She seemed dull, timid, and withdrawn. She was the good little girl, who seldom smiles, never laughs, works with conscientious scrupulousness—an old mind in a young body.

I prescribed some of the powerful ovarian extracts which we have at our disposal these days. This treatment had some success, albeit very uncertain.

One day, a long time afterward, I spoke to her of my religious experiences. I told her that in God's presence every one of us can shine the light into his own soul. Then she confided in me and told me of an attempt at rape of which she had been the object. One can guess the moral anguish this experience must have aroused in her, and its connection with the amenorrhea. One can see too the reason for the way Lucienne behaved—her conscientiousness in her work and the stifling of her youth. For a long time I still had to prescribe organotherapeutic preparations and tonics; but from that day on, with a changed environment, Lucienne began to develop and to put on weight. Her periods returned—and so did her smile.

Dyspepsia, asthma, and amenorrhea are functional disturbances in the genesis of which the part played by the patient's morale is incontestable. I propose to show in this book that our personal problems also play a considerable part in organic diseases. We all know those patients who no longer respond to any treatment, who gradually become weaker in spite of all our efforts, and so we say: "What do you expect? Since his wife died he has just let himself go."

The patient who comes to consult the doctor is interested only in the illness from which he is suffering—that is to say, in a dominant symptom, from which he would like to be freed.

If the doctor questions him about his mode of life, his moral attitude, his behavior as regards the other members of his family, he does not at once see the possible relationship between these matters and the illness from which he is suffering. And if he accepts the technical treatment undertaken by the doctor, he is the less willing to follow his advice about his manner of life. Indeed, he hopes that medicine, thanks to its technical progress, will make it unnecessary for him to change his life, so that he can go on living in accordance with his whims and passions, counting on some wonder-working pill to rescue him from their awkward consequences.

The doctor, on the other hand, recognizes that technical progress in his art is held up by disorder in men's lives. He has wonderful diagnostic methods and therapeutic weapons at his disposal today. But he sees that before they can bear fruit the reform of men's lives must make as much progress as that made by medical and surgical technique.

The doctor of a hundred years ago knew many fewer things than his modern colleague does, but he worked in more favorable conditions. He traveled peacefully in his hansom cab, and had time to think about his patients. He knew the whole family and could offer, at the right moment, a judicious word of advice, which was even more gratefully received than was his scientific knowledge. He was familiar with his patient's "temperament," knew "what was right for him," and he was more willingly listened to when he pointed out the things in the patient's way of life that were compromising his health.

Many doctors nowadays feel with a certain sense of bitterness that the results of their efforts are not in proportion to the technical methods at their disposal.

One sign of this is the renewed interest being taken in the idea of the "terrain." Following upon the discoveries of Pasteur, a great hope arose among doctors—that the specific germ of each disease would be determined and subjected to laboratory study so that the proper means of rendering it harmless might be discovered, and in this way victory over every disease would be assured. It seemed that the human organism would be found to be a neutral battlefield on which the war against the microbes and their toxins would be waged. This hope has in part been realized, in the defeat, for example, of diphtheria, smallpox, and rabies. But there has been much less success with most infectious diseases, especially chronic ones. Microbes are tough and widespread. But they do not gain a foothold in every organism. And even if they do gain entry, they develop only insofar as they find a favorable (i.e., weakened) terrain. Pasteur himself, in spite of his belief in the specificity of the microbe, recognized on his deathbed the importance of the environment when he murmured: "Claude [Bernard] was right!"[1] Since then the importance of the powers of resistance of the human organism has been fully recognized. Indeed, if a man does not frequently encounter microbes in the normal course of his life, he is in much more serious danger when eventually he is attacked. In World War I, for instance, colonial troops from parts of Africa where tuberculosis is unknown were decimated by the disease.

And then in practice we are constantly coming upon patients who fall victims to the most varied diseases, one after another. Scarcely have they recovered from pneumonia when they are attacked by phlebitis; this is followed by a sharp liver attack, nephritis, or cardiac failure. Faced with a clinical picture of this sort, one must conclude that the important thing is not the various types of diseases, but the deficiency in the patient's powers of resistance which is manifesting itself in all these different ways.

Pharmaceutical advertising has imposed on the public the idea that the best safeguard to health is the use of medicaments. It has in this

[1] A. Thooris, *Médecine morphologique* (Paris: Doin, 1937), p. 81.

way helped to lessen reliance upon the body's natural forces, which can be brought into play only if one's mode of life gives them a chance. A spiritually oriented medicine puts more faith in the organism, because it involves belief in God who implanted these forces in the body. Consider how far the surgeon in fact relies on these mysterious God-given forces in the consolidation of a fracture.

In the normal state we are constantly reacting against those things in our external environment which would tend to harm us. For example, diarrhea is aimed at the rapid elimination of a defective alimentary product. This same phenomenon in a slightly more marked degree becomes a disease, but the transition from a defensive reaction of the healthy organism to the pathological symptom of the diseased organism is not clear-cut. Many symptoms may in this way be seen to be exaggerated forms of normal defensive reactions. We may say, then, that they are abnormal *qua* disease, and normal *qua* defensive reaction.

What *would* be abnormal would be for the organism not to defend itself. When staphylococci invade a sebaceous follicle, they provoke on the part of the organism a defensive reaction in the form of a boil, which we term a disease. But clearly it would be much more abnormal if the organism did not defend itself against the staphylococci, and allowed them to penetrate further and set up septicemia.

So there are maladies that help to preserve health.

In spite of all our efforts our manner of life is never what it ought to be. Our failures mount up, either through indiscipline in feeding, or through overtiredness, against which the organism reacts with a crisis in the form, perhaps, of a mild attack of fever, which is put down as "flu" in order to give it a disease classification. In fact it is a natural means of renewing the tissues. Experience shows that the vast majority of these mild seasonal attacks of so-called "flu" pass over without needing treatment, apart from fasting and a purgative which, together with abundant liquids, help them in their eliminatory role. If, however, one tries to "reduce the fever"—that is, to stop the spontaneous defense reactions of the body—by means of one of the remarkable products which the chemical industry has produced in such numbers, the result may be a difficult convalescence and prolonged debility. Similarly, an attack of nerves is doubtless a providential discharge, protecting the organism against more serious ills.

The technical progress of medicine, then, cannot of itself safeguard health, if men by wrong modes of life compromise their powers of resistance. What, in fact, are the factors making for a deficiency in the resistance offered by the "terrain"? There is first the hereditary factor. If one thinks about this, one sees that this is referable to the wrong living of preceding generations. Syphilis and alcoholism in the parents, and especially conception in a state of inebriation, are clearly concerned with what we are calling personal problems. And then in the person's own life, there is excess in eating, either from gluttony or because it is the fashion, overwork through ambition or greed, a life that is too comfortable, which saps both physical and moral stamina, sexual abuses and violent passions, anything that causes gnawing anxiety, and lastly fear, rebellion, and remorse. All these things comprise our personal problems.

"The great thing," a young man writes to me, "is our resistance to disease, and that resistance depends directly upon the quality of our living. . . . My physical life, like my intellectual and spiritual life, depends directly on my obedience to God's commands, and on the total sovereignty of Jesus Christ over my body, mind, and spirit."

Some examples of patients with tuberculosis will assist me in showing the relationship that there is between personal moral problems and those of health.

Concerning Tuberculosis

Here, in outline, is the story of a patient whom I shall call Claire.

At the age of four Claire lost her dearly loved father. This shock, in spite of her tender age, had a profound effect on her whole childhood, not only from the emotional point of view, but also on account of the moral and material consequences of this bereavement in a family life that up to then had been perfectly happy. For years her sorrow led her to rebel against God and against what she considered to be injustice on his part. So as not to add to the sorrow of her mother, who bore her grief without complaining, Claire used to weep in silence every evening in her own room, and often the idea of suicide seemed to be the only answer, but her fear of hurting her mother, whom she loved, saved her from this course.

With the advent of World War I, the financial difficulties that beset their middle-class home were increased, and were met with secret sacrifices. In her desire to ease the family burden, Claire assumed the heavy task of running the home. To this she added dressmaking, late nights, sports, and mountain walks. The family was a very united one, but they never spoke about their difficulties for fear of causing each other distress. Claire wanted to seem strong, not only out of pride, but also because of her need to relieve the others of a burden which she felt was too heavy for them. But she did not truly accept her life, and was hard on herself in order to justify her own self-pity. Revolt, spiritual isolation, overwork, sorrow—all these are personal problems which are linked one to another.

She married a man of whom she was very fond, hoping to find in him the support she had lacked throughout her childhood and youth.

But her husband had not himself achieved a balance in his personal life, and was seeking compensation for his own inferiority complex in the artificial strength and assurance of his wife. How many mental failures have their origin in this situation: Two people who feel weak in face of the difficulties of life seek mutual support in each other, instead of drawing their strength from God. Misunderstandings, disillusionment, and head-on clashes are inevitable.

Difficulties of all kinds grew daily, and Claire, with her acute sense of responsibility and duty, attempted to face up to all the troubles, took upon her own shoulders all the burdens, and sought to find a way of surmounting all the material and moral complications. She lived a life of privation, and excessive fatigue, whereas her husband never had the courage to adapt himself to the harsh family and financial necessities of their situation. Faced with the collapse of her hopes, Claire felt inwardly broken, but she braced herself once more against her misfortune. A year later she had a hemoptysis, and the doctor confirmed the existence of a developing tuberculous condition. She was sent into the mountains.

By means of correspondence, and helped by their separation, husband and wife found each other again; each felt full of good will, and real happiness seemed within their grasp. Claire gained strength, and the doctors, a few months later, allowed her to return home—too soon.

On her return she found awaiting her innumerable difficulties which her husband had concealed from her. Years of moral and material misery began again; and during this time she toiled unceasingly, underwent privations, and suffered from not having the children she longed for. Once again she began to spit blood, and realized that she must get further treatment, but did not wish to do so for fear of adding still more to the material burden her mother had to carry.

It was then that she realized the impossibility, in spite of her efforts, of achieving harmony with her husband, and of going on with married life in the way they were. They separated. This gave Claire some relief, morally speaking; but her physical condition betrayed her once more, and she had to stay in bed and take care of herself. She felt then that everything in her life would always turn out badly and collapse even further, as long as she did not pray. But this, in her rebellious pride, she would not do. If God granted her some happiness, she thought, then she would thank him.

She was taken to a state sanatorium, and there she was horrified at all the tragedies and the lingering death she saw around her. Her instinct for self-preservation reasserted itself, if not entirely on her own account, at any rate for the sake of her mother, who was waiting and hoping for her return. But she felt she could not face the painful prospect of the future that would be hers after her mother's death, living alone, childless, with no one to love; the thought made her decide that she would commit suicide on the day her mother died.

Then she had appendicitis, with complications, which endangered the whole course of her cure. Her condition became worse, and she felt convinced that she was going to die, and told herself that she was not sorry, since she no longer expected anything from life, and death would put an end to all her sufferings. Not even the thought of her mother's grief now gave her strength to fight back. Her general condition deteriorated rapidly, and her early death seemed inevitable.

Then, for the first time in her life, she felt that all bitterness, all longing, all will, and all rebellion were disappearing within her. And suddenly, in the solitude of her sickroom, without her calling on him, God was there. She quite clearly felt his presence, and understood that he was saying to her: "It is a sin to want to die. It was I who gave you life, and I will take it back when it seems good to me to do so. You must will to live; even if your mother were to die, I could give you a full life." Then, quite simply, without even understanding or realizing what it would mean to her, Claire said Yes to God.

From that day her general condition improved; she became gentle, disciplined, and amenable; she submitted to all the measures adopted for her treatment, and permitted a pneumothorax to be established. She went up into the mountains, full of an inner joy which, however, she kept to herself for fear of not being understood.

She did not yet know that God does not enter into men's lives in order to remain hidden, that his presence will escape us if we selfishly try to keep him to ourselves. Her need for affection made her seek her own satisfaction and not solely the divine will. She soon realized, to her despair, that God's presence was no longer real to her. She prayed, but could not find him again. She felt that God had withdrawn from her, that she would never be able to reach him again, and with this her distress was greater than any she had ever known. She had thought that she had found happiness, but it had escaped her again.

For a year her physical condition remained stationary, and all her new-found joy was gone. But when God has laid hold on a person he never lets go, and one day she came across a book, *For Sinners Only*, by A. J. Russell.[1] She was quite overcome, and underwent a new spiritual experience as she realized that God was once more showing her the path she must follow, and that only her own willfulness had caused her to stray from it. She dedicated herself afresh to God, allowed him to come into her daily life, and accepted that life. Her health improved.

Claire bore witness to her faith. She had found that harmony which can be brought about in each of us only through real contact between the Creator and the creature. When her mother fell ill, God gave her day by day the strength she needed to look after her and to surround her with loving care. Then, two years later, when the mother who filled her whole life died, she remained serene, able to bear her grief without rebelling, and also able to help and encourage her family.

Claire has fallen ill again, but she accepts this new trial in the realization that the life even of a sick person can have a positive meaning if it remains in close contact with Christ. She hopes to get better.

The reader will have been struck by the indomitable self-will that Claire displayed, and which had to be broken before she could come to a decisive spiritual experience. I have noticed how frequent is this

[1]London: Hodder & Stoughton, 1932.

proud and easily offended strength of character in those suffering
from tuberculosis. I remember a young woman who was not one of
my patients, but with whom both my wife and I had profound discussions on religious matters.

The child of divorced parents, beset by tremendous difficulties that
stemmed from her mother's nervous state, imbued with a lively faith,
but wild, independent, and critical, she too reacted by tensing herself
against adversity. For many years she overworked, sleeping only a
few hours every night, and cutting down on food in order to meet her
financial burdens, in spite of the first signs of failure in her general
condition.

And when the lung infection revealed inself, she accepted it with
all her usual pluck, but without throttling her lively and independent
spirit, and filled with pride when by some subterfuge she could disobey the doctor's orders.

As soon as she felt a little better she longed to return to an active
and adventurous life, and accepted the demands of her treatment only
in the hope of enjoying the compensations that such a future would
afford.

I brought to this sick girl the Christian message of total acceptance
of disease and abdication before God of all self-will.

Just as my wife and I were leaving her room she called us back to
say, in a voice that was filled with emotion: "You are right, what I
need is to abdicate more thoroughly. I knew God was asking me to
take some fresh step, but I did not know what it was."

Some time afterward she wrote to us: "I have truly accepted my
illness—its spiritual as well as its physical suffering. There is no
rebellion left in me. God has given me such peace that people have
been asking what is the cause of the change that has taken place, and
that has given me an opportunity to witness to my faith. . . ."

A sanatorium nurse once said to me: "The first condition of success in the treatment of our tuberculosis patients is that they should
accept their disease. Without that they are constantly thwarting the
efforts of the doctor because of their spirit of independence." In our
daily practice we all know these lively and undisciplined patients
whose attitude constantly compromises their recovery.

Blanche was a patient who put herself in my hands for a time, then left me and consulted a number of other doctors, called me in again, only to leave me once more. She began all kinds of treatments but never kept them up. She argued over every prescription, refused pneumothorax, injections, and so on.

Without going into all the causes of this ceaseless rebelliousness, I record that she was the daughter of a brutal and selfish drunkard of a father and a sentimental mother. From childhood she had been unsociable, independent, and impulsive, a dreamer. The disease made its appearance following upon a serious shock—the death of her fiancé in an accident just before they were to have been married.

For a long time she refused to go up into the mountains. When she did decide to go she went into a boarding house, where she had more freedom than in a sanatorium. Three months later she left, against the doctor's advice. She took up work again in order to be independent, and I had to argue with her for several months in order to get her to leave it. She married a mild-natured man, and dominated him. Various courses of treatment were tried, each one prematurely broken off or compromised by her indiscipline. She argued about everything, accepting this, refusing that, flying into a passion, and even undergoing several religious experiences—but always she refused to accept the necessity of a radical abdication of the will before God. And this was just what she needed most. She said she would rather die than give up her independence. And in fact she did die, after a long period in which her illness got worse. I was not treating her when the end came. I hope that one of my colleagues was able to help her to find acceptance, peace, and abdication.

All my fellow doctors could tell of similar cases, where their efforts have come to nothing against the patient's capricious impulsiveness. It is clear that this "personal problem," a wild and independent nature, is met with over the whole field of medicine. One can have no idea of the number of patients who run after all kinds of doctors without completely obeying a single one, who take a delight in setting one against another, who are always looking for one that will allow what the other has forbidden, or who exclaim, when one comes to the essential prescription: "Ask anything you like of me, but not that!"

The same applies to the many patients who obstinately refuse to allow themselves to be taken to hospital when their treatment requires it. It is only rarely that they admit their secret motive. One man is afraid of being made the subject of scientific experiments; another is afraid of being forced to eat food that he dislikes. A woman who has been unable to establish an atmosphere of real confidence in her home is afraid of being supplanted while she is away. Another is merely afraid that her cat, for which she has an exaggerated attachment, may not be properly looked after by someone else.

But one person's whims may harm other people's health. I know a young woman who had married a commercial traveler. She could not accept his continual traveling, and soon there was an emotional scene every time he had to go away. For the sake of peace the husband decided to change his employment. But he found it very hard to put up with the sedentary life of an office. His health was affected, and a trivial illness suddenly took a serious turn.

When the wife prayed about it, she realized that she had allowed her whim to take precedence over the need to let her husband follow his own aim in life. When he recovered she asked him to forgive her, and invited him to take up once more his occupation as a traveler, which was more suited to his temperament.

All doctors know how difficult it is to get discipline and submission from a capricious and self-willed personality. It is no use exhorting, blaming, or issuing orders. The whole being of the patient must undergo a real revolution.

Returning to the subject of tuberculosis, one ought to mention the innumerable borderline cases of everyday practice, the little fibrous tuberculoses, the old quiescent lesions. The doctor knows very well that these patients are less in need of technical treatment than of adopting a real discipline of life, of learning to rest in time or to adopt a more healthy diet.

Armand was a patient whom I treated first for depression. Failing to discover the moral cause, I confined myself to medication and routine psychotherapy.

A year later hemoptysis occurred and I diagnosed a developing tuberculosis. I sent him up into the mountains. Was there a "synthesis of the case," a cause common to the psychological depression and the physical malady which succeeded it? Questioned on this point, the medical superintendent of one of our big sanatoria replied without hesitation: "I am convinced that if one went systematically into the psychic antecedents of our inmates, one would find that in half of them, at least, a depressive phase preceded the development of their tuberculosis."

As far as Armand was concerned, it was only long after, when he and his wife talked frankly with me, and I began to be interested in their life problems, that I learned what moral defeats and difficulties lay behind these psychological troubles.

Their marriage was not going well. Mutual lack of understanding, and incompatibility between their very different characters, had gradually driven a wedge between them.

Armand was weak-willed, and had soon given way to temptation and sought in dangerous passions and attachments to fill the void in his heart. The injured wife had shut herself up more and more inside her attitude of being the innocent sufferer, and this only drove her husband even further away. He was leading an increasingly undisciplined life, with late nights, overwork, and domestic quarrels. He was miserable.

And so he fell victim, first to psychic depression, and a year later to tuberculosis.

When things have gone wrong in a person's life, so that his personality is deeply disturbed, this shows itself first in nervous troubles, for it is our nervous system which is the most fragile.

But very soon, if the warning of these nervous accidents is not heeded, if the doctor does not succeed in tracking down the personal problems which are their underlying cause, physical disturbances will follow, since the power of resistance is lessened. In accordance with the personal predisposition of each, one will fall victim to pulmonary tuberculosis, another to enterocolitis, yet another to phlebitis or some other organic disease.

Armand, naturally, took up with him to the mountains his unresolved personal problems. He was a rebellious patient, constantly taking liberties with the rules of the sanatorium, which he left prematurely in order to go into private lodgings where he had more freedom. The enforced idleness of the treatment in the mountains only increased the patient's moral indiscipline. This idleness was to continue when Armand returned to the plain, since he had been dismissed from his employment for fear of infection.

Besides, the idea that one must "take it easy" if one is delicate does not stimulate a patient of this kind to look for work. And if he has neither a professional code nor religious convictions that might give him true inner discipline, it is easy to see that the errors in his way of life have the effect of fatiguing more than resting him.

Idleness and unemployment did more than anything else to bring about the relapse which obliged me to send Armand into the mountains for the second time.

It was this realization of the harmful effect of idleness on the sick that prompted Dr. Rollier, of Leysin, to found his workshop-clinic. In this way he demonstrated that invalids who are given the opportunity of doing work commensurate with their strength—even while still under medical care—recover more speedily. Here we have a concept of medicine in which treatment of the person is complementary to technical treatment.

Meanwhile, I had formed a deep attachment for Armand. He had realized that the solution of our moral problems is of prime importance as far as our physical health is concerned. As a result, his second sojourn in the mountains was quite different from the first. Armand had become a willing patient. His condition improved rapidly. On his return he was able to re-establish harmony in his married life. He looked for employment without delay, and this time his work helped to confirm the moral reformation that had taken place in him. Since then his health has been good.

I met him quite recently in the street, with his wife. Their attitude left no room for doubt about their refound love and happiness.

A colleague and friend of mine, who runs a sanatorium, told me recently that at the last meeting of sanatoria medical superintendents, the discussion turned to the important question of relapses. It is a great disappointment for the specialist who has obtained a good result with high-altitude treatment to see his patient return to the plain and take up his normal life again, only to be back a few months later. Several of the doctors at the meeting therefore suggested that patients should be kept in the sanatorium for a longer period. But it is obvious that a patient whose tuberculous infection has cleared cannot be withheld indefinitely from returning to his normal life.

And my colleague, in the light of his personal religious experience, affirmed that this was not the real problem. If it too often happens that the patient's return to the plain leads to a relapse, this is due to the fact that in returning to his family and his social environment he has gone back to all the problems whose solution he had been unable to find before. So, added my friend, it is not enough to cure a tuberculosis patient; it is necessary at the same time to help him to acquire that quality of life which will assure his victory over his passions, his power to resist temptations, and true discipline.

The medical superintendent of another sanatorium once remarked to me, on this subject: "You are surely right, but we specialists are too wrapped up in our technical work. What we need is a doctor alongside us to treat the souls of our patients." But would it not be better if every doctor, however specialized, treated the whole "person" of his patient? This would be the true answer to the disadvantages of overspecialization.

The influence of the patient's morale on the physical course of the disease explains the more or less constant proportion of successful cures of tuberculosis obtained by every new method of treatment whose fashionableness stimulates the patient's confidence. Charles Baudouin points this out,[2] attributing it rightly to the laws of suggestion. But he himself recognizes the limitations of the effects of suggestion. At the slightest doubt or difficulty, a negative suggestion arises to compromise the favorable results obtained at first.

A true spiritual experience, on the contrary, has not only a tonic effect on the person who undergoes it. It has concrete results in his behavior, it corrects his faults of character, and puts an end to the conflicts which trouble him.

[2] *Suggestion and Autosuggestion*, trans. Eden and Cedar Paul (London: G. Allen & Unwin, 1920), pp. 97-99.

Here is one final case which seems to me to be very significant in this respect.

Sonia was a lively, happy, expansive child. But at the age of twelve she lost her mother, to whom she was very deeply attached. This was a great shock to the child. Her father was gloomy, pessimistic, and uncommunicative. His grief drove him even further into himself. She had no contact with him. He remained a widower for two years. Sonia was very lonely. She looked for emotional support to neighbors who had a bad influence on her. The remarriage of her father made matters worse; she rebelled against this stepmother who was intervening in the household just when she had begun to take a responsible share in running it. She criticized the stepmother, escaped whenever she could, and was thrown into a state of complete inner confusion.

At the age of fourteen she had pneumonia. At fifteen she was seriously ill with influenza.

Sonia wished to become independent in order to be able to leave home. She entered a teacher-training college, and threw herself into the work in spite of repeated bouts of bronchitis. She was gloomy, quick to take offense, and anxious. At the age of nineteen she had her first attack of pleurisy, in the middle of her examinations. She took very little care of herself, and entered an institute to earn a living. She had a second attack of pleurisy. Alone, and in the throes of an acute moral crisis, she was fighting a fierce, exhausting, and losing battle for purity against the difficulties of her own imagination. Her spiritual life was equally chaotic, shaken by repeated crises, efforts, and doubts. After a third attack of pleurisy she was sent to a sanatorium. At the age of twenty-three, in order to be able to stand on her own feet, she accepted a post as schoolmistress in a little village in the mountains, where the climate was severe, with no sun all winter, in a dilapidated and icy-cold school.

She lived a sad and friendless life, gnawed by anxiety for her family, from which she was morally isolated. Soon a serious attack of bronchitis brought her back to the sanatorium. This time there was an early tuberculous infection. But on her return from the mountains she fell into the hands of a doctor who contested the diagnosis, criticized his colleagues, and applied his own methods of treatment. Her life dragged on miserably, with fleeting periods of improvement, but with her general condition deteriorating and her nervous state getting worse.

An intestinal inflammation suddenly took a serious turn, and revealed itself as a new seat of tuberculous infection. The state of her lungs was no better, and for the first time Koch's bacillus was found.

Sonia was now in the hands of a distinguished specialist who urged her to give up for good her work in such unfavorable climatic conditions. But she was afraid of the future and took up her post again. A fresh crisis: she had to undergo an emergency operation for an ulcer in the cecum. The enteritis became worse. She was filled with rebellion and despair, and her doctor obliged her to ask for leave to go south for the winter.

It was then that a friend of hers suggested that she should come and see me on her return, in order to examine with me the whole problem of her health. On my side I was forewarned by a friend, who told me that he considered her to be as sick morally as she was physically. And indeed it was a miserable creature whom I saw come into my consulting room, a hopeless wreck. Though I found the state of her lungs to be surprisingly good, her general condition and her state of mind were deplorable. I will not go into the details of the thorough physical check which I carried out. She did not find it easy to talk about herself. Her story came out only bit by bit. She was obviously loath to reawaken all her unpleasant memories.

I pointed out to her I felt convinced that the worse our physical and moral condition, the more we stand in need of a frank and victorious spirit to sustain the body.

Our conversation went gradually deeper. To the outline of her life which I have already sketched here she added further details into which I will not now go, since they partook of the nature of confessions. Long silences marked her struggle against resistance within, but the picture was becoming more and more complete.

Then at last a smile lit up her face in quite a new way. One was aware of a great sense of relief in her. I thanked her for her confidence and her courage. We prayed together. When she left she was deeply moved, but her eyes were shining.

Next day I expected to find her relaxed. But the opposite was the case. So I said gently: "You have surely something more to tell me, something harder to confess than anything you told me yesterday."

Then I witnessed one of the greatest spiritual battles I have ever seen. She told me at once that she had had a terrible night: She knew very well that if she did not confess all there was to tell, that would be worse than if she had told me nothing at all. But it took several hours before her liberation was complete. She still had on her mind a childhood fault which had burdened her whole life. She went on: "I felt I would never be able to get rid of it. Everybody thought me irreproachable, and I was haunted by the memory of this thing, and I did not dare to confess it to anyone. Twice I tried to do so. I went to see some Christian friends, but came away again without any of them realizing what the true purpose of my visit was. When I was in the South and I was advised to come to see you, I thought that this was my last chance that God was giving me to let the daylight shine right into my heart. For several months, before coming North, I prayed day after day for courage to confess it all to you——"

Sonia added that for several years she had realized that the righting of her physical condition depended on her spiritual liberation. She felt that the weight on her mind was compromising all the devoted efforts of her doctor to treat her. At the time of her operation she had wished with all her heart that she would never come round from the anesthetic. At last she exclaimed: "For ten years I have been afraid of living. How could I have got better?"

That same day, Sonia consecrated her life to Jesus Christ.

The months that followed were not easy. For a long time still, she told me that she did not feel God's forgiveness. And then the current of her spiritual life, freed from the great obstacle that had obstructed it until that time, began to carry along with it lesser debris which she had to bring to me each time she came to see me. She began to explore her life, and to understand better the measure of the moral distress of her family, blaming herself for her critical attitude toward it. All this was tiring and testing for her. Her health was not robust. I almost wondered if I ought not to have waited until it improved before I let her get caught up in such a spiritual revolution.

To set one's life and one's soul in order is no light matter. It requires great and fatiguing efforts before it leads to an improvement in health.

Nevertheless, after some months Sonia's physical and nervous state was improved, and at the same time her spiritual life was growing and developing.

She was willing to follow her doctor's advice, to face new difficulties, to face the future with confidence. And when she learned that the education authorities were insisting on her resignation—the thought of which formerly had frightened her so much—she accepted the decision quite simply and calmly.

She is not yet cured. She has not been preserved from further trials. But her physical condition has improved in spite of everything. And then she has experienced God's forgiveness; she has begun to exercise a spiritual influence on those around her, to be a pillar of strength to her family, and to help souls to find Christ.

Concerning Other Physical Diseases

What I have described in the case of tuberculosis is true of all infectious diseases, the prognosis of which always depends primarily upon the subject's power of resistance. One type of patient who is discouraged by life, weighed down by family problems which he has been unable to resolve, or whose health is undermined by alcohol, can die from an ordinary attack of influenza. Efforts of the doctor to bolster up his general condition and to stimulate his defensive reactions will meet with little response. And then he sleeps worse and finds digestion more difficult because he is worried. It becomes necessary to rely more on tranquilizers, which lessen his resistance.

I do not need to dwell on the influence of personal problems on those who suffer from the arthritic group of diseases. In these patients a large number of factors are mixed up together. First, there are the hereditary factors—one might say that what may be called the "arthritic terrain" is traceable to wrong modes of life of previous generations; and second, personal factors, both physical and moral.

Among wrong physical modes of life, alongside overwork and lack of exercise, wrong eating plays an important part: diets that contain too much meat or too many sweet foods,[1] or that are too acid; or overuse of alcohol—in short, diets governed by gluttony. In God's plan of creation there is a proper diet for man, and man cannot neglect it with impunity.

But moral faults also play a considerable part. Dr. Swain, of Boston, who runs a clinic specializing in the treatment of arthritic affections, spoke of 270 cases in which the patient was cured on being freed from fear, worry, and resentment. He came to the conclusion that at least 60 per cent of arthritis cases have their origin in a moral conflict.

I shall have occasion later to refer to a most instructive case of diabetes. I could cite a large number of cases of neuritis. In one, the neuritis showed itself shortly after a bereavement which left the patient in a rebellious state of mind. Since I first began looking systematically for moral factors in neuritis, I have not met a single case in which their importance did not at once suggest itself.

One of my patients, as I write these lines, is a woman suffering from neuritis in the right radial nerve. I shall call her Clotilde. She is slight, thin, and dried-up, an ascetic who has always "lived on her nerves," as the saying goes. Instead of turning to God for the moral strength she needed in order to stand up to the difficulties that have been her lot in life, she has drawn on her own nervous energy. Getting on in years, she has had to face a host of new difficulties—financial losses, her husband's unemployment, and the failure of her son. This time her reserves of nervous energy were not enough for the demands she made on them, and she fell into a nervous depression. It is like a commercial firm in difficulties: It borrows, and borrows again in order to maintain an appearance of prosperity, until the day comes when the hole to be plugged is too big, and its credit is gone.

Clotilde realized that only God could give her the confidence and serenity she needed in order to bear her trials without being overwhelmed by them. She has made great progress. She has rediscovered peace, she takes pleasure once more in her work, and sleeps without sedatives. Now she is suffering from a localized neuritis which I take

[1]Paul Carton, *Traité de médecine, d'alimentation et d'hygiène naturistes* Brévannes, 1931), p. 527.

to be a fixation of her nervous discharge. Just as in septicemia a localization of the infection is the first step toward healing, so a localized neuritis is a symptom of the healing of a nervous depression.

Genevieve suffered from rheumatism. She happened to live in Geneva, and having heard me speak at a conference some years before, came to consult me.

From childhood she had been obsessed by the desire to succeed, to be independent—and then when sickness overtook her, by fear of the future. She would have liked to continue her education, but her parents kept her at home to help with the work of the house. After a number of difficult years she went abroad and found a certain happiness as a children's governess.

Then an industrialist whose children she had been bringing up because his wife was an invalid, proposed to her after the wife's death. She accepted, not so much from love, as from a desire to ensure a secure future.

Love is blind, they say, but fear is even more so. On their return from the honeymoon she found that her husband's firm was in deep financial trouble. Complete bankruptcy soon followed, and the husband fled the country, leaving Genevieve to face trouble and debt. And so she, who so longed for independence, found herself compelled to accept assistance from her family and to take up another post in the hope of being able to support her husband—if she could find him.

Soon her health gave way: an attack of angina was followed by rheumatoid arthritis. A Christian lady who had heard of the trouble she was in invited her to a religious conference, but she was afraid to go for fear of losing her job.

However, she had to leave her job in order to spend several weeks looking after her mother. A fresh attack of arthritis obliged her to take the waters at a spa, where the doctor, seeing her state of mind, and acting according to his lights, said to her: "What you need is a boyfriend."

This only exaggerated the moral crisis through which she was passing, and things were made even worse by her disappointment at finding the conditions in a new job so bad that she left it after only three days.

She told me all about it, and then, after a moment's silence she added that she was well aware of the fatal influence on the course of her life of her desire to succeed, to be independent, and also her fear of the future. For a long time now, she said, she had had the feeling that the only answer to this fear would be real faith in God. But how to find it? While the lightning flash of faith may tear apart in a moment the clouds that have gathered over a person's life, a long apprenticeship is needed for the Christian life to mature and for all the clouds to be blown away.

I sent Genevieve to a Christian friend who spent three successive afternoons with her and encouraged her by telling her about her own spiritual experiences. Then, during a lengthy stay in an institution directed by a pastor, Genevieve learned to give herself entirely to God, to ask her family's forgiveness, to forgive her husband, and to begin to see the possibility of reconstructing her life on a basis of faith. Only one post was available for her, one which seemed of no great interest to her, as well as being beyond her strength. But she accepted it in a real act of confidence, and God soon led her further along the path she had chosen. I saw her some months later. She was manageress of an important firm, well thought of by both her employers and her colleagues, practicing a quiet time every day, liberated from her fear of the future and considerably improved in health.

Let us now turn to the subject of arteriosclerosis, which plays such an important part in general practice and sometimes puts the doctor's patience cruelly to the test. These are, in fact, frequently patients who have behind them a long history of digestive and moral indiscipline, with which they have the greatest difficulty in making a break.

So long as they have not found the inner source of true renunciation, they continually contravene their doctor's orders, preferring to ask him for a medicine which will make it unnecessary for them to reform their lives, and are impatient when the medicine does not afford the desired relief. They are active people who have heaped on their shoulders responsibilities and cares from which they cannot now extricate themselves. From long habit they have come to enjoy the excesses of diet their strong constitution has allowed them to indulge in. One cannot but point out how embarrassing to the doctor these patients are, with the endless little "exceptions" they allow themselves, but rarely admit, compromising their health daily.

In these people, there are always moral factors as well as physical ones. As I write these lines I am called to attend a specific case of arteriosclerosis. In spite of the improvement brought about by the treatment the patient has received, he has suffered another serious attack. Clearly the disease has an organic basis, and at one time I should for that reason not have bothered to question those with whom he comes into contact about his behavior. But now I am told that he has recently been subject to daily outbursts of violent anger.

Fahrenkamp, in his book, *Die psychophysischen Wechselwirkungen bei den Hypertonieerkrankungen*, has demonstrated this continual intermingling of psychological and physical factors in cases of hypertension, and K. A. Menninger[2] stresses the tremendous influence of the state of mind on the condition of those suffering from high blood pressure. Their inner conflicts, their moods, and even their confidence in some medicine that has been prescribed for them—all affect their blood pressure.

Thus high blood pressure often seems to be a sort of physical expression of a moral hypertension which parallels it. This is the case with a woman whom I shall call Albertine.

A year ago her doctor discovered that she had a maximum pressure of 270 mm. He gave a careful treatment consisting of dieting and medicines. She lost over thirty-five pounds in weight and now shows a pressure of 200 mm. Auscultation reveals a clanging second aortic sound and an extrasystolic doubling of the first sound.

On hearing her life story, one realizes that under affliction she has become tense and hard. Her first husband was murdered. The second went off to the war. She adopted an orphan girl and poured out all her affection upon the child, only to find that when the girl was in a position to leave home she showed a sudden hostility toward her foster mother.

Since then Albertine has lived in a state of perpetual agitation, unable ever to relax, rushing about, incapable of slowing down, impulsive, irascible, living on a fourth floor with no elevator, unshak-

[2]*Bulletin of the New York Academy of Medicine*, April, 1938.

able when she thinks she is in the right. A believer, she goes to church every day, but she trusts no one and has no friends. She is imprisoned in a grim inner tension. As well as the medical treatment aimed at the reduction of her blood pressure, what she stands most in need of is an inner relaxation of tension which will reopen her heart to trustfulness and tenderness.

At the beginning of this century, medicine, with its tendency toward organicism, tried to give precise anatomicopathological definitions of angina pectoris, corresponding to no less precise theories of pathogenesis. The problem was, it seemed, proving wonderfully simple. Unfortunately, there were quite a number of patients who did not fit into these theoretical categories—and these were the very patients in whom moral factors played an obvious part.[3] The organicists found an easy way out by declaring that these were cases of "false angina pectoris." It is clear that this attitude is completely arbitrary, and takes little account of the complexity of the problem. For the patients with "false" angina suffer just as acutely as those with "true."

Happily, it is possible to discern a reaction in our own day against the oversimplifications of organicist medicine. Lian reminds us[4] that angina pectoris is merely a syndrome, susceptible of being provoked by various causes, moral as well as physical—and often both in combination. Thus the notorious distinction between "true" and "false" angina pectoris, which has troubled so many patients, has no meaning as soon as one stops looking upon it as a disease in its own right.

In his turn Laubry takes up the whole question,[5] the cautiousness of his conclusions being in marked contrast with the rigidity of former classifications. He stresses the complexity of the factors involved, and speaks of the pathogenic role played by the "thousand injuries of life."

The liver reacts readily to one's state of mind. Common expressions such as "to feel liverish," "to take a jaundiced view," attest this

[3]See the account of an "epidemic" of angina pectoris on board the *Embuscade* in the *Gazette des hôpitaux civils et militaires*, 1862.
[4]C. Lian *L'Angine de poitrine* (Paris: Masson, 1932).
[5]*Presse médicale*, Dec. 17, 1938.

fact. Whereas one person suffers from migraine at the slightest vexation, another will have a "bilious attack." In accordance with his theories one doctor will tell a patient that his liver attack comes from an imbalance in the involuntary nervous system, and another that all his ills "come from his liver." The reader would be surprised at the number of patients who tell us that a doctor has told them that they have a weak liver, and who have consequently imposed upon themselves serious dietary restrictions. The truth is that in most cases the trouble, whatever its symptomatology, comes simply from the vexation the patient has experienced. To expect to be insulated from all annoyance would be utopian. The truly Christian response to the "thousand injuries of life" is to accept them.

Some patients know quite well that they have a bilious attack, experiencing pain and swelling of the liver, violent headaches, and vomiting every time they take alcohol or are involved in a family quarrel. But instead of disciplining themselves and trying to establish a new atmosphere in their family life, they go on the round of the specialists, try every kind of "liver pill" recommended by the neighbors, in the newspapers, or over the radio, and have themselves X-rayed.

There is much truth in the following lines on this subject, taken from an article on "Sin and Sickness" by Professor E. de Greeff:

We do get sermons from time to time on the radio. But what we hear daily is, "You are irritable, you are sleeping badly, you are dissatisfied with yourself, people don't know you. . . . take Enver's little liver pills." . . . An honest man does not seek to make illness an excuse, but he does expect that some medicine or expedient of hygiene will bring him inner peace, without any effort on his part. . . . How many lazy people honestly imagine that their stomachs are to blame for their spoiled lives! . . . Pathology and physiology, useful and comforting as they are to man, are not what people vainly think them to be: they will play their part only in so far as men are willing to do their best to put their lives right. Little liver pills cannot take the place of personal effort.[6]

Doctors of course know this already, and they do attempt to reform their patients' lives. But many of them experience the mortification of seeing that their advice is seldom followed. The aim of this

[6] *L'Homme et le péché*, collection "Présences" (Paris: Plon), p. 50.

book is to point out that every life can really be reformed if the problems are tackled at the roots. For want of believing in this complete transformation, doctors content themselves with half-measures. I know one such patient whose doctor, aware of the part played by the psyche in her liver troubles, had recommended that she seek relaxation

For relaxation she listened to the radio. Unfortunately the radio is not always soothing. And when this patient, who nursed in her heart a keen resentment against certain foreign statesmen, chanced to hear them making speeches on the radio, she was so upset by it that another attack of her liver complaint was the result. It is clear that the true solution would have been found not in "relaxation," but in being set free from all the resentment that was poisoning her mind.

Every doctor could give any number of examples of this kind from his own experience.

I shall confine myself to quoting from a letter:

From the age of ten until I was forty-two I enjoyed magnificent health. At forty-two, when I left industry to take up an administrative post, I experienced for the first time in my life feelings of hate towards two of my superiors, who had subjected me to a series of gross humiliations. These humiliations were all the more difficult to take because I had previously been spoiled by the success of my life abroad, by the situation I occupied there, and because I had imagined up till then that I could get on perfectly well with anybody.

As a result of these humiliations, which I could not become reconciled to, I began to suffer from liver troubles. I had never before experienced the least pain in my liver. My hate of my superiors, and my dislike of this new life which I thought I should never be able to get used to, provoked several serious bilious attacks.

From the very day when I tried to listen in silence to what God had to say to me, I realized that I must get around to praying for my superiors and loving them. There took place a violent struggle within me that time. Nevertheless, a day came when I felt that God had removed all feeling of hate from my heart: from the day God accomplished that miracle, not only have I had no further pain in my liver, but also I have met with no further difficulties in my relationships with my superiors.

But I must be careful not to refer only to the role of moral factors in liver conditions. There are physical factors as well—and they too are connected with problems of life, especially with gluttony. Every bad habit in a man's way of life has its cause in his inmost heart.

In this connection, gluttony plays an important part. It is the commonest cause of the dietary excesses whose effects the doctor observes daily. Too many richly cooked foods, too much meat, especially pork; too many sweet things, chocolates and fancy cakes; gluttony over spices, coffee, alcohol, or tobacco. In our Western countries there are many more people eating too much than eating too little.

Gluttony is not, of course, confined to food, for any exaggerated predilection can be described as gluttony: idleness, too great a love of one's bed; the intellectual gluttony of those who revel in ideas and never use their hands or their feet; the gluttony of sentimentality, self-pity, or of sex; the gluttony of ambition with its greed for fame which imposes on so many people a life of overwork that is out of all proportion to their capabilities and their temperament; and lastly, the lust for money.

A sick person will fairly readily take medicine. But how many prescriptions about a person's manner of life are followed? How many smokers are capable of doing without a cigarette? How often can the alcoholic forgo his aperitif, or the person who overworks stop rushing about?

I remember once lunching with a friend, who whispered to me as he ordered a plate of pork, "I always feel a bit of a heathen when I eat pork."

"Then why eat it?" I asked.

"Because I like it," he replied.

I recall a liver sufferer of whom I could also say quite a lot from the psychological point of view. When she sincerely tried to think what it was that was spoiling her life she had to recognize that it was purely and simply gluttony, rather than all her moral complexes. The slightest overeating had repercussions on her physical and mental state lasting several days. She said to me one day: "I see that I must become disciplined down to the last mouthful."

Everyone has his own problems. We always feel that other people's problems are easier to solve. One man, who knows only intellectual passion, cannot understand how another is unable to resist his greed for some particular food. But whether one is to be able to lead a disciplined life often depends on a concrete, specific victory of this kind. I have seen people's lives suddenly develop richly both physically and spiritually from the day they become liberated from a passion for tobacco or chocolate. Wherever discipline is found to be most difficult, that is the battlefield on which the reformation of a person's life must be fought out.

Gluttony, however, is not the only cause of bad eating habits. Fashion, social prejudices, self-conceit, and laziness play an important part. It is because a diet with a large meat content goes along with a position of social ease that nutritional and plethoric complaints are so frequent among the rich. Doctors know how often diabetes is found among businessmen, whose digestion is attacked both by their business worries and by their "business dinners."

There are plenty of people who never have meat in the evening in the ordinary way, but who feel obliged to serve it when they have a guest who, if the truth were known, would also like to do without it. Similarly hotels, especially high-class hotels, are obliged to provide for their customers menus which are by no means good for their health, with several meats at the midday meal, lots of sauces and side dishes, correspondingly little in the way of vegetables and fruit, and meat again in the evening. It is odd to see how many people there are who feed themselves quite sensibly during the remainder of the year, and yet overwork their digestive systems when the holidays come along. These "holiday upsets" in the digestive system, caused by over-rich foods in hotels or else by the "local specialty" which simply must be tried, are well known to all doctors.

And there are poor people who on payday indulge in indigestible fancy meals, as if to have their revenge for their poverty and all the privations it inflicts on them toward the end of the month.

A certain doctor's daughter told me once that as a young girl she had suffered acutely from being crossed in love. Her father had at that time discovered that she had albuminuria. Had she not been a doctor's daughter, no one would ever have known whether or not this condition was anterior to the unfortunate love affair. For it so happened that, shortly before, her father had made an analysis which revealed no albumin.

The same thing could be demonstrated in the case of phlebitis, which usually occurs in subjects who are physically and morally fatigued. I am thinking of a patient who was immobilized for several months by phlebitis. It was followed by pneumonia, a sure sign of the weakening of his powers of resistance. Nevertheless, the pneumonia healed rapidly, and the patient was convalescing very satisfactorily when the phlebitis recurred. This happened just when he was having a serious disagreement with his employer, who was thinking of dismissing him because of his long illness. Everyone knows the strain caused by situations such as this.

It would be very interesting to conduct systematic research into the moral problems of those who suffer from chronic skin diseases. The patient care of the doctor achieves some betterment, and then all at once, just when the victory seems to have been won, and without any obvious cause, there is a recurrence and within a few hours the skin erupts again. It is only rarely that the patient will reveal to the doctor what is happening in his inner life at such moments.

I shall refer later to a case of dermatosis in a patient troubled by a hopeless conjugal conflict, who recovered rapidly as a result of religious conversion. I can think of another patient, suffering from chronic eczema, whose life was beset by serious emotional troubles.

Of the various types of dermatoses, without doubt furunculosis is most clearly connected with problems of life. More often than is generally thought, recurrent furunculosis owes its tenacity to some secret worry. This does not relieve us from the necessity of using vaccines. But neither must we use the vaccine as an excuse for not seeking to discover and solve the patient's problems of life.

A patient whom we shall call Sigismund came to me to be treated for a carbuncle on the back of the neck. While I was dressing it I asked him if he had any serious worries or difficulties. He replied that he had none. He said he was happy and confident.

I mentioned then that I myself had on two occasions started boils just after having lost my temper without justification, and that these boils burst as soon as I frankly recognized the underlying cause.

Sigismund at once exclaimed: "Oh, then that's just like me! I get a new boil every time I have an argument with my wife. I had noticed it, of course, but I didn't like to say anything about it because I thought it couldn't be anything but a coincidence, since boils are caused by germs."

What Sigismund did not know, because popular science does not mention the fact, is that the staphylococci which give rise to the boil are very common germs which we all have on the surface of our skin all the time, without suffering any infection as a consequence. And so to say that the staphylococcus causes the boil is an improper use of language. It is the agent, but the real cause is whatever is diminishing the subject's powers of resistance and thus encouraging the active development of the germ.

This case reminds me of a girl whom I attended for a long time, and whom we shall call Mariette. She suffered from an obstinately chronic furunculosis. At last I began to wonder whether she might not be subject to some secret worry which was diminishing her powers of resistance. She was in fact sad, reserved, and morose. But she never allowed anything to be seen of what was going on in her heart.

One day, a friend of hers had the courage, out of affection for her, to take the bull by the horns and advise her to make a clean breast of the mystery to me. It proved very difficult. She was extremely shy, and lapsed into silence whenever one tried to press her. She was at a real emotional impasse, incapable of seeing what she ought to do.

I did not try to dictate to her what line she ought to take, but rather to bring her into God's presence so that she might then herself be inspired. Her smile reappeared and the boils ceased. But she suffered a relapse a few months later. I did not know what to think, and then I learned that she was experiencing new difficulties, about which she had once again lacked the courage to speak to me. She had a few more small boils, which soon burst. Her shyness had still to be overcome, and the full development of her natural powers of resistance would still be dependent upon further progress in her moral development.

About the same time I was treating two other women and a man for furunculosis. They all spoke to me about their serious private troubles. One of the women had marital difficulties, the other was worried about the desperate condition of her husband, while the man was having trouble in his job.

One last example will permit me to show the importance of personal problems in heart disease. I do not, of course, need to insist on the part they play in functional troubles of the heart: palpitations, cardiac neurosis, extrasystoles, and cardiac erethism—all this is well known, not only to doctors, but also to the general public.

But the exact frontiers between functional and organic troubles are not always easy to establish in everyday practice! One is often amazed at the remarkable way in which the body can bear serious organic disorders, while other very minor disturbances obtrude themselves on the attention because of the functional troubles they trigger off. One can say that very frequently the outcome of an organic disorder of the heart, or of a state of imbalance and asystole, depends more upon the state of mind of the subject than upon his anatomico-physiological condition; aside from the fact that a liberated mind is able quite differently to accept the restrictions imposed by the disease upon the person's activities, and is much more disciplined in following the doctor's advice which is aimed at regulating the patient's life in accordance with his cardiac resistance. It is noticeable that those patients whose condition makes them most rebellious and upset, the ones who are most anxious about its outcome, most avid to get well, are the persons who most often endanger their cure by their constant disobedience of the doctor's orders.

I am called to an old lady of eighty-six who has tachycardia, a state which cannot be classed as a cardiac neurosis. We shall call her Félicienne. On her table is a bottle of digitalis, prescribed some days before by a Poor Law doctor. She confesses that she has taken three times the amount of the prescribed dose, in the hope that it would work better! Thinking that she has had enough digitalis, I put her on quinidine and give instructions that all excitement must be rigorously avoided.

On my next visit I find her heartbeats quite regular, and put it down to the beneficial effects of the quinidine. But I have the curiosity to ask my little old lady, now that she is easier to talk to, if there is perhaps some moral factor behind her heart attack. She at once exclaims: "There is indeed! They killed my cat! And it was on that very day that my palpitations started!" She had taken good care not to mention the fact to the first doctor, who would perhaps have prescribed a modest sedative instead of digitalis.

I do not claim to have exhausted the subject in the course of these few pages. I have wished simply, by means of a few examples taken from very different fields of medicine, to show the importance of personal problems. If this is so great in the case of patients suffering from organic diseases, it is even greater in those afflicted by functional and psychical disturbances. I shall now touch upon this aspect.

Functional and Psychical Disturbances

The terror of past centuries was the scourge of great epidemics such as cholera, plague, smallpox, and puerperal fever. In this field, and I cite only a few typical examples, the success of medicine is a veritable triumph. Unhappily, a new specter menaces humanity today—its nervous state. The number of minor psychopathic conditions, of functional disturbances, of neuroses and psychoses has increased catastrophically over the last hundred years. This increase, says Dr. Alexis Carrel, can be "more dangerous for civilization than infectious diseases."[1] Again, he says that "mental diseases by themselves are more numerous than all the other diseases put together."[2] And, leaving aside mental illnesses properly so-called, sufferers from "nerves," with a vague and fluctuating symptomatology, constitute a good half of the patients that make up a doctor's usual clientele. Faced with this constant stream of neurotics, the doctor finds himself more or less at a loss what to do. Trained in a medical age dominated by pathological anatomy, he is almost annoyed with himself at not being able to place these patients in any precise category, and at seeing them come back again and again, each time with some new complaint, improving with every course of treatment, but never being cured

[1] *Man, the Unknown* (Penguin Books, 1948).
[2] *Ibid.*

completely. He senses that they are not so much diseased as the victims of the physical and moral disorders of their own lives and those
of the set in which they move. They have more need of advice than of
remedies, but do not follow the advice he gives them. What they need
is to find a spiritual axis for their lives rather than any sort of medical
treatment. But the fact is that present-day ideas are against the doctor's venturing into the spiritual domain, which he feels to lie outside
the province of medicine. And when he sends on the patient to his
spiritual director, it is often with a certain skepticism over the latter's
competence to deal with a psychogenic problem.

He realizes that the increase in the number of nervous complaints
is due to a general moral recession. This recession, in fact, with its
consequences in family, professional, and social life, increases the
number of problems that are due to marital, family, and social conflicts, to emotional shocks, to uncertainty and fear, to the falling off
in honesty and trust, to worry and immorality.

Of these sufferers from nervous complaints, most are women, for it
is the social and moral position of women that has undergone the
most radical change during the last half-century. When, of old, a
woman was married by her parents to a man whom she did not love;
when she was the victim of the egotism and authoritarianism of a
husband to whom she was a domestic servant, and who was unfaithful to her, she did indeed suffer, but she accepted her lot because the
social conventions offered her no hope of escape. Nowadays she can
contemplate divorce. And from the moment the idea occurs to her,
her sufferings seem more unbearable, her conflicts with her husband
become more serious, so that she finishes up suffering more acutely
still. In a society governed by undisputed moral principles, life was
relatively simple; their collapse increases the number of moral "problems" in face of which the individual is left bewildered and powerless.

I wish to be very careful to avoid all misunderstanding on this
subject. We must not look for the restoration of social conventionalism which was often moral only on the surface. This formalism of
principles, even when it appeared to accord with Christian teaching,
was too much imbued with the spirit of the Pharisees, against which
Christ inveighed with the utmost rigor. However, our own age suffers

because it has cast aside formalism of principles without putting any genuine morality in its place. The adolescent of today who rebels against paternal authoritarianism is more at sea than used to be the case, unless he finds within himself the source of a true moral discipline able to take the place of the old framework of "principles." And the greatest misfortune of our age is that it is one of transition: the old formalism is not dead, whereas a truly Christian society is as yet unborn. Parents, feeling that their children lack any spiritual axis to their lives, try to impose upon them what is left of the old external morality, so that they are torn between their desire for liberty and the formalism from which they are unable to escape. That is why there are so many neurotics in strict families, among the children of pastors, and where social conformity rates high. This must be clearly and frankly recognized. The majority of our "cases of nerves" reveal the pathogenic role played by a formalistic upbringing. In liberating such people we are hard put to destroy the conventionalism with which they are still so strongly imbued despite all their rebellion against it.

But formalism is not Christianity. One might even say that it is essentially the negation of it. It was what crucified Christ. So then, if in this book I state my conviction that what the world and medicine stand most in need of today is a moral and spiritual renewal, this does not mean that I am advocating a return to the formalism of the beginning of the century, but rather the building of a new civilization in which the spirit of Christ will be the inner source of personal, family, social, and individual conduct.

I have already referred to a case of asthma directly connected with a personal problem, namely, fear of a father. I shall mention others later, for asthma is one of those functional disturbances through which the inner anguish of a person's life is expressed, in cases where there is a predisposition toward it. I recall a patient, whom I shall call Albert, who spoke very frankly about himself to me. The hereditary and personal factors were extremely complex in this case, and I cannot deal with them in detail: his father an alcoholic, family troubles, rebellion against the career mapped out for him, the loss of his wife after one year of marriage, marital conflicts in a second marriage, financial difficulties.

He had undergone psychoanalysis, and had improved considerably, but since then a large number of new problems had arisen to beset him. He had a typical bronchial asthma, which was a great burden to him. One day, brought face to face with Jesus Christ, he opened his heart to me, not only concerning the misfortunes of his life, but about his faults, about the sources within him of his failures in life. This religious experience brought about a noticeable improvement in his physical condition.

But a religious experience, however profound, does not at one blow solve the problems of a person's life. For several years I followed the advances and retreats in Albert's inner development, which were expressed, so to speak, by improvement and worsening in his asthmatic condition. Every time he examined his conscience he found once more the inspiration which relieved the tensions amidst which he struggled. His physical condition reflected this. But each new obstacle, each new inner resistance, was marked by a bronchial relapse.

In describing such a case, I mean to show the complexity of the problem raised by the "medicine of the person." Experience will not permit an oversimplified approach, as if some flight of the spirit were all that was necessary to ensure a moral life free of difficulties, and unblemished physical and nervous health. But experience does nevertheless show how closely a person's physical and psychological state depends on victories which are won only in the realm of the spirit. Quite recently I have learned that after years of uncertain development Albert has been led by his faith to establish his home again and to find true happiness in consecrating it with a religious blessing which he had formerly refused to accept.

Naturally I could cite many cases of gastralgia, hyperacidity, and dyspepsia that were connected with personal problems. One of my colleagues said once to a patient: "It's not a stomach disease you have, it's a foreman's disease." In fact his hyperacidity dated from the time of his promotion to foreman in the factory where he worked, and he was afraid of the responsibility involved in his new duties.

The following is from a letter I once received.

Ten years ago, just when I had taken on a difficult teaching assignment, I began to get violent stomach pains, and feelings of sickness which I found it difficult to describe precisely. The doctors could find nothing physically wrong with me, so it was one of those so-called "nervous diseases" which are nevertheless devilishly real. . . . Since I have given my life to God, the pains have almost completely disappeared. I get slight recurrences of it very occasionally, but always after I have been overworking or overeating.

I could not say what caused the trouble: fear of responsibility? Fear of losing my mother, who was ill at the time? Fear of the future or of being shown up in my true colors? I don't know. All of these things at the same time, doubtless. . . . Something else that has been put right—I am not late for school anymore. That's a pretty big miracle in my life! I get up in time to say my prayers and have breakfast, whereas before I used to swallow something without even sitting down, sometimes as I ran. . . .

Another case is that of Naomi, a young woman in her early thirties. She suffers from chronic nervous gastralgia. She is endowed with an energetic temperament and this has helped her to bear the misfortunes of her life. While still quite young she lost her mother, and took on responsibilities in the running of the house and also in her father's business. She was still adolescent when her father died. She succeeded him in the business. Indefatigable and full of pluck, she took on further social tasks, on top of her already overloaded timetable. For years she took no holiday, straining at her work. Instead of resting when the gastralgia appeared, she sought relief in a diet that was not adequate for her energetic temperament. An excess of starchy food set up a stubborn condition of constipation.

Constipation, the importance of which is so great in medicine because of all the autotoxic complications it brings in its train, is (surgical cases excepted) related to personal problems, wrong diet, lack of exercise, or even a bad habit of laziness over regular emptying of the bowels.

But there is more to it. It sometimes appears as a physical symbol of a negative mental attitude to life.

Philip, a young man who suffered for a number of years from constipation in a particularly recalcitrant form, came to realize that it was spasmodic: a physical image of the tension in his mind. His life was overshadowed by a serious quarrel with his family.

And in fact two years ago, when he submitted his life to God and became reconciled with his family, the constipation disappeared as if by magic.

It had brought on a chronic state of enteritis which still persists, but is gradually being attenuated.

Furthermore he was, if I may put it so, constipated in life, withdawn, hesitant, aimless, and lacking in energy. Now he is full of vigor, he has found his way, and everything is going well with him.

Virginia was another patient suffering from "symbolic" constipation. So bad was it that it resisted strong purgatives for nearly a week. When one knew her psychological history and her state of mind, it was seen to be a sort of "hunger strike" in reverse, in the words of the colleague to whom I entrusted her for re-education.

She was contradictory, impulsive, capricious, independent, undisciplined. The fact that a serious conflict had separated her from her parents from the age of twelve was no doubt due to her character as much as her character was due to the conflict. This process of mutual cause and effect had been projected thereafter into her whole life. Her school life was marked by idealistic "passions," and then she energetically took up the study of medicine, only to drop it on an impulse just before she was due to sit for her final examinations. In everything else she acted in the same way—given to a sudden about-face, rejecting all advice and constraint, experiencing difficulties in her life, but stubbornly resisting any serious attempt to guide her.

This rebellious and disillusioned psychological state could not fail soon to have repercussons on her physical state, particularly on her endocrine balance. There was a serious ovarian insufficiency, coupled with amenorrhea which had lasted three years, and obesity. For the last eight years she has traveled from clinic to clinic all over Europe, cutting short every course of treatment the moment the doctor tried to overcome her resistance and re-educate her.

She came to see me because, under the influence of a foreign lady whose acquaintance she chanced to make, she had undergone an unexpected religious experience, through which she suddenly came to see that a physical cure depended on a radical change in her attitude to life. Since then she has known many "ups and downs," moments of despair and of self-examination. But the spiritual flame lit in her has never been extinguished. And I have seen her again recently, healed physically, serene and assiduous in her work.

The connection between personal problems and functional troubles of the heart such as palpitations, or nervous troubles such as insomnia and neuralgia, is so well known even to the layman that it is unnecessary for me to cite actual cases here. The daily exercise of our profession provides plenty of examples. The same is true of migraine and other periodical headaches. Whatever their particular symptoms and mechanism, involving endocrine, neurovegetative, hepatic, and neuropathic disturbances, they are fundamentally bound up with personal life problems. A lawyer of whom I inquired what had been the consequences of his spiritual reawakening on his health, replied at once: "I used to suffer from migraine. Now I am free of it."

The reader may object, however, that everybody comes up against difficulties in life—disappointments, remorse, injustice, conflicts—but everybody does not fall ill. The truth is that we all experience functional disturbances in varying degrees of intensity and persistence. If we examine closely the psychological reactions which are interfering with the normality of behavior in a neurotic, we are compelled to recognize that they are not of a different kind from our own, but merely more intense: They are still fear, jealousy, susceptibility, anger, dissimulation, self-pity, sentimentality, erotic desire, and depression. What characterizes the neurotic is the fact that the very intensity of his reactions sets up a vicious circle from which he is unable to escape on his own. His fear, for example, destroys his self-confidence, and his lack of confidence feeds his fear. He is afraid of himself, afraid of being ill, and it is this fear which is making him ill. The psychoanalysts have demonstrated that all the unconscious reactions of neurotics may be observed in the daily life of healthy persons.[3] I entirely share their views on the continuity between the normal and the pathological in the case of psychoneuroses. All the behavior traits of the neurotic may be seen in our own false reactions

[3] Sigmund Freud, *The Psychopathology of Everyday Life*, trans. J. Strachey (London: The Hogarth Press, 1960).

to the problems of our lives. One goes a considerable way toward helping these sufferers in showing them frankly that one has reactions similar to theirs, since this takes away from them their feeling of isolation in being different from other people. As a result of an insult, an injustice, a disappointment, we, like them, suffer from insomnia, anxiety, palpitations, displacement of affect, or overcompensation. In any case, these motor responses constitute a sort of self-treatment, an emotional discharge. Everyone knows that weeping brings relief. By means of this motor response, and also through the effect of the passing of time and through the instinctive forces of life and balance "gaining the upper hand," the reaction is gradually diminished. This is what I shall call the "minor liquidation" of the shock received, for rather than really healing it, it covers over the wound, to which the subject becomes resigned. Should there come a fresh insult, for example, from the same person, the memory is at once reawakened, and the accumulated animosity from the past heightens the degree of the fresh reaction.

It is in fact by means of this "minor liquidation" that we neutralize by far the greatest number of our emotional shocks. But there is another course, which I shall call "major liquidation." It is the spiritual way. If we bring an insult or a disappointment to God, we can be delivered from it. What takes place then is a true liquidation, for then hate gives way to love, rebellion to acceptance.

The greater a moral injury is, the more difficult its minor liquidation becomes, and the more a major liquidation of it is called for. It is seldom that parents who have lost a son or daughter in the flower of childhood, for example, can find inner peace apart from the experience of God's grace.

And the more sensitive a person is, the easier it is for him to cross the threshold into a state where minor liquidation is impossible. A psychological vicious circle is set up, in which the intensity of the person's reactions, due to his oversensitivity, in turn increases his sensitivity. To take an analogy from physics, it is like the difference between damped and undamped waves. In a normal person a slight emotional shock becomes attenuated, like a series of damped waves, whereas in the neurotic the psychical vicious circle maintains the reaction in the manner of an undamped wave. In neurotics we always find that great sensitivity coincides with extraordinarily difficult personal problems, so that minor liquidation of them is rendered impossible. It was this that made me say once to an oversensitive woman: "You can only be either ill or a saint." Saintliness here does not of course signify moral perfection, but seeking to liquidate every problem of life through a spiritual attitude.

Beatrice was a young woman whose life was nothing but a tragedy of poverty. Abandoned by the father, living on public assistance, the little family had suffered the continual affronts involved in living on charity. For instance, poor children were issued by the authorities wooden clogs, which were cheaper than shoes, but served to distinguish them immediately from the other schoolchildren. This young woman was still overcome with violent emotion in my counsulting room at the memory of the noise of her clogs, advertising to the world at every step her social humiliation. Humiliation it was indeed, for the family was of noble origin, and therein lay the whole tragedy. "We were too poor," she said to me one day, "to mix with educated people, and we felt too great a need for refinement to feel at ease among people as poor as ourselves." She used to seek relief in music, only to be told by a welfare organization investigator, "When one is in the situation you are in, one doesn't play the violin." An atmosphere of wounded pride, of rebellion, and of sentimentality enveloped the family, and this exacerbated the child's natural sensitivity. She had to put up with the insults of the tradesmen to whom she was sent to make purchases on credit, and was shocked at her own behavior when she greedily ate a bar of chocolate after days of living on nothing but black coffee and cups of tea. The family was sent back to their native canton, the language of which she did not know. The canton authorities, in order to assist the family more cheaply, placed them in an institution for abnormal persons, where the children were among epileptics and mental defectives. It is hardly to be wondered at that all kinds of psychological troubles made their appearances in this sensitive and timid girl.

At the age of puberty she went through an extremely difficult phase. Her need to react plunged her into violent scenes with her mother, even though she herself felt that these scenes were out of character with her true nature. This naturally made her afraid of herself—because she felt in a confused sort of way that there was within her another self which she was unable to control. And this fear impelled her in spite of herself into further scenes. She would spend whole nights in tears, incapable of breaking the vicious circle in which she was being caught. Or else, in the dead of night, she would be overcome with a terrible feeling of remorse. She would go and awaken her mother to ask her forgiveness. But when her mother kissed her, she was afraid that it was just in order to get rid of her. Next day the struggle would begin again, to end, as always, in defeat.

She was beset by the terrifying thought that she was sliding down an inevitable slope, that she was lost, and under a curse.

She saw herself, she said, as a ladybug on the ground in the full light of the sun. She was at one and the same time the beetle and the spectator of the scene. It was always the same scene: An ill-disposed gentleman—the world—used to come along and crush the ladybug simply for the pleasure of killing it. Then the unpleasant gentleman would have a twinge of conscience, and turn the insect over with his foot to see if it were still alive.

At this time she made several attempts, in secret, to do away with herself. When, shortly afterward, she began to suffer from functional digestive troubles, she thought that this must be a punishment from heaven for having attempted suicide. The awful remorse that this thought caused had the immediate effect of aggravating and consolidating those troubles.

I shall pass over sexual difficulties and their unconscious link with digestive troubles, since the sex appetite is also a mysterious inner being, crying out for food, just like the pangs of hunger that gnawed at Beatrice amidst the privations of her poverty. And like all monsters, this one demands more, the more he is fed.

I hope, by means of these few notes, to show the reader what I mean by a psychical vicious circle, this unbreakable chain of cause and effect in which problems of life are linked together, each exacerbating the other. I could set down many more details in a case like that of Beatrice, showing all those chains of reaction—problems causing reactions, and reactions leading to new problems. And so, sensitive and artistic as she was, she was unable to accept being compelled by poverty to choose a livelihood that did not satisfy her nature.

For Beatrice the road to health, the breaking of her vicious circles, was the spiritual acceptance of her lot, of her social condition, of her sensitiveness, and of her occupation.

I am reminded of another patient, whom I shall call Muriel. About her birth there was some mystery which she never dared to discuss with her mother who, however, surrounded her with love and solicitude, and devoted herself to a life of hard work in order to bring up the girl.

When there is between mother and daughter some subject that neither can discuss openly with the other, their intimacy, however great, can never become really deep, joyful, and spontaneous. There is a certain constraint running through every facet of their life together, however hard they may try to make up for it by demonstrations of affection, sacrifices, and mutual solicitude.

This mystery naturally set up in Muriel feelings of inferiority which were only made worse by the fact that she hid them away in her heart. They were aggravated during her time at school when she heard her schoolmates talking about their fathers. Her sensitive imagination went to work, and soon she had invented a romantic story to explain the mystery. The story became fixed in her mind, so that she began to forget that it was fiction: She was to some extent the dupe of her own imagination. A vicious circle of distrust was set in motion, for the more one suspects a child of lying, the more does he seek the compensation of his fictions.

Furthermore, the mystery in Muriel's life impelled her to look everywhere for a support to take the place of the paternal support which she lacked. Her moral isolation also increased her fear of life and her need for support.

For lack of finding this support in God, who alone could give it to her fully, she looked for it in music, dancing, and gymnastics, and in her youthful enthusiasms for those who taught her these arts. All her moral and mental endeavors were directed toward these artistic activities, which she engaged in alongside her daily work. The result was severe overwork, leading to a sudden illness on the eve of a big display for which she had been feverishly preparing. She went on directing the rehearsals for several days, despite a temperature of 102°. She felt that the bottom would fall out of her life if she had to give them up. And the very fact that she found herself in this moral vortex, in addition to overworking, made her illness worse: A quite ordinary infection degenerated into bronchial pneumonia with one relapse after another over a period of several months—months of revolt and distress, made worse by her feeling of being a burden on her mother.

From that time her tremendous need to find a solid support attached her to her doctor, who tended her with the greatest care. Behind all this was a fear of life, which was delaying a cure. Neuropathic disturbances made their appearance—intense tachycardia and functional paraplegia.

People were not slow to find fault with her attachment to her doctor, particularly as it was so emotional in character. The effect of these suspicions, however, was to complete the vicious circle in which she was imprisoned. She adopted an attitude that was an unnatural pose.

The result of this inextricable tangle of reactions in neuroses is always a loss of naturalness. One of my women patients once said to me: "It can't be natural with anyone any more because I am always pretending to myself as well, and I can't get out of the habit. I have no idea myself how far my attitudes, reactions, thoughts, and fears are true or false. I played the part of an invalid in front of the doctor because he was playing the part of the doctor in front of me, and neither of us could help it. Nobody acts naturally with me; I'm treated as abnormal, and that prevents my being normal."

It is true that it is hard to be natural with a neurotic. If one treats him as "normal," if one blames him for making too much fuss, one is demanding of him an effort which he is no longer capable of making. If one is afraid of his reacting too sensitively, one is treating him as an invalid, and merely making him more neurotic. I spoke about this once with the daughter of another patient whom I shall call Noelle.

She said: "Yes, it's true, we have never acted naturally toward her. The moment she comes into the room, the subject of conversation is changed. Because she is ill, without noticing that we are doing it, we hold her at arm's length, outside our affairs and interests, when they are the very things that would help to draw her out of herself. We never talk politics or anything serious."

This lack of naturalness made Noelle a person apart—and at the same time she was being tacitly blamed for having no interest in anything but her own illnesses and worries. Spoiled by her father, she had had a childhood that had been too easy, and was not prepared to face the difficulties of life. A pretty girl, and much sought after, she had finally married (without loving him) the one among her admirers who was best suited to the social conventions of the circle in which she moved. Then trouble came. While still young she lost her husband. Her material situation became difficult. Brought up to enjoy life, she saw her life slipping away without happiness and without love. The serious illness of one of her children turned her worries into obsessions.

Those about her, sorry for her at first, soon tired of her continual complaining, considering it to be exaggerated. So a barrier was set up, isolating her still further, crystallizing her oversensitive reactions, turning her in upon herself, and preventing her acting naturally.

And then there was the vicious circle of treatments, clinics, and medicines, with their hopes and disappointments.

Faced with this situation, I realized that it was no use adding one more fresh treatment to all those that this patient had already been subjected to. What she needed was to be readapted to her natural environment, to be taught once more to behave naturally in it.

I sent a young woman to live with her who combined experience of the sick with a deep Christian faith. Her task was simply and naturally to live with Noelle in her own background, to take an interest in those things that naturally interested her, to grow flowers with her, and to live with her the fashionable life she was used to. This program of readaptation to a "natural" life, though it had its origin in our concept of man as a spiritual being, was of course not intended to turn Noelle into a religious person—that she had never been. What was needed was rather to recreate in her a taste for the life of society that she had been used to in the past. I took a hand in it myself by showing an interest in her activities and in her parties. The life of fashionable society may be the sphere in which one learns to give oneself to others, and to forget self.

If one looks closely into it, one realizes that there is no disease, however "physical," so to speak, which is not complicated with an element of neurosis. In her book *Servitude et grandeur de la maladie*,[4] Mme. France Pastorelli makes a penetrating analysis of the psychological complexes which are inevitably set up between the patient and those around him—the family, the nurse, and the doctor—and which can be resolved only on the spiritual level. It is impossible completely to avoid all affectation when faced with a sick person, whether it be the harshness of incomprehension, sentimental commiseration, calculated optimism, worried pessimism, veiled irritation, or helplessness. And the trouble is that every failure to act naturally brings into being an element of neurosis, which in its turn compromises the treatment and inhibits spontaneity.

A doctor finds it particularly difficult to behave naturally toward his wife when she is ill. It is for this reason that so many doctors are unable to treat their wives, while being quite able to deal successfully with patients not so closely connected with them.

My own experience is that in following Christ one can learn to act naturally once more. He pointed this out himself when he said that in order to enter the kingdom of God one had to become like a child. It is characteristic of the child that he is natural. He can be natural even with people who are not acting naturally, and whom he thus helps to be natural again.

In communion with Christ the person suffering from nerves can rediscover the childlike mind, simple and uncomplicated; he can break the vicious circles of fear and rancor, and dare to show himself to others as he really is, without hiding his weaknesses, without asking for pity; he can learn to accept the difficulties of his life, his sensitiveness, and lack of understanding on the part of other people.

In communion with Christ the doctor steps down from his scientist's pedestal, approaches his patient man to man, and is enabled to act naturally toward him.

⁴Paris: Plon, 1933.

The Knowledge of Man

A few years ago, one of the most famous doctors of our time, Alexis Carrel, wrote a book which has had a profound effect: *Man, the Unknown*. Dr. Carrel was the surgeon who introduced the technique of continuous irrigation with Dakin's solution, which has saved countless lives. It was he too who conducted at the Rockefeller Foundation the successful *in vitro* laboratory experiments in survival. In *Man, the Unknown* he gives a general outline of the extraordinary progress in the study of man that has been made possible by scientific techniques. But his book shows at the same time the anguish of the scientist who realizes that true knowledge of man eludes all his scientific achievements, that the mystery of man always escapes him.

Science, in fact, works only by analysis, by dividing *ad infinitum* the object of study. It is like cutting a cake, first in half, then into quarters, into eighths, into sixteenths, and so on. In this way it is able to make continuous progress, to enter into ever minuter details, without any real enlargement of the field it embraces. Furthermore, what happens then is like what happens when we separate a jigsaw puzzle into its five hundred pieces: The over-all picture disappears. This is the state of modern medicine: It has lost the sense of the unity of man. Such is the price it has paid for its scientific progress. It has sacrificed art to science.

Its discoveries are true; that is to say, they reveal valid and important facts. But they do not lead to a true understanding of man, because he is a synthesis. We shall not come to understand man by adding up all the items of analytical knowledge that we possess of him, but by comprehending him as a unified whole.

I am careful not to set the two sources of knowledge over against each other. The whole sense of this book is, on the contrary, to show that a "medicine of the person" is made up of the combination of these two methods. The scientific teaching of the medical faculty prepares the doctor well for the analytical study of the physicochemical, physiological, and psychological phenomena of man. There can be no question of doing without these techniques. I have often been consulted in recent years by students desirous of fitting themselves to practice a medicine of the person. I have always urged them to acquire during their years of medical training the most thorough scientific grounding the university can provide. But the doctor who wants really to understand men must add to this knowledge an experience of a spiritual nature. As Duhamel wrote, the doctor's art is essentially a "singular colloquy with the sick person," a confrontation of two men who can really understand each other on a spiritual level.

Man is not just a body and a mind. He is a spiritual being. It is impossible to know him if one disregards his deepest reality. This is indeed the daily experience of the doctor. No physiological or psychological analysis is sufficient to unravel the infinitely complex skein of a human life. He sees how little his patients understand themselves, as long as they do not examine themselves before God; how apt they are to close their eyes to their own faults; how their good will is held back by circumstances, discouragement, and habit; how little effect his advice can have in reforming a person's life when the patient's mind is torn by an inner conflict.

When I decided to devote all my energies toward acquiring this deep knowledge of man, the first precondition seemed to me to be the necessity of giving more time to each of my patients, and in order to do so, to accept a smaller number. The way our profession has developed has had the effect of turning the modern doctor into a man in a hurry. Many of my colleagues suffer from the sort of life they have to lead, in which too many patients troop through their consulting rooms, generally without leaving the doctors time enough really to get to know them. The development of social welfare plans and the standardization of doctors' fees have largely contributed to this state of affairs, which is one that must be put right.

The result is that patients see their doctors very frequently—or even a large number of doctors—without ever having time to seek the hidden cause behind the ills they suffer from. The diagnosis is arrived at after a clinical or radiological exploration, or a laboratory investigation. The patients are given advice and medicines. They recover successively from a number of illnesses. But why their resistance is weakened, why they have so many diseases in succession, why they lack the strength to live as they ought to live in order to be in good health, they only rarely have time to go into with their doctors.

To understand a person's life, to help him to understand it himself, takes a long time.

A thing that had struck me in the Paris hospitals was the consummate art with which the Masters, the heirs of the best French clinical traditions, conducted the interrogations of their patients. These interrogations were long and profound, always throbbing with human interest, full of penetrating insights into the drama of human life. They knew how to "make the patient talk," or to cajole him into a feeling of confidence so that he would say what was on his mind, in his own often very expressive language. Such interrogations often sufficed to enable the doctor to make a firm diagnosis—and he never failed to underline this with a slightly disdainful remark to the effect that the "gentlemen in the laboratory" could not but confirm it.

But these interrogations often went beyond the diagnosis and gave the complete outline of a person's life, showing where things had gone wrong, throwing a searching light on the secret problems that had played a decisive part in the development of the disease.

Thus it seems to me that the doctor's first task is to draw up a balance sheet of a person's life. Once upon a time, because of my very zeal to help people in their difficulties, I concerned myself chiefly with what I ought to say to them. While they were speaking to me, I was worrying about how to answer the problems of their lives. Today

I realize that it is more important to listen to them with interest than to think about what my answer should be. And it is no artificial interest—there is nothing more fascinating than to understand a human life. I have often felt that to listen in this way with patience and interest is the beginning of a treatment; many patients, even before I have said anything to them, have already been able to see themselves in a clearer light, and to see what has to be done to mend their lives, simply because they have for the first time had to look at their lives as a whole, rather like viewing some great fresco. There are so many people who have got themselves caught in a hectic whirl of life and have never had the time, or the courage, to take a straight look at themselves!

And then, understanding human lives demands that we devote some of our time to meditation. The doctor who can no longer find time in his day for prayer and the inner life, time to prepare for his consultations in the presence of God and to seek his will for his patients, cannot bring them the spiritual climate that is necessary if they are to open their hearts to him. Driven on by his devotion to the needs of his practice, he leads a fatiguing and unsatisfying life in which only more and more rarely does he find those peaceful moments of intimacy when he can provide what the patient most expects of him.

This climate that the medicine of the person requires is only fully established when the doctor comes down from his scientific pedestal and meets his patient as man to man, finding spiritual communion with him.

I shall make this clearer if I tell the story of a patient with diabetes. Louis came to consult me, complaining of mental fatigue, loss of memory, palpitations, and dyspnea. A urine test showed the presence of sugar at the rate of 93 grams per twenty-four hours. I told him that all his troubles were caused by diabetes.

Being satisfied in my mind at having "made a diagnosis" I did not bother to do anything much in the way of further investigations. He did tell me that he had business worries—but everybody had them, hadn't they?

One day I was called urgently to his home. I feared a diabetic coma, but I found him to be suffering from acute depression. He was prostrated, and most unwilling to talk.

"I don't know what trouble you are in at the moment," I said to him, "but I do know that there are moments in a man's life which may be decisive turning points. Moments of crisis, in which he may be tempted to run away from himself, to add one more defeat to his life in order to hide other defeats; or else he may, on the contrary, begin to be really honest with himself, have the courage to make a frank reckoning of his faults, to accept their consequences, and to mend them in order to start again with an entirely new life."

I spoke to him of my own experience—of how in the sight of God I was able to examine my own life clearly, to admit to myself and to others the compromises which I was hiding from both myself and them, and to find the strength to set my life in order, so as to give it a quality which must still be purged daily before God, but which provides the solution to the problems of my life.

Slowly Louis began to open his heart to me. He had lost his father while still quite young. He started to work in order to help the family. Courageously he made his own way in the world, and succeeded. But the loss of his father had left an irreparable emptiness in his life. Success made him bold. He began to take risks and to play fast and loose. And when as a consequence of illness financial difficulties arose, the temptation was there. His chief did a lot of traveling away from the office, and trusted him. Louis had begun to engage in certain irregularities, always with the intention of regularizing the position in time. But in fact one thing led relentlessly to another, and the hole grew bigger. From then on his life was nothing but worry, moral isolation, and fear of discovery.

It was then that he had come to see me, and I had informed him that the functional disorders from which he was suffering were due to diabetes. For years I had treated him from the physical point of view, in the classic fashion. Until the day came when it was no longer possible for him to hide the irregularities in the office. . . . Now he needed several thousand francs if he were to buy off his chief, to avoid a complaint being lodged, which inevitably would be followed by arrest and dishonor.

I was deeply moved as I sat there in front of that man. I was fond of him. He had been in my care all that time, and yet I had seen only one side of his life, so to speak, and now suddenly I was discovering the other side.

We went on talking together for a long time. I spoke to him of my life, of my own shortcomings. I told him that real amendment of life was not the same as running away from trouble and getting off lightly. If he were willing to rebuild his life on new foundations, I could help him.

A fortnight later he came back to my consulting room. He told me that he had decided to make a clean breast of the whole thing. He made a complete confession to me of his whole life. The reader will understand that I must not set out here all the details—which in any case I have largely forgotten. But since medicine is our concern here, I cannot omit to stress the completely new light that was thrown on the causes of his diabetes. Abuses and lack of self-discipline had prepared the way for it for years, both physically and morally. Cases like this show the superficiality of the information gleaned from the usual kind of interrogation we make of our patients. We should require a complete confession from each of them if we were to have a more reliable idea of the causes of disease.

When Louis left my consulting room that day, he had really encountered Christ and found the grace of God. He was ready to face the justice of men, and saw that the first manifestation of a new life, based thenceforth on honesty, would be the acceptance of the consequences of his past faults.

Then he was arrested.

When I saw him again, at the trial, I was able to tell the judge that I was confident of the amendment of this man's life.

As a first offender he was set free, to face the long trial of unemployment and poverty, for society does not make it easy for those who have slipped to rebuild their lives. But this man, without family or home, resources or work, went on growing spiritually day by day.

Soon he was helping other people to find the courageous solution to their difficulties.

One day I sought his help on behalf of another of my patients, whom I shall call Mark. He was a depressive, the victim of distressing insomnia, upon which strong doses of opium had no effect. He had given up work several times on account of nervous exhaustion. He suffered from extremely painful gastric disorders which resisted even the severest dieting.

I had a long talk with his own doctor, who had known him for many years. He showed me that this patient was the victim of his own scruples. He was a model husband and employee, devoting himself to his work with a zeal that led him to overwork. He was employed on administrative work, and found the peak periods at the end of the month extremely fatiguing. In spite of being moved to another branch of the work and having several periods of leave, his health was show-ing scarcely any improvement.

I talked at length with Mark about my experience of nervous dis-orders, saying that more often than we think, they are connected with personal problems in our lives. When I spoke of secret troubles he could no longer hide his anxiety. His digestive symptoms became worse and he hardly slept at all. I was tempted myself to have doubts about the course I had adopted with him.

It was then that I asked my former patient, Louis, to go and see him and to tell him of his own experience.

One hour later Louis was at my door, overwhelmed with intense emotion. In talking with Mark, he had hardly reached the central subject of his story—that of the irregularities in his business dealings —when Mark had taken him by the throat, shouting: "Stop! That's not your story you're telling me! It's mine! How did you find out that I have been embezzling money at the office? Be quiet! It's too awful!"

But Louis had gone on quietly telling his story, about our meeting and his own liberation when he had decided to refound his life on honesty, to accept that his past should be brought to light.

Mark was now a miserable, broken man. I found him weeping, his head in his hands. I went quietly up to him. In a feeble voice he said to me: "Oh, if only I could never have met you! I am a lost man now." Then I spoke to him of Jesus Christ, who always comes nigh those who see themselves as they really are. There was not much said between us. I cannot remember now what it was we said to each other. But half an hour later he was on his knees, devoting his life to God. When he arose his eyes were shining.

The days that followed were still hard to bear. Louis helped him. Other friends also helped. Soon a new life was beginning in that home which had been for so long under the shadow of the terrible secret that was preying on the husband's mind and coming between him and his wife.

There is a saying that there are three men from whom one should hide nothing: the priest, the doctor, and the lawyer. The truth is that there are few people who hide nothing, even from the priest, the doctor, and the lawyer!

When I compare what I used to know about my patients' lives with what I know of them since I have learned how to enter into real spiritual fellowship with them, I realize that only before God can we get rid of the formidable barriers which prevent a man from speaking frankly about his shortcomings, even to his doctor.

It is not difficult to imagine the quite new light that is thrown on the origin even of organic diseases by such knowledge.

Man—body, mind, and spirit—is a unity. The life he lives in his body corresponds with the life he lives in his mind and the life he lives in his spirit. Everyone understands what is meant by body, but I must make clear the distinction between mind and spirit. Mind, the psyche, is the domain of psychology: the will, intelligence, feeling, moral sense, etc. The spirit expresses itself through all these, and also through the body, but it is neither the mind nor the body. It is concerned with the personal relationship of man with God, and fashions the mind and the body in accordance with that relationship. The difficulty of the concept of the spirit lies in the fact that one can speak of it only in the same terms as are used to designate the motions of the mind. In itself it is indefinable; it is known only by inward experience. One can study psychology, even moral and religious psychology, without ever coming near the domain of the spirit. It is reached only when one is face to face with God.

Furthermore, these three realities—body, mind, and spirit—are not just three elements by whose juxtaposition a man is constituted. They are three aspects of one and the same unity: man. Once again it is Alexis Carrel who insists on the error of a mechanistic conception of man which sees him as a collection of separate pieces which when put together form a complicated machine. From the first moment of his existence, when he is a simple cell, man is a unity. Whatever the subsequent differentiation that takes place in his tissues, functions, and faculties, he remains a unity.

So the much debated problem of the relationship of mind and body is an artificial one, invented by our mode of thought which makes an arbitrary distinction for the purposes of analysis between the various aspects of the unity of man, and then wonders what are their mutual relationships. The philosophical theories (all of them unsatisfactory) which have been put forward—materialist monism, spiritualist monism, and dualism—are in marked contrast with the Christian concept of man, which is that of incarnation, "namely that the human mind cannot be completely defined except in relation to the body which it animates and together with which it forms a real and substantial unity."[1] There is no mind except a mind which expresses and manifests itself in a body. Similarly there is no body unless it is animated by a mind. And again, there is no soul except one that is incarnate in a body and a mind, and no body and mind without spirit, that is to say in personal relationship with God.

Despite all our desire to be objective in our investigation of man, we cannot avoid polarizing our inquiries in accordance with our own concepts. The doctor who believes only in material factors makes a systematic search for physical factors in a tuberculosis patient, for example—heredity, contacts, attacks of pleurisy, and so on. In this way he forms a materialistic idea of the causes of the disease. The doctor who believes in psychological factors will add to this research an investigation of the patient's mind. In this way he will bring to light moral factors and psychological complexes, and will form a

[1] A. D. Sertillanges, *Saint Thomas Aquinas and His Work*, trans. Godfrey Anstruther (London: Burns & Oates, 1933).

more complete picture of the pathogenesis. The doctor who believes in the soul discovers that the spiritual development of his patient is not without a bearing on his psychological and physical development. He observes that physical and psychical disturbances are related to disturbances in man's personal relationship with God.

The physical problems of a person's life correspond to his psychic problems, and both these kinds of problem correspond to spiritual problems. One cannot tend the body without tending the mind and the spirit. There is no physical reform possible without moral reform. And there is no moral reform without spiritual renewal.

Thus the examination of a person's life must include, besides history-taking, a detailed physical, psychological, and spiritual examination. In practice, I follow for each patient a *pro forma* outline which I have drawn up, and which includes hereditary and personal antecedents, the examination of each organ, laboratory tests, notes on psychology, anthropometry, physiognomy, graphology, and so on, and the patient's spiritual history. This helps me in making a general examination of each patient. It should be common practice in hospitals, but is too easily skipped in order to save time.

Daily practice often reminds me of the teaching of Leibnitz, who saw the body as a symbol of the mind. We are constantly coming across examples of physical attitudes that seem to be symbolic of mental attitudes. This, of course, is the basis of the study of human morphology, which I shall refer to later.

There was the case of Ginette. I was called in for an ordinary condition, and observed a pronounced curvature of the spine which the school doctor had already noted, and for which he had sent her to an orthopedist who had had a leather corset made for her. Radiography showed that there was no lesion in the vertebral column. The doctor had said to her: "You hold yourself badly; you must straighten yourself up. You see, we are forced to fit an appliance on you so as to stop your lungs from being compressed all the time."

I had a talk with her mother, intrigued by the question as to why the child should stoop like that.

I learned that the parents got on together very badly. The father was in the habit of causing noisy scenes at home. Not content with taking it out on his wife, he bullied his children, and the little girl was terrified of him. She no longer dared to speak to him, and withdrew into a corner like a hunted beast.

I realized then that the physical attitude of the girl was but the reflection of her moral attitude of fear. Instead of developing happily as a child of her age should, holding her head high and breathing deeply, she shrank into a worried stoop. Look at people whom you know, and see how their attitude, their gait, and their way of standing and sitting reflect their state of mind.

All these false attitudes, these bodies which stoop because their minds are closed up, have more influence on health than we think, on the intensity of the respiratory process, on physical vitality and resistance to disease. They will not, however, be corrected merely by the use of leather corsets, exhortation, or even by physical exercises. They call for a doctor who, in addition, concerns himself with the solution of the personal problems of the patient's life.

The work of psychoanalysts has provided many other illustrations of this symbolization of the mind by the body. This is the "meaning" of the symptoms of neuroses. A hysterical paralysis is the materialization of a refusal to move forward in life.

In the same way body and mind are a symbol of the soul, of a man's attitude to God.

But while the study of the body and the mind is pursued along analytical, technical, and objective lines, that of the spiritual being eludes all extrinsic investigation. It is for this reason that it is the key to a synthesized knowledge of man.

God has a purpose for every man. To live in accordance with this purpose is man's normal life. To depart from it physically, morally, or spiritually is what I have called "wrong living," which has harmful repercussions on health. The task of the doctor, therefore, is to help men to see what is God's purpose for their lives, so that they may succeed in living the lives that are normal for them.

"Materialist doctrines," Claude Bernard once wrote,[2] "are errone-

[2] *Leçons sur les phénomènes de la vie communs aux animaux et aux végétaux* (Paris: Baillière, 1879).

ous, for there is as it were a pre-established design for each being and each organ."

Whether or not we realize it, we always judge even the least important facts in relation to an ultimate end, philosophical in kind. In bourgeois society this ultimate end is reason, utility, and comfort. In a "normal" society it would be the will of God. By making this search for God's purpose for each life its main object, medicine would contribute to the establishment of this normal society.

Men, of course, differ greatly one from another. All those from Pythagoras onward, who have tried to correct men's lives, have been led to the study of this diversity. For if God has not made us all alike, this is doubtless because he has a different purpose in life for each one of us. The blacksmith's hammer differs from that of the upholsterer or the carpenter because its purpose is also different. But man is a living being, so that his temperament is also, in part, determined by his behavior. Let us call it, for example, a "digestive" temperament, with a clear predominance of the abdominal segment over the other segments of the body. We can see in it an innate tendency which has predisposed the man to gastronomical excesses and laziness. We can also see in it, equally clearly, the morphological consequences of his gluttony and idleness.

Thus there is a mixture in a person's temperament of factors which come from God and factors which derive from wrong living. By means of prayer and meditation a man can distinguish what things in his temperament are God-given, and must be accepted, from what comes from wrong living and must be corrected.

Such are the thoughts that have led me to do research into temperaments, which I am going to touch upon now. I do not claim that the views I set down here are original, since the statistical data which I have begun to collect are still insufficient. I shall confine myself to setting out the principal classifications of temperaments that have been suggested, their concordances, and a few suggestions of lessons that can be learned from them with respect to the medicine of the person.

Temperaments

The difficulty of a classification of temperaments is the same as is inherent in all biological classifications. "This is what has given rise to the remark that species have been thought up for the convenience of the scientists," writes Schreider, "and that in reality there exist only individuals." One either oversystematizes, reducing the infinite diversity of men to a restricted number of types, or else one admits so many types that for practical purposes their classification becomes useless.

Hippocrates himself had been struck by the predominance of certain segments of the body, and had recognized four fundamental temperaments, corresponding to the four "elements" of ancient science:

The choleric temperament (C), where there is a predominance of the osteomuscular system and of the members as opposed to the trunk, corresponding to the element "fire" and the bodily humor "bile" or "choler," marked by a tendency to motorial excitement.

The melancholic temperament (M), with a predominance of the nervous system and the cephalic segment as opposed to the trunk, corresponding to the element "earth" and the bodily humor "atrabile," marked by emotional sensitivity.

The sanguine temperament (S), where the respiratory and circulatory systems and the thoracic segment predominate, corresponding to the element "air" and the humor "blood," and characterized by an expansive optimism.

Finally the phlegmatic or lymphatic temperament (L), in which the digestive system and the abdominal segment predominate, corresponding to the element "water" and the humor "lymph," marked by a tendency to passivity.

This classification, whatever one may think about the ideas of the time on the "elements" and "humors," is still the best. Proof of this is that with only minor variations numerous authors make what is basically the same classification into types.

For a fuller discussion of the subject, which is too technical in its details for our purpose, the reader may refer to the works of Halle, F. Thomas, De Giovanni, L. Rostan, Viola and his pupil Pende, Allendy, Sigaud and his pupils Thooris and MacAuliffe, Biot, Carrel, Schreider, Corman, and Kretschmer.[1]

The reader will see for himself that with slight differences almost all these classifications correspond in large measure with the Hippocratic classification, which shows that they get near enough to the truth.

Carton took upon himself the reinstatement of Hippocrates' classification, supporting it with a large number of clinical observations, psychological and philosophical considerations, and morphological researches. I cannot do better than refer the reader to his books *Diagnostic et conduite des tempéraments,*[2] and *Art médical.* His great merit is that besides considerations of general morphology, to which I shall return presently, he gives a series of clinical indications for each tendency of the temperament, so that objective diagnosis is facilitated. He also provides physiognomical, chirological, graphological, and other indications. I have investigated these systematically

---

[1]Allendy, *Les tempéraments* (Paris: Vigot, 1922). A. Thooris, *Médecine morphologique* (Paris: Doin, 1937). L. Mac-Auliffe, *Les tempéraments* (Paris: N.R.F., 1926). R. Biot, *Le corps et l'âme* (Paris: Plon, 1938), chap. 2. Alexis Carrel, *Man, the Unknown* (Penguin Books, 1948), pp. 224-25. Schreider, *Les types humains* (Paris: Hermann, 1937). Louis Corman, *Visages et caractères* (Paris: Plon, 1932). E. Kretschmer, *Physique and Character,* trans. W. H. Sprott, 2nd ed. rev (London: Kegan Paul & Co., 1936).

[2]Paul Carton, *Diagnostic et conduite des tempéraments* (Brévannes, 1926).

for the past three years, and on most points my experience confirms that of Carton. Furthermore, he gives not only the physical signs of each of the basic tendencies of the temperament, but also the dominant qualities, the most frequent failings, and the environment and employment that suit them best.

Thus, according to Carton, the choleric (C) needs activity and movement, the melancholic (M) needs company and ideals, the sanguine (S) air and space, the lymphatic (L) water and solitude. He makes clear-cut distinctions between their different types of behavior, maintaining that C decides, executes and leads; M seeks, combines, and stimulates; S imagines, discovers, and stirs up; and L compares, regulates, and curbs. C undertakes, M becomes agitated, S flares up, and L stands still. C organizes, M thinks, S improvises, and L attends to details. C explores, M inspects, S dashes about, L watches. C is influenced by firmness, M by reasoning, S by sentiment, and L by gentleness. C feels the need to be accepted, M needs tranquility, S moderation, and L energy.[3]

One of the most useful things in Carton is the simple method he adopts for the notation of intermediate cases. Thus a CMSL represents for him the perfect masculine type, the type who possesses primarily the tendencies of the choleric, to a lesser degree the tendencies of the melancholic, in an even more attenuated form the tendencies of the sanguine, and to a slight but definite degree those of the lymphatic. On the other hand Carton considers MLCS to be the feminine type.

And again, for example, a CS combines the decisiveness of the C with the activity of the S. Such would be a leader, full of initiative and authority. The danger with him would be authoritarianism and impulsiveness; he would lack calm thought (M) and patience (L). I could give many more examples, and the clinical cases that I shall be citing later will form useful illustrations of these general considerations.

Carton's chief mistake seems to me to be the inclusion under the single designation M of both the intellectual and the sensitive types, who in practice are seen to be very different. The true intellectual,

[3] *Ibid.*, p. 30.

abstract and cold, is not at all sensitive, while the sensitive nervous type, whom Carton states to be predisposed to intellectual work, is frequently not so. It seems to me that the intellectual corresponds to the combination CM, and the sensitive, artistic type to SM or LM.

It remains for me to give an outline of the morphological indications of temperament. The measurements which I use systematically, after Carton, are weight, height, the spread of the arms, the length of trunk, the height of the sternal fork and that of the base of the xiphoid appendage, the length of the arms, the strength measured by dynamometer, the thoracic circumfererce, the cranial diameters, and the circumference of the neck.

These measurements show the main relationships between the various segments of the body: In the average man the arm-span exceeds the height by 4 cm. (1 cm. in a woman); the lower members equal 85 per cent of the trunk; the cephalic segment and the abdomen are equal and exceed the thorax by 12 cm.

An arm-span of greater length is a sign of endurance. In the choleric, the members are longer. In the melancholic the head is larger; in the sanguine, the thorax; and in the lymphatic, the abdomen.

Of course all these dimensions and indices require a critical interpretation, into the details of which I cannot enter here.

The face, furthermore, is full of valuable indications for the determination of temperament. The upper segment of the face, above the bridge of the nose, predominates in M; the middle segment, nose and cheekbones, in S; the lower segment in L; and a balance of all three segments indicates a C temperament. The last thus has a rectangular or square face, the M type an inverted triangle, the S a hexagonal face, while that of L is egg-shaped.

The expression is anxious in M, hard in C, lively in S, and calm in L, and so on.

In the same way the hand affords a number of indications, as do the lines of the hand, which depend on habitual gestures. The relation between the length of the fingers and that of the palm corresponds noticeably with that between the face and the cranium.[4]

L has a large stumpy hand, flabby and featureless; S has a plump

[4] L. Corman, *op. cit.*, p. 153.

hand with a well-developed thenar eminence; M's hand is long and triangular, with bony fingers; that of C is rectangular with thick square-ended fingers. The tips of the fingers in L are markedly double-jointed.

Finally, graphology provides valuable indications with which I have not the space to deal adequately here.

All these researches are based on the fact that our behavior, our gestures, our habits, and our states of mind have a permanent effect on our bodies, to a certain extent determining their shape. Conversely, our morphology has also a certain influence on our behavior. I referred to this above, in speaking of the mind being symbolized by the body.

This all refers to straightforward types, and Mac-Auliffe rightly stresses the beauty of these straightforward types, which "is an assurance of the solidity of their construction."[5]

In practice, however, one more often finds complex or even contradictory types, such as, for example, a round body with a flat hand. These morphological divergences imply an inner struggle between contradictory tendencies. I remember a young woman whose measurements were quite paradoxical. It seemed that her natural development had been disrupted by obstacles, like a river pouring in torrents over a barrage instead of following its course. A detailed examination of her life confirmed these views.

The study of temperaments opens up interesting perspectives into what might be called the medicine of the healthy.

"Prevention is better than cure," people say. And yet doctors rarely see the healthy. Most people go to the doctor only when they are afraid: afraid of disease, of infirmity, or of death. I have had an increasing number of physically healthy people coming to see me over the last few years. Their motives in coming to consult me were quite different. For the love of God, out of a desire to obey him and to devote to his service the best of their health, strength, and talents, they were seeking to know themselves better, so as to organize their

[5]*Op. cit.*

way of living, their food, and their rest in accordance with his will. It is a great joy to the doctor to be able to help a healthy person in this way to make himself even healthier, and to improve his usefulness to society. It is, in a way, to help him to build up positive health: not a health whose sole aim is to help him to avoid disease, but one that will help him to render better service. It is a great joy too for the doctor sometimes to meet a well-built man, full of possibilities. In our study and practice we hardly ever see a normal man.

Michel was one such whom I examined recently. He was the type of the fast athlete. His arm-span exceeded his height by 9 cm., and his skeletal index was 96. His body was long-limbed, trim, and harmonious. The normal man is beautiful. This qualitative notion of beauty was the medicosocial norm of the ancients. As science has become analytical, it has looked for quantitative norms of health in laboratory figures. A man who finds this "positive health" which brings the solution of his problems of life and spiritual development, becomes beautiful, whatever his morphological type. Mac-Auliffe rightly maintains that beauty is a sign of health.

Michel exhibits a harmonious temperament: CMSL, Carton's masculine type. He has vowed his life to God, and leads a wandering and adventurous life in his service. It is as important to encourage a man by showing him the riches of his gifts, so that he may make them bear fruit, as to correct his faults.

One interesting detail insisted upon by Carton as well as by Thooris and Mac-Auliffe is the evolution of the child. While still at the breast man is scarcely more than a digestive tube, insensible to the outside world; this is the digestive age, or L. In the second stage of childhood the thorax develops; this is the respiratory age, or S. In adolescence, the rebellious age, his limbs grow long; this is the muscular age, or C. Finally, in adulthood man experiences his full cerebral and social development; this is the cerebral age, M.

In the same way, both L and the small child are liable mainly to digestive troubles; both S and the older child to respiratory affections, adenoid growths, etc.; both C and the adolescent to diseases of the bones and joints; and lastly, both M and the adult are chiefly predisposed to nervous affections. In S the burden of the person's worries is borne by his circulatory system, and high blood pressure results, whereas in M the result is nervous depression; in C it is rheumatism, and in L digestive disorders.

Hippocrates says that S subjects are "more ill in the spring," M "in the autumn." In C "big changes to warmer weather in the various seasons cause many maladies." Lastly, L subjects are "more disposed to illness during the winter and spring . . . in old age, and as it approaches, they are full of infirmities."[6]

As Peter says, "we fall the way we lean"; and Mac-Auliffe adds: "The study of our temperament gives us precise information about our destiny, our aptitudes, and our weaknesses."[7]

This is why Descartes writes: "The mind depends so closely on the temperament and the dispositions of the bodily organs that if it is possible to find some means of making men generally wiser and cleverer than they have been until now, I believe that it is in medicine that it must be sought."[8]

Reference to numerous cases to show the value of the study of temperaments to general medical practice would lead me into technicalities outside the scope of this book. The reader may refer to the works of the authors I have quoted. The light thrown on the problem of social misfits is of more general interest.

Every civilization constructs its own scale of values as between the four fundamental tendencies of temperament. Whereas Hindu civilization is characterized by the contemplative and affective passivity of L, and Greek civilization was dominated by the artistic creative genius of SM, in our Western civilization C is normative: the man of action is the typical man. This is what has given western man his leading position, and caused the development of commerce, industry, technology, applied science, colonial expansion, and comprehensive social organization.

The choleric—energetic and domineering, imagining little but achieving much, seeing things as black and white rather than in

[6]Paul Carton, *L'Essentiel de la doctrine d'Hippocrate* (Brévannes, 1933) pp. 58-59.
  [7]*Op. cit.*, p. 269.
  [8]R. Biot, *op. cit.*, p. 130.

shades of gray, insensitive and hard-hearted, but leading a life of toil as severe on himself as on others, preferring quantity and speed to quality and depth—finds himself quite at home in this technological civilization. He occupies the positions of authority in political, economic, and even intellectual life, and imposes his faster temperamental rhythm on the social machine.

And so it is from among the sensitive, the artistic, the phlegmatic types that this society recruits its social misfits. The choleric sets the tone, and the conscientious but passive phlegmatic looks like a failure.

But in making men different, God meant every man to have his equal place in society, and the present crisis in our civilization demonstrates that this elevation of the man of action to the rank of social norm can lead only to an impasse. All our effort and activity, all our standardization and organization end in political, economic, and psychological crises without precedent.

Creative imagination, calm thought, artistic production, the gentle things of life, the things of the heart and the soul have been strangled in this race to achieve and produce more and more. And humanity has no idea what to do with all its material wealth and all the products of its activity. It suffers from sterility amidst its granaries. It has looked for profits and can no longer even sell. For in a civilization in which action and technical progress have become the norm, money is king, and material return the only criterion of value.

And our mental hospitals are filled with people whose natures are artistic, gentle, and intuitive, crushed by the struggle to live, incapable of keeping up with the speed of the men of action, incapable of earning their living, defeated by the wounds inflicted on their sensitivity, stultified by their feelings of inferiority and social uselessness, discouraged and lacking faith in themselves. For though the phlegmatic is passive he is by no means insensitive—quite the contrary. But his sensitivity is not externalized in lively nervous reactions; it turns in upon itself and leads to depression and melancholy. Thus, in C sensitivity leads to authoritarianism; in S to anger; in M to a nervous crisis; while in L it produces depression. Here is an example:

If there is one organism that is characteristic of our Western civilization, it is the modern factory, where in order to succeed one has to be shrewd and keen, where work is standardized and speed is more important than quality, where the man who wants to get to the top must sacrifice his family life to his passion for work, where financial return is the supreme criterion, where men may work together for years without ever having time really to get to know each other. René is a factory engineer. His temperament is LMS, with a total lack of the tenderness of the choleric. He is thus the inverse of Carton's masculine type. His arm-span is 4 cm. less than his height; short in the arm. [There is a notable predominance of the abdominal segment over the cephalic and thoracic, and also of the lower segment of the face; he is loose-jointed (dorsal reversibility of the ungual phalanges, and feminine angulation of the elbow fully extended); his skin is soft, pale, and cool; he has a gentle expression, slow movements, large appetite, liking for comfort and tranquility, horror of strife, feminine tenderness, love of children and their games, is conscientious to a fault, inhibited when harassed, and so on.] He corresponds fairly exactly to Corman's eighth or "moon" type.

This man suffers, to the point of illness, from the hectic atmosphere of the factory. When he has a technical problem to solve, he studies it methodically and in detail, following up every wearisome possibility with scrupulous perseverance, incapable of making a superficial judgment. Academically he is brilliant, for lymphatics are good scholars, disciplined and conscientious. But they are lost in the hurly-burly of life. René has an academic outlook in a pragmatic atmosphere. The modern factory takes little account of the academic virtues, and prefers the keen type who gets through his work quickly without losing himself in a maze of details.

René begins to lose confidence in himself and in his ability. He becomes withdrawn, takes refuge in daydreams, wastes his time, and becomes worse the further behind he drops in his program of work. He is appreciated by humble folk, by the workmen who call for his help when some difficulty crops up, sure of his understanding and his kindly and patient help, and of being able to understand his methodical explanations without being made to feel his superior education.

By taking a kind and profound interest in René, by allowing myself to become attached to him, going in detail into his schedules of work in order to help him to distinguish the essential from the secondary, and to realize the real services he renders, I have helped René to improve his output on the job and his self-confidence. But clearly the solution of a psychological problem of this nature is bound up with that of the problem of industrial civilization itself. I am struck by the fatal consequences for industry of this preference given to quantity over quality. In order to find a way out of the present crisis, the factory has the greatest need of men such as René, upon whom one can count without reserve to produce conscientious work, and whose kindly qualities are such as to transform the atmosphere of the work-shop. But for want of fulfilling their proper social function, people with temperaments like his become ill, misfits, unhappy, and unpro-ductive.

As is well known, psychologists distinguish two forms of thought: clear, logical or apperceptive thought, and intuitive or spherical thought, by free association. The choleric knows only logical thought, concrete and definite reality; and the rational civilization in which the world has been involved for three centuries suffers from poverty of creative imagination. All that is truly creative in man—intuition, art, spirituality—derives from spherical thought and is foreign to this rational civilization, which therefore characteristically despises it. Kretschmer himself, who stresses so strongly the importance of spher-ical thought in creative activity, speaks of the religious conception of the world as deriving from an outmoded "era of gods and heroes." He boasts of the progress represented by the "scientific conception" characterized by "national and international organization." When one looks at the present state of the world it is permissible to doubt the advantages of this progress. Having lost their awareness of God, men have lost the awareness of their rich diversity. In a society in which God once more occupies his proper place, C types will indeed render the services to be expected from their positive go-getting attitude, but the M types will also be able to bring forth the fruits of their sensi-tivity, the S types those of their imaginativeness, and the L types those of their conscientiousness.

So then, man's temperament is a factor which, like everything he possesses, is neither good nor bad in itself. Each temperament has its dangers: authoritarianism in the choleric, negativism or gluttony in the lymphatic, falsehood or day-dreaming in the sanguine, and egoism in the melancholic. Each temperament has also its treasures.

The reason for our study of temperaments is that we may learn better to know ourselves and what God wants of us. It is in order to submit and consecrate our temperament to God, for him to use in accordance with his purpose.

The temperaments characteristic of artists are LSM or LMS, which combine the tendency to passive dreaming of their L-dominance with the tendency to imaginativeness of their S-dominance and the sensitiveness of their M-dominance, with a total lack of C-dominance, that is to say a lack of aptitude for action.

These artists in other times, as for instance in the Renaissance, would have been appreciated as the elite of humanity, but now they are no more than jetsam, tortured by their need for peace, for the opportunity for original creation, which modern society denies them.

In the last century they still had their niches in the bohemian way of life, and could still follow their destiny, although dying of hunger. But the further society advances along the road of technical progress, utilitarianism, speed, and standardization, the more does it ride roughshod over them.

A painter asked me to examine his two sons. When I told him that I found in the second, as well as in the first, the characteristics of an artistic temperament, he muttered with a frown: "Ah, so he is an artist as well! What are we going to do with him?"

His reaction made me think how mistaken our civilization is. The richest periods in history have been those in which artists have been looked upon as an elite. Today the utilitarian bias of our sterile civilization has so impregnated our way of thought that even a painter seems almost disappointed to learn that his two sons are artists. I thought of the thrill of joy and pride with which a Renaissance painter or an ancient Greek sculptor would have welcomed the same discovery!

The Cartesian era, with its famous hypothesis that only what is demonstrable to the reason is normative of thought, relegated art to the position of a social luxury, as it did the spiritual life. Artists themselves are imbued with this notion that they are superfluous cogs in the social machine. They have lost confidence in their mission and have a feeling of inferiority as regards the world of affairs and of the intellect.

But artistic genius is like an inner demon which, if it is not exteriorized in some creative work, gnaws at the vitals of the mind. This is why one finds so many artists among the social misfits who consult the psychiatrist. I am reminded of a young patient with whom I had reached a "dead end." She had come to understand her own mind, and realized everything that had been distorting her psychological behavior, but this understanding did not suffice to give her the courage to live and strive. I reflected then that what she lacked was a vocation, a positive lever for her effort. Knowing that she painted and that a certain painter had seen her timid attempts, I went to see him. To my inquiries he replied unhesitatingly: "She not only has talent, but genius. But I have not dared to say so to her because she is ill." I replied in my turn: "Her appearance of illness is no doubt due to her vague feeling that she has this unexpressed genius within her. To recognize it will be to strengthen it." Since then the painter has been giving her lessons, and her psychological improvement has gone hand in hand with the development of her talent. Her first study was an "Annunciation"—the biblical scene in which a woman received from God her creative vocation.

At the same time I was treating a poet whose whole inner tragedy was poured out in plays which were never staged but which were of enthralling interest to a doctor; and a young woman whose whole soul was put into children's songs which she did not dare to show to her teacher; and an architect.

We will call the architect Emile. There are two sides to the life of an architect: There is the artist who uses his creative imagination and sketches a frame for men's lives, a frame which will have an enormous unconscious influence upon them. Then there is the commercial side, that of the building site, the man who must be able to give instructions to contractors, compete for orders, and hustle on the work.

Emile had a typical LMS temperament. With the sensibility of the artist he combined the passivity and sensuality of his dominantly lymphatic character. He suffered also from digestive and hepatic auto-intoxication due to overeating, in which he sought compensation for the injuries inflicted on him by his commercial life. He was easily taken in by unscrupulous people, trampled upon by people in a hurry, and inhibited in the struggle of life by his feelings of inferiority. He was as softhearted as a woman and had a tremendous need for affection. He was weak, rather self-centered, and punctilious. He ought to have been born in more tranquil days, when artists were more appreciated. He had married a strong-willed woman who thought she was helping him by exhorting him and urging him on, which only paralyzed him more than ever. He had some sort of religious life, but it was vague and sentimental, and unrelated to his concrete life.

Carton wrote that the phlegmatic must be won over by gentleness and kindness. I have always found this to be so. To challenge them, tell them they ought to try harder, or to accuse them of laziness, so far from stimulating them, only makes them more discouraged. If one makes friends of them—which is not difficult, because they are very friendly—if one is patient, affectionate, and trusting with them, one sees them regaining confidence in themselves and overcoming the difficulties which have been paralyzing them. In their turn these practical victories, however slight, do more to encourage them than any rest cure or advice.

In connection with Emile I alluded just now to religious experience in its relation to temperament. I cannot omit to return to a fuller discussion of this subject because of the misconceptions which are prevalent in regard to it. Many believe that there are some temperaments more religious than others. It is true that timid, unpractical, scrupulous people, and those who find the struggle of life too much for them, are more ready to take an interest in "religious matters" than the big, strong, strapping, practical types. But the former are the very ones who too often get tangled up in their own religious arguments and their moral scruples, and miss the true spiritual experience which would transform their attitude to life. It is possible to spend one's life discussing theology without ever coming face to face with Jesus Christ. It is also true that one can experience this confrontation without being in the least predisposed toward it by an interest in spiritual matters.

Look anywhere in the Gospel story and you will see that those whose lives were decisively transformed through their contact with Christ belonged to the most varied categories of temperament: the shy and the impulsive, the humble and the proud, the practical and the intellectual. Alongside them, people of all classes of temperament —and among them, be it noted, many theologians fond of religious arguments—were able to brush past Christ without having any religious experience at all. They saw and heard the same things, which got no further than the surface of their minds, and were never integrated into life. Therefore, though in this book I stress the medical importance of a true decision for Christ, I am careful not to confuse it with a sentimental inclination toward religion.

One might similarly think at first sight that confession would come more easily to an extrovert than to an introvert. The former, with his easy jovial manner, readily talks about himself. "The thing about me," he says, "is that I hide nothing. If anything, I am too frank." But this is a more apparent than real self-revelation. It leads to no spiritual experience so long as it does not get beyond the flood of easy confidences to the thin trickle of real confessions. The problem of the human heart is the same for each of us, and is independent of character. The road to Christ is not easier for some than it is for others. It is difficult for all.

In the same way also optimism can be mistaken for faith. I am by nature optimistic, whereas my wife is pessimistic. I am confident, she is apprehensive. For a long time I reproached her for her pessimism as indicating lack of faith. For my own part I prided myself on my optimistic outlook as if it came from my faith and not from my inborn disposition. One day, when we both had a great act of faith to perform, I realized during my quiet time that I was being less than honest in confusing faith and optimism, to my own advantage. The truth was that real faith was as difficult for me as it was for my wife. And so I was much better able to help her to overcome by faith her natural pessimism than when I used to contrast it with my thoughtless optimism. It helped me also to see what it was that was making my Christian witness sterile as far as timid, skeptical, and pessimistic people were concerned. For as long as they felt that in what I said about faith there was more of natural optimism than of real faith, they tended to think that that was "all right for confident people," but that it was not for them.

So then, the study of temperament ought to help us to live in accordance with our own true nature, to cultivate the talents which God has shared out to us, instead of comparing ourselves with other people, envying their gifts and being thrown into despair because we feel inferior to them. God loves each person equally and knows well that no one man is more valuable than another.

I am reminded of a young man with an LC temperament, most of whose brothers and sisters were of the sanguine type. His slowness and passivity were accentuated by the feelings of inferiority aroused in him by the more extroverted qualities of his brothers and sisters. But while the sanguine is more imaginative and brilliant, taking much upon himself, and spreading himself more readily, the LC's aptitude is for a humbler kind of work, but he is more persevering and profound.

It is of course between husband and wife that this mutual comparison is most frequently made and is most dangerous. For it leads to a progressive accentuation of the dominances of each temperament, which may eventually lead to what it is fashionable to call "incompatibility of temperament." Perhaps I may be permitted once more to make myself clear by quoting my own experience, since this psychological phenomenon is not the monopoly of marriages that are "on the rocks"; it is found in the happiest families. The more apprehensive my wife became, the more I tried to counterbalance her fears by adopting an air of confidence, even overdoing it sometimes, in order to cover up my own fears, for fear of encouraging hers. But the more confident I showed myself, the more my wife expressed her fears, in order to save me from falling into culpable overconfidence. The more advice she gave to the children, the more silent I became. And the more silent I was, the more advice she gave. One day she complained to me about my silence, and in my quiet time I saw that my behavior, instead of being regulated by a desire to obey the will of God, was in fact controlled by my natural temperament and my wish to counterbalance that of my wife. There was nothing to stop this vicious circle from growing worse and worse, unless it was broken by a change of attitude. And I saw at once that if I were to take my own responsibility toward the children more seriously, my wife would be able to sit more lightly to hers. Medical experience has taught me that there is no home that escapes this law of conjugal counterbalance. It manifests itself in a thousand different ways—loquacity and silence, expansiveness and reticence, optimism and pessimism, intellectualism and materialism, vivacity and gentleness, a love of solitude and a liking for society, conventionality and fantasy. It lies at the root of countless personal problems, or at least exacerbates them; and it can lead to well-nigh insoluble marital conflicts.

Among all the personal problems to which I have made it my purpose to refer in this book, there is no doubt that there are none which have more importance for the physical and psychological health of mankind than marital conflicts.

Conflicts

I remember once in Paris, when I was studying under Professor Laubry, he discussed with us the case of a divorced woman suffering from functional heart trouble. "There is always some reason for a woman to have nervous troubles," he said; "when she is unmarried, it is because she wants to get married; when she is married, it is because she wants a divorce; and when she is divorced, it is worse still." This epigrammatic remark expressed the great specialist's sad experience of human life, namely that the best-regulated treatments are constantly compromised by unresolved personal problems.

I have just examined a woman with a view to her admission into a convalescent home. She is still young, but her general condition is poor. When I questioned her about the underlying moral causes of all her troubles, she replied without hesitation: "I am divorced, and it is since then that my health has been bad." She had had liver troubles. She had had to undergo a gall-bladder operation. But the tissues lacked vitality and the scar had torn open. This in turn had brought on further complications. And then she began to have attacks of neuritis.

A young girl whom I shall call Paulette suffers from disorders of the autonomic system. A physical examination reveals no organic disorder and I am able to reassure her mother, who has been very worried about her health.

A very ordinary case, of no great interest medically. But the fact is that such cases make up a good part of the work of the general practitioner. Paulette's parents are divorced. Her mother, who has been given the care of the children, is a nervous type of woman, which is quite understandable.

Paulette is quite simply suffering from the divorce of her parents, both of whom she loves, and young as she is this is already showing itself in the form of functional disorders. Furthermore, the mother has transferred her injured affectivity to her children and is surrounding them with a possessive love which harms their development.

Geneva, with a population of 125,000, contains 5,000 children of divorced parents, all of whom are no doubt suffering in their physical, nervous, and psychical health from the divorce of their parents and all its consequences. And how many doctors are there who cannot put up an effective fight against the extension of divorce because they are themselves divorced? The hope that divorce will resolve psychological difficulties is an illusion. The number of psychoneuroses has never been so great as it is now; divorce has never been so widespread heretofore.

Whereas in Switzerland at the beginning of this century there was one divorce in every eighty-five marriages, there was in 1936 one in ten marriages, and last year in Geneva, one in four.

And for every divorce decree that is pronounced, how many couples are there whose divorce proceedings are taking place, dragging on for months to the detriment of their health, with repercussions on the children, attempts at reconciliation, lawyers' statements, and spying by detectives?

And for each couple whose divorce is going through, how many must there be involved in serious marital conflicts, or living side by side like hostile or indifferent strangers, kept from getting an official divorce only by a vague feeling of concern for the children's welfare; or again, how many more living with no real harmony and no intimacy, in acrimonious bitterness or resignation?

And then behind marital problems there are sexual problems. A vicious circle is set up between them: Sexual problems are not, as many people think, problems of a separate category which can be resolved on their own by some special psychological technique. They are the mirror of an individual's personal problems. It is because he has not arrived at a normal attitude to life that he is unable to achieve harmony in this most delicate domain of the mind, soul, and body. And it is also because his sexual life is warped that his attitude to home and society is also warped. Thus general conjugal difficulties have an effect on sexual harmony, and sexual difficulties affect conjugal life and the children.

The mystery of sex is generally the first thing to make a breach in the complete confidence existing between children and parents and to erect moral barriers between them. It is often because they have not found the solution of their own sex difficulties that parents are embarrassed on this subject in front of their children and incapable of giving them a good sex education. Sometimes their complete silence leaves the child a prey to unhealthy curiosity, and often to exhausting masturbation, followed by precocious sexual abuses. In this way young people, through having made a bad beginning in their sex life, spoil their happiness forever. Sometimes, on the other hand, parents approach the subject in a spirit of conventional moralism which presents the whole subject of sex as sinful, says nothing of its divine aspect, sets up countless stubborn complexes, and plunges the young into a sterile and obsessive struggle against impurity which is as exhausting as sexual abuse, and undermines their confidence in themselves.

And then there are all those unmarried people who never succeed in developing their personalities to the full because they never manage to come to terms with celibacy, while others, whether married or not, ruin their health in sexual excess. And there is the lifelong wearing down of physical and moral resistance by unreal imaginations, unhealthy reading, sexual selfishness, and the double life led by so many married people whom their guilty secret prevents from discovering the tonic force of true sexual harmony. The experience of the doctor shows him how few men and women there are who enjoy the physical and psychical powers which full and proper sexual development can bring.

There are also venereal diseases, with their delayed-action complications—not only for the patient but for his descendants and for the race. And then abortion with its physical and psychological complications, and also sexual perversions properly so-called. All this has incalculable repercussions on health.

All this too has no solution except on the spiritual level, as I shall show later. For the moment I wish once more to emphasize, in accord with my medical experience, certain aspects of the problems of married life. Many people think that when faced with a couple whose marriage has gone wrong one must decide who is to blame, to act as a sort of umpire in the conflict. The couple involved, moreover, try to make one do so by describing how they suffer and appealing to one's sense of justice. And when friends and relations come and take up the cudgels for one or other of the pair, telling him or her that *they* would not put up with what is going on, they only make matters worse.

What I always feel, however, is how impossible it is justly to apportion blame in a marital conflict, and that both husband and wife are equally in the right if one really tries to understand them. Their grievances are always perfectly well founded, and one could wear oneself out reproaching each for what the other has revealed about his conduct. But these grievances are not generally all of the same kind. In the great majority of cases one of the spouses has formal right on his side or her side. The husband has not been unfaithful. He has not slipped up. He is esteemed by all. He gives his wife everything to make her happy. He has even agreed several times to forgive and forget her indiscretions, and if this time he refuses to do so, it is because of his principles, for the sake of the children, or even because softness on his part would involve moral complicity. But when one listens to his wife, his fault is that he is always right. She is suffocating in this atmosphere of social conformity, with this husband who has no imagination, who gives her everyhing except what she needs in order to live—the feeling that she is really understood and loved.

This situation resembles that which obtains in conflicts between nations. There too the ones who are strong and rich are on the side of law, and accuse the others, in the name of justice and right, of disturbing the peace by their exorbitant demands. But the others appeal from law to equity, and protest against this law which bars the way to life, and which they are forced to break if they are not to be strangled.

It is as difficult to arrive at mutual understanding between members of a family as between nations.

Marital conflicts are even more difficult when it is the woman who is the stronger of the two. I mean strong not only in character but also in virtue. Among the couples who have come to me over the last few years, I could point to a large number whose problems are basically similar in outline.

A strong wife, who faces up to every obstacle, suffers every misfortune, complains endlessly, always says she is "at the end of her tether," but nevertheless sets the pace; and a weak, indecisive husband, retiring, downtrodden, lacking willpower, who because of his failures piles up difficulties for himself, and these difficulties in their turn make the marriage problem worse. All these women say—and say it sincerely—"I would like nothing better than that my husband should take the lead." And all the husbands say that they have never felt sufficiently confident of themselves to speak their mind and assert themselves. They heap up failures—acts of conjugal unfaithfulness, financial disorders, debts, gambling, drink, idleness. And if the husband confesses any of this to the wife, she replies: "If you had only told me all about it at the time I could have helped you." And it is just because they know that their confessions are always answered by reproaches, simply because their wives always say: "You ought to be like me, faithful, disciplined, orderly, reasonable," that these husbands do not dare to confess their faults, but instead become more deeply enmeshed in them.

Strong wives are thus constantly called upon to try and cope with the difficulties brought about by their husbands' weakness, acting in their place, paying their debts, and taking complete control, so that their lives are a continual burden.

Saint Paul remarks on how difficult the strong find it to understand the weak.

A miracle from God is needed. I have seen it happen in a sufficiently large number of cases to be able to affirm here that God has a solution to all these conflicts. But I have known also of sufficient failures not to underestimate the difficulties, and to know that apart from a miracle from God there is no answer to these marital vicious circles.

Leah was one of these strong wives, with a robust temperament, a will of iron and boundless energy, full of vitality, domineering and independent. She had early emancipated herself from the rigorous conventionality of a strict and careful upbringing. In a fit of rebelliousness she married a weak and sentimental young man, against the advice of her parents, who had "heard things which were not to his credit."

Later on she did not want it to be said that she had made a mistake, and so for a long time concealed from her relatives the difficulties she had to contend with because of the weakness, and then the deceit, of her husband.

However, following upon a religious experience, Leah realized where she herself was at fault. She realized that she had ridden roughshod over her husband, and she asked his forgiveness and told him she wanted to help him in a different way. An extraordinary renewal of confidence and joy resulted. For a time I thought that final victory had been won. But her family and friends described the wife's new attitude as "weakness," and in spite of everything the couple did not succeed in establishing that true spiritual communion which alone could have surmounted every obstacle.

And when I asked the husband why he had tried to conceal his new lapses by lying once again, it was once more his "fear of his wife" that he used as an excuse.

This case ended in divorce and the departure of the husband, and I have reported it in order to make it clear that our faith is not naïve. We are under no illusion about the crushing determinism of the psychological vicious circles which I am describing. Breaking them is no easy matter. It calls for an extremely rich, profound, and sustained religious experience. Far too often we content ourselves with an insufficient religious experience, and whenever I have to do with a failure like that of Leah's marriage, I have an acute sense of my own personal responsibility: If I had had sufficient faith, sufficient boldness, sufficient love to help this couple to make their experience of spiritual resurrection more radical in their lives, divorce would certainly have been avoided, and at the same time husband and wife would have been enabled at last to help each other to overcome their "strength" or "weakness."

I have, moreover, seen a number of wives and husbands who, after undergoing a powerful spiritual experience, have been so eager, in the first flush of their enthusiasm, to push their marriage partner along the same road, that their very insistence has acted as an obstacle. So long as one's aim is to show a person his faults and that he needs religion to put them right, one is maintaining an attitude of criticism and superiority in regard to him, which repels him instead of attracting him.

It is only when a husband and wife pray together before God that they find the secret of true harmony, that the difference in their temperaments, their ideas, and their tastes enriches their home instead of endangering it. There will be no further question of one imposing his will on the other, or of the other giving in for the sake of peace. Instead, they will together seek God's will, which alone will ensure that each will be able fully to develop his personality.

In every argument between a husband and wife there are apparent causes: conflicting ideas, opinions, ideals, and tastes. But behind these apparent causes there are real ones: lack of love, touchiness, fear, jealousy, self-centeredness, impurity, and lack of sincerity. Indeed, one may say that there are no marital problems; there are only individual problems. When each of the marriage partners seeks quietly, before God, to see his own faults, recognizes his sin, and asks the forgiveness of the other, marital problems are no more. Each learns to speak the other's language, and to meet him halfway, so to speak. Each holds back those harsh little words which one is apt to utter when one is right, but which are said in order to injure. Most of all, a couple rediscovers complete mutual confidence, because, in meditating in prayer together, they learn to become absolutely honest with each other.

Such honesty is very difficult to achieve. One always feels that if one makes a total confession, if one reveals all one's secret thoughts, one must lose the confidence of one's partner forever. The truth is quite the contrary. A union founded on complete mutual frankness is notably more solid than one which is thought to be safeguarded by prudent reservations. This is the price to be paid if a man and a woman are to cease living side by side like strangers, to come out of their spiritual solitude and create a climate of normal mental life.

This is the price to be paid if partners very different from each other are to combine their gifts instead of setting them against each other.

A man whom I shall call Victor has the rectangular face of the good administrator, of the "earth" type, the CL temperament. Imperturbable, unruffled in any situation, his mind works slowly but methodically and comprehensively. He enjoys robust health, is full of energy and capable of putting out a considerable physical effort. He is conscientious and active, but finds it difficult in his job to make contact with other people.

His wife, whom I shall call Victoria, is just the opposite: imaginative, intuitive, sensitive, versatile, and passionate. She weeps for nothing at all, and is full of enthusiasms. In company she has a knack of saying the right thing to break the ice and put everybody at ease. Her fits of enthusiasm alternate with periods of discouragement. Her health is precarious, her energy soon exhausted; in the morning she experiences great fatigue, which she tries to counteract by drinking coffee as a stimulant. Hers is very much an M morphology.

The recording of her blood pressure shows a curve similar to that of a child, with tiny oscillations.

Her childhood and youth were characterized by the incessant "ups and downs" of her impulsive nature. A disappointment in love at the age of eighteen had a profound effect on a nature as sensitive as hers. She married shortly afterward, largely out of fear of remaining a spinster if she missed this second chance.

She found great difficulty in accepting the very different nature of her husband. His steadiness of character she looked upon as mediocrity; at the same time it made her ashamed of her own mercurial moods. She wanted something out of life that was more romantic, more passionate.

Victor too had difficulty in understanding and accepting his wife's fragile and unstable temperament. Not knowing how to take her, and feeling himself thoroughly inferior in intellect, intuition, and emotion, he buried himself more deeply in his passivity, which she described as selfishness.

But after several years during which these difficulties of mutual adaptation had their effect both on Victor's temper and on his wife's health, they have found the road to a solution in a deep spiritual communion. For they are made to complement each other—Victoria to provide the inspiration, her husband to put it into practice. Their feeling that they understand and can be useful to one another sustains and enriches the love of this couple, so rich already in the extreme diversity of their natural gifts.

A marriage that is a real union is always a miracle. Only God can make it, and he requires perseverance in faith.

I received an urgent call to go to the bedside of a young woman —whom I shall call Cecile—whose husband had already been my patient. She was in an extreme state of agitation, and the concierge, who had not dared to leave her until I came, whispered to me: "She tried to do away with herself, but somebody smelled the gas in time and stopped her. I hope she's all right, but she's very unhappy. Her husband has been giving her such a bad time for ages. . . ." I was left alone with this poor little wretch. Little by little she became calmer. Monotonously she repeated: "Why didn't they let me die? Next time I'll manage it better."

I felt that I ought to give this young woman something other than medicines or words of advice, blame, or comfort. I knew practically nothing about her beyond the fact that she was of foreign origin, a Catholic, and unhappy, whereas I was a Genevan, a Protestant, and prosperous. But that was not the point, was it? The point was what was the matter with her life, that miserable life that she had tried to end because she could bear it no longer.

But she appeared to be disinclined to talk about herself. To question her just then would only have made her shut up all the tighter. "There is a solution other than death," I said calmly. "I do not know the details of your troubles, but I know that whatever they are they can be turned into joy. God has an answer for all suffering, for all men, for all women, for all situations."

Gradually she took more part in the conversation. She was looking at me in surprise, with the life coming back into her eyes. But she said that all this was not for her.

Then I spoke about the Cross. I told her that the way of Christ consisted in accepting everything, bearing everything, enduring everything without ceasing to love and to forgive, and what was more, to seek still—whatever injustice one was subjected to—to discover one's own faults. It was an extremely painful road, but all those who resolutely set about following it to the end found joy.

We talked together for a long time. When I left the patient, the concierge came in and asked me what I could have found to say to her to bring about such a change. A slight smile, though still a very sad one, was faintly visible on her face.

That face of hers was ravaged, as was her whole body, by dermatosis, the nature of which remained obscure, despite all the efforts of the skin specialist who had been called in, which makes one think that it in fact had something to do with the moral sufferings of the patient.

However, the treatment I was following for the dermatosis provided an opportunity for further conversations and further spiritual progress. Some years previously, Cecile had broken away from the Roman Church. Her marriage to a Protestant meant that she had forsaken the childhood religion she had known until then. God had no further place in her life, and it had not entered her head to turn to him in the midst of her disappointments and rebellions.

When the dermatosis was healed, she told me how sorry she was that the cessation of the consultations meant also the end of our conversations about religion. She was afraid of backsliding in the new road along which she had begun to travel.

At this point I asked a friend, a lady who was a Christian, to go and visit her.

A few weeks later, Cecile consecrated her life to God, and I heard her tell of the profound joy which filled her heart.

But months of severe testing were to follow. The matrimonial situation was no better. The contrary, in fact, was the case. The husband seemed to find it very convenient to have a wife who was ready to put up with everything and accept everything without ceasing to love him. His attitude toward her reminded me of a cat playing with a mouse. He would leave her and then come back to her without a word of regret, take advantage of what she had earned, and then leave her again. Despite her communion with God, the poor woman had more sorrow than joy.

Fifteen months went by in this way without the wife's gentle acceptance seeming to have any effect on the husband.

One day, however, he met one of my friends who knew the whole story. A providential day: The husband had in his pocket the memorandum which he was taking to his lawyer to start divorce proceedings. They fell into conversation, and talked for a long time. That same day the memorandum was burned.

A few days later it was Easter Eve, and I was in a little church in the Canton of Vaud at the wedding of two of my friends. Cecile and her husband were there as well. An inspired florist had decorated the church. In the middle he had placed a vine, with the new shoots on it, and all around he had disposed branches of cherry. The effect was stupendous. During the service a mother read the thirteenth chapter of St. Paul's first Epistle to the Corinthians, in which the Apostle speaks of the love which "bears all things, believes all things, hopes all things, endures all things."

After the service, on a little mountain track I came upon Cecile and her husband. They were walking arm in arm, their faces alight with joy. The husband said to me: "It really is Easter for us—the resurrection of our home and our happiness. That wedding just now —it was as if it were our own. We had built our home without God, and it is God who has remade it now."

It is clear that what I have just said about matrimonial conflicts could also be said about all the other conflicts which divide individuals and groups. There are first the conflicts between parents and children. In a considerable number of clinical observations it is noticeable what a lasting effect such childhood conflicts can have on a person's life. This is true not only from a psychological point of view. The need to defend their independence against very authoritarian parents, to assert their liberty beneath the weight of convention imposed on them by parents who are too bourgeois, or the need to evade their vigilance if they are too jealous, leads children into the worst kinds of alimentary, moral, and social faults. Others are the victims of the unorthodox ideas of their parents in regard to food and to abstinence. The reader will find in this book several cases in which a parent-child conflict has dominated a person's whole life. It is almost always the consequence of the parents' own personal problems.

And then there are the conflicts between brothers and sisters, dramas of jealousy, or feelings of inferiority with regard to a favored sibling. And later on, collective conflicts, quarrels over inheritances, wars of many episodes, which can divide a family into two opposite camps for decades, and absorb the best energies of worried, rebellious, and broken men and women.

Here is an example: a patient with neuritis of the right radial nerve. We shall call the patient Arlette. I look for the causes of her malady. There are no constitutional antecedents, and no history of overwork, except perhaps too much knitting, which may have favored the localization in the arm. No dampness in the house, no intoxication of any sort.

"Have you any private worries?" She dissolves into tears. For five years she has been quarreling bitterly about some minor financial matter with her husband's daughters whom she brought up and of whom she is very fond. She is literally ravaged by this conflict, which haunts her day and night.

Her friends dissuade her from making the first step toward reconciliation. They keep reminding her of all the injuries done to her by her stepdaughters, and represent any attempt at a *rapprochement* on her part as a violation of justice, a reward for wickedness, an act of weakness. Meanwhile, she is the one who suffers!

Of course I prescribe the proper medical treatment, but I tell her at the same time that Christianity consists in forgiving, forgiving even those who do not come to us and eat humble pie; and that following in Christ's footsteps, far from abasing us, on the contrary ennobles us. She leaves me, having made up her mind to take the first step toward a reconciliation.

And there is also the common case of the weak man caught between his mother and his wife, who are fighting to maintain their influence over him. I recall one such who came to see me believing himself to be the victim of this sort of conflict. He did not take long to see how much he was himself responsible for the situation, because of his weakness, his negative attitude, and his self-pity, which gave rise to this struggle to influence him. His self-pity was doing injury to his love for his mother just when that love was the only thing that could disarm her.

I have not mentioned conflict between a child and an unjust schoolmaster or governess. But then I could not possibly list all the conflicts which spoil men's lives. There are all those connected with work—not only between employers and employees, but more often still between foremen and workmen, between jealous workmen, between competing employers. And there are all the social, political, and international conflicts. I do not need nowadays to emphasize the consequences of these on the lives and health of countless men, women, and children.

There, as in the family, only a return to God can bring a true solution—reconciliation between employer and employee, between competitors, between political opponents, between nations, and between races. I should be overstepping the limits of my book if I were to cite examples of this that are known to me.

8

Flight

The reader will have noticed, in the cases I have quoted so far, that personal problems are interconnected like the links in a chain, that a matrimonial conflict, for example, may bring in its train rebelliousness, laxity, alcoholism, and dishonesty. For when a man does not feel strong enough, when he despairs of solving some vital problem in his life, he tries instinctively to conceal his defeat by running away. And this flight creates a new problem which makes setting right his life more difficult still. Sometimes he is aware of this, but more often the flight is unconscious. In order to demonstrate the considerable part played by flight of this kind in men's lives and health, I wish to cite some examples of it in greater detail in this chapter and the next.

There is, first, flight into dreams. Real life is harsh. It is constantly injuring our sensibilities. The temptation to escape from it by flight is the stronger the more sensitive we are: We run away in order to protect our sensitivity, to escape the conflict which wounds it. The land of dreams is close at hand, so that one can escape into it at any moment, far from these painful realities. The escape often takes the form of a continuous story, a novel in many episodes which a person tells himself, going over the episodes again and again, and which absorbs his mental energy. It is a secret treasure into which he pours the best of himself. It is his way of turning the tables on harsh reality.

He composes for himself a life in which he is always winning victories, and this compensates for the defeats he sustains in real life. In his fantasy he always plays the star part, he is always loved, esteemed, understood; he is always in command, he is free to sacrifice himself nobly.

Of course I am not criticizing imagination, which can be a creative force in the mind of a poet. But the sort of dream of which I am speaking here is sterile and ineffective. It is fatiguing rather than restful. Above all, it aggravates the divorce between the ideal and the real. We are the more ready to take flight on the wings of dreams the more mediocre reality is, and reality seems the more mediocre the more we compare it with some idealistic dream. There is thus a cleavage in an individual's personality, which is divided between a dream that he does not live, and a life whose reality he dislikes. The consequences are not only psychological: I could cite the cases of many people who for years add to the fatigues of their day by spending hours every night feverishly writing a "private diary," which no one will ever read, in notebooks which pile up in a secret cupboard, and are like a dead weight on a person's life.

There is also flight into the past. Many people have their eyes turned constantly backward. They relive their Golden Age, a distant era in which they were happier, amid successes and joys. In this way they escape from the problems of the present, which they no longer try to solve, and savor the joys of the past.

Moreover, it is not only joys that are involved. Regret and remorse can act equally dangerously as a flight into the past. The scrupulous mind which is constantly going over the past, taking a somber pleasure in analyzing it, is escaping into unreality quite as surely as the one which goes back to its brighter pages. For the center of gravity of a person's life to be behind him is the opposite of true living, which is a march forward. Thus a person's existence becomes sterile and incapable of providing solutions for his problems.

And then there is flight into the future. Escaping into the future, constantly making plans, is another form of flight into dreams, another way of escaping from the imperfections of the present. In its extreme form it becomes what is called the flight of ideas. Thought follows thought in such rapid succession, jumping continually ahead, that they become ineffective, leading to no sustained action.

I myself used to have a tendency toward living in the future. I was always forming fresh projects which seemed to me to be finer than what I was engaged upon at the time. My wife, on the other hand, lived in the past. She only really enjoyed a journey after it was over, when she could be certain that no unforseen event would spoil it. Happily, we have met together in the present, to live truly together.

Living with God means living the present hour which he gives us, putting our whole heart into what he expects of us in that hour, and leaving the past and the future to him, to whom they belong.

I wish now to record a case which shows that even accidents may sometimes, medically speaking, have their origin in personal problems. Many accidents are the result of alcoholism, a factor whose role is obvious. But in this case there is a more subtle psychological cause.

Freud recalls that the Romans would withdraw from an undertaking if they stumbled on leaving the house, considering it a bad omen. He rightly maintains that this so-called superstition conceals a profound knowledge of the laws of the unconscious. A false step or an awkward movement does not only result from inattentiveness because of an inner conflict, or from a lack of self-control, but also very often betrays the secret opposition of the unconscious to the projects of the conscious, and represents a symbolic act of sabotage on the part of the unconscious.[1]

Octave is a young man of weak will and lymphatic temperament, whose development has been inhibited by the authoritarianism and coldness of his family upbringing. In the evening at home the father reads his newspaper, the mother knits, each in his or her own corner, and the hours go by without a word of conversation being exchanged. Octave seeks in vain for some response to his need for affection.

Having started work in a large concern, he attaches himself to the first man who knows how to speak to his heart. This colleague, who is older than he, and a homosexual, finds him a defenseless victim. This is the beginning of a liaison which becomes ever more demanding. Dominated by his close friend, Octave drifts further and further away

[1]Sigmund Freud, *The Psychopathology of Everyday Life*, trans. J. Strachey (London: The Hogarth Press, 1960), p. 259.

from the moral influence of his parents, and because of this becomes more and more passive in his resistance.

Every time he has a day off, he and his friend take motorcycle rides which he would like with all his heart to refuse. And the lack of understanding on the part of his parents, who grumble at him without consideration, thrusts him more firmly into the power of his colleague.

There comes a day when this inner conflict has reached the limit of endurance. As they are returning from one of their rides, he is driving the machine, and his friend is on the pillion-seat. In a moment of aberration, without his realizing properly what is happening to him, he hurls himself against a tree at the side of the road, as if he were drawn toward the obstacle.

The symbolic character of the accident is clear. Finding himself in a moral impasse, tortured by an impotent desire to rid himself of this friend who dominates him, Octave is betrayed by his unconscious into a violent solution. It is a kind of flight.

The accident, though serious, is not fatal—and successfully accomplishes its purpose. It provides the long-awaited opportunity for Octave finally to refuse to start the Sunday rides again, and for a breaking-off of the friendship.

But this does not mean that the moral problem has been solved. In fact a fierce hatred takes the place of the dangerous friendship between the two workmates. This daily war is no less destructive of the personality of Octave, who soon becomes a prey to obsessions and thoughts of suicide. He withdraws further and further into himself. He suffers from palpitations, insomnia, and increasing debility. A doctor talks to him of an "overstrained heart," gives him tonic injections, and tells him to rest.

It is in these circumstances that the young man is sent to me. I talk to him of how before God one can see oneself as one really is, and speak about oneself without any fear of being misunderstood.

By the third visit confidence is sufficiently established between us for him to be able to tell me all that is troubling him. He is no homosexual, and this is without doubt what has been aggravating the psychological and moral situation. A homosexual would have been able to accept the liaison more easily because he would have been a consenting party. Octave has not long been married, he loves his wife, and it is only his secret which has caused his depression.

From this time onward his condition rapidly improves. He smiles again, his eyes regain their old sparkle. He is no longer afraid of his onetime friend, and is able to reoccupy his place in the same office. All his hostility has gone. He is able to adopt a natural attitude toward him. This is the sign of his recovery, which is soon complete.

What struck me in this case was that he was perfectly well aware of the importance of his motorcycle accident. Right from his first visit he had dwelt upon it. But it was only later that I realized what its hidden meaning was.

If he had found God sooner, his unconscious could have been able to do without the accident, which in any case brought no real solution.

I am called to see a man who is suffering acute abdominal pain. Before I go into the bedroom his wife says to me: "I have called you without telling him. He doesn't want to have a doctor." I diagnose a hernia of a kind difficult to reduce. But my interest has been aroused by this "fear of the doctor" which his wife has mentioned, and I begin to talk more seriously with the couple. They do not get on well together, and are leading a terrible life. The deplorable nervous state of both is one of the factors in the conflict, and the conflict in its turn aggravates their nervous state. It was in the course of a violent quarrel between them that the husband "ruptured himself." I hand him over to be treated by the surgeon, but my job is not ended there. I must seek to gain the full confidence of both husband and wife to help them to resolve their conflict.

The reader will have some idea of how much might be said about flight into disease. The fact is too common and well-known for me to need to dwell on it. No one escapes it. Time and time again in my own case self-examination has shown that a sudden feeling of fatigue, a headache, or an attack of indigestion is really a trick played on me by my own unconscious. A difficulty or a disappointment had interrupted the smooth flow of my work; a difficult letter to write, a puzzling case to sort out, or a disagreeable task to be undertaken had held me up, and so my unconscious was furnishing me with a good excuse for postponing it. All functional disturbances and, *a fortiori,* all neuroses, may be seen to involve thus a secret flight into disease. This, of course, is not to say that the disease is therefore "imaginary." A serious injustice is done to people suffering from such disturbances if they are accused of inventing their troubles as an easy means of escape. The feeling of not being understood, of not having their troubles taken seriously, from which they so frequently suffer, prevents these people from coming out of their unconscious refuge. In order to be able to come out of the tiny shelter that they have built against the storms of life, they need to feel that they are understood, loved, and supported.

Just as a dream makes use of elements taken from the experience of the preceding day, and turns them into a story with a meaning, so the unconscious makes use of real functional disorders to create a disease whose underlying significance is that it is an escape. And it is because it is an escape that it fixes as a disease, appearing in the same form at every obstacle. How many women there are who have a migraine every time they receive an invitation to visit their hostile in-laws!

When one helps patients to search honestly among their childhood memories for the first manifestation of their functional disorders, a fair number of them remember their parents, who normally gave little sign of their affection, making a tremendous fuss over them the moment they were ill. The result was that soon illness seemed pleasanter than good health, and they half-consciously emphasized their smallest complaints in order to obtain those marks of the affection they thirsted for. In others, only illness could hold in check their parents' strict rule, and give them a chance of avoiding the lessons, visits, and formalities that were forced upon them.

It is very difficult to be quite fair to patients whose illness appears to be a form of flight. Generally those around them are at one moment too hard on them and at the next too soft, neither of which attitudes is just. The illness is only made worse both by weak emotionalism and by harsh reproof. In reality this habit of flight sets up a great inner struggle, between the tendency to run away and the desire to stop running away.

Here is what a former woman patient of mine writes:

Being obliged to stay in bed, and thus dependent on others for a period of several months, as the result of a serious accident, I soon realized the risk I was going to run if I remained merely passive in bed. In fact, as soon as one gets inside the hospital one's state of mind changes. Without suspecting it one assumes that one is the center of everything, of the whole world. It is *my* accident, *my* doctors, *my* nurse, *my* injections, *my* toilet, *my* meals, *my* digestion, *my* thermometer. In this way everything gradually becomes exclusive, and of the first importance. Then it is *my* case, unique of its kind, and soon everything revolves around the possessions which events have made mine, and I become something really interesting. My visitors, finally, make me believe it.

Having realized this lamentable state of mind, one fine morning I decided to change my attitude completely and to make an all-out effort to stop thinking all the time about myself. The chance soon came. In the next room there was a man seriously ill, whose groans and complaints I had often overheard, and in fact I had decided to ask to be moved to a different room. But that morning the decision I made was not that one. I no longer wanted to be a mass of egoisms, but a living being, with a mind and heart escaping out of the prison of self.

My room was full of flowers—my flowers! A regular garden; only the day before I had been given a pretty cyclamen. There slipped into my mind the thought that in the next room there were certainly no flowers—I never heard any visitor going in. So I asked the nurse to take the cyclamen to the poor lonely patient. "Yes," she told me, "it's a little old man. He has only one son, who comes to see him from time to time. He has no flowers."

He was pleased to have the flowers. He even imagined that he knew me, and sent in his thanks. From then on I felt I had a responsibility to pray for him.

I paid no more attention to his cough: it didn't worry me any more. When I heard him complaining I prayed that God would ease his pain. A few days later I heard no sound from the next room, and asked about him. He had gone out like a lamp. Near his old head the nurse had put the cyclamen which had brought a little love into his room.

One of the most distracting things in a clinic is the bells. There is a great ringing of bells, in the morning especially. There is the slow patient who keeps his finger on the button. There is the nervous woman who has slept badly, and who rings twice or thrice to make sure that someone will come quickly. There is the discreet little tinkle that is afraid to disturb, and the peremptory ring. After a little while one gets to know from the sound which patient is calling. Then there is the operating theater bell, insistent and serious, calling to their proper places the nurse, the patient, and all those who have to be present at the operation. "The theater is ready," it says, "we are waiting for you, do not keep the doctor waiting."

Then comes the sound of the rubber wheels of the trolley as it is pushed towards the elevator, muffled footsteps, low voices. One can see the relatives walking in the garden as they wait in anxious silence.

It was at this point that a new responsibility began for me: to pray for the surgeon, that God would give him understanding and guide his hand surely; for the patient, that he would grant him confidence and peace; for the relatives in the garden, that they might have hope. All this, too, was something important, and meanwhile my pain, my doctor, my injection, and all the other personal things were no longer occupying my mind. I was glad at heart, with a feeling of duty done, and the certainty that God would hear my prayers, to which I didn't fail to add: ". . . but God's will be done . . . the God of love, who knows better than I what is best for each of us."

Another vicious circle is set up in all those who become the slaves of habitual medicines. And quite often the remedy, the treatment, the stay in hospital or in a health resort are themselves forms of flight. It should be clearly understood that I am not decrying medical therapeutics, physiotherapy, or psychotherapy. It is yet another form of flight to deny oneself their valuable services.

But therapeutics can become a danger if they concentrate on symptoms and permit the avoidance of a courageous investigation to see if there are faults in a person's manner of life which he ought to make an effort to put right.

A man comes and asks his doctor for a tonic because he is run down, as if a drug could take the place of a prudent regulation of his frenzied activity to economize the energies he is overtaxing because of ambition or anxiety.

A highly strung person who is in the middle of a family quarrel and who has been unable to sleep asks his doctor for sleeping tablets.

Man's need for religion is so great that if the true one is taken from him, he makes up others for himself. There is a religion of the medicine bottle, and there are others, more naïve still. It is surprising to see how many strong characters, who reject all recourse to divine help in life's difficulties as being the relic of an outmoded past, fasten their hope of salvation on some drug simply because it is the product of scientific progress. Having been told that this progress has no bounds, that it would make it possible to conquer all disease, men have been imbued with the fallacious hope that, thanks to science, they will be able to live completely disordered lives with impunity. It is time they were reminded that health cannot be bought as a bargain.

Trousseau, one of the greatest of French clinical specialists, writes:

> Thus it is that a doctor goes on writing prescriptions in spite of himself. I have no objection if what this doctor is doing is to use medicine for the purpose of consolation—if, for example, he contents himself with restoring her peace of mind to a distracted mother. Provided he safeguards his position, this is always permissible. But if the doctor gives a medicine to a patient, who recovers a few days later, and then he attributes his patient's recovery to this medicine although it has had nothing to do with it, this is what I complain of.[2]

Trousseau's skepticism in therapeutical matters is shared at bottom by the majority of doctors, who have much less faith in medicine than the public, the nurses, or the pharmacists. I wonder how many doctors there are who when they fall ill take as much in the way of medicine as they would prescribe for one of their patients.

It is not my intention to suggest that the reformation of our patients' lives can take the place of the prescription of medicine. But neither is it true that the latter, which is the easier of the two, can take the place of the former.

Many doctors have complained about abuses in pharmaceutical advertising. Quite apart from direct advertising to the public at large, the amount of advertising to the medical profession is unbelievable. Vincent has some very useful things to say on this subject in his book *Vers une médecine humaine*.[3] My old teacher, Professor Roch, compiled a list of the items he received in the course of three months. There were 20 small gifts of various kinds (pencils, notepaper, calendars, etc.), 101 free samples, 20 letters, 96 free periodicals, and 363

---

[2]René Dumesnil, *L'Âme du médecin*, Collection "Présences" (Paris: Plon, 1938), p. 88.
[3]Collection "Esprit" (Paris: Aubier).

catalogues, folders, cards, and brochures. One can imagine the situation had he returned all the free-sample coupons attached to these items. "All this must cost a great deal," he said, "much more, I think, than the value of the patent medicines I have allowed myself to be led into prescribing in any three months of my career."[4]

The accounts of the Scholastic Insurance Fund of the Canton of Geneva showed that in 1937 its pharmaceutical expenses exceeded those of 1936 by 4,000 francs, although the sum paid out in respect to medical fees had gone down by nearly 18,000 francs over the same period. These pharmaceutical expenses, compared with those of 1925, showed an increase of 51 per cent!

Recently I found in a free magazine sent by one of the most reputable drug houses in the world an article on the treatment of pruritus. The author suggested to doctors no less than forty of his firm's products. He added naïvely: "The number of therapeutical methods is perhaps a little confusing. . . ."

In making these remarks I am not intending to condemn the use of medicines. I prescribe them myself, and I am of the opinion that some naturists, carried away by their polemical fervor, go too far in excluding the resources of pharmacy. But the best therapeutists, those who know their *materia medica* best, have not ceased to protest against the widespread abuse of drugs in our day, quite apart from drug addictions properly so called. This abuse is, it seems to me, but one consequence of the scientific paganism and the moral regression of the modern world, as well as the weakening of the professional ideal in a large number of doctors.

The abuse of medicine brings us to that of stimulants, which is always a form of flight. Naturally it is chiefly those who suffer from weak nerves who seek in this artificial stimulus a deceptive compensation for their distress in face of life's difficulties. Occasionally it is poverty: A cup of black coffee is an easy means of hiding the weakness due to undernourishment. The habit of taking stimulants soon becomes uncontrollable, and takes away one's pleasure in normal meals. In some people this process goes so far that they take scarcely anything else. I know a young, high-strung girl who is in conflict with her father. She almost lives on strong tea, which she drinks from morning till night. Naturally, she is constantly ill, in spite of the efforts of the doctors. If she does not admit her toxic habit to them, it is because she is afraid that they will deprive her of it, and she is doubtful whether she has the strength to give it up.

It is unnecessary for me to deal at length with the more serious addictions to narcotic drugs, the harmful effects of which are well known.

The same is true in the case of alcoholism. Statistics in plenty could be quoted from any of the journals published by temperance organizations. We know the effect of alcoholism on the mental health of our population. It directly occasions almost one quarter of the admissions of men for treatment by our psychiatric services, and more than a quarter of the psychopaths admitted are the descendants of drunkards.

The part played by alcohol in hospitalization is equally important. "A third of our patients," writes Professor Roch, following upon an inquiry conducted in his hospital in Geneva, "would not have entered hospital if they had not been alcoholics." Alcohol, in fact, prepares the way for many illnesses—to say nothing of accidents!

Finally, there is the effect of alcohol on the mental health of the population. In Geneva, 37 per cent of the divorces granted over a period of ten years were due to alcoholism. More than 30 per cent of the juvenile delinquents sent to Swiss reformatory schools were the children of alcoholics.

Though ordinary drunkenness is on the decline, there is a great increase in the kind of alcoholism prevalent in fashionable society, particularly among women.

All this is so well known that I need not dwell on it.

I treat a woman who is suffering from disorders attendant upon the change of life, showing the symptoms typical of Basedow's disease. I give her a course of diiodotyrosine, but at the same time I pursue my investigations into her moral condition. The whole of her childhood has been lived under the shadow of her father's drunkenness. All her brothers and sisters are high-strung. And her married life is poisoned in its turn by her husband's alcoholism and all the material poverty and moral conflicts it brings in its train.

I then see the husband. He is full-blooded, and suffers from high blood pressure, an enlarged liver, mild glucosuria, and an aortal systolic murmur. Naturally, I forbid him to take alcohol, and put him on an almost vegetarian diet. But I well know that this will scarcely be effective if I limit myself to the negative aspect of my task. I must apply myself to gaining his confidence, taking an interest in his home and his job, and help him to regain confidence in himself and realize the kindly qualities that lie asleep in his heart. It is not long before there is a change in him. The matrimonial conflict is resolved, and the signs of goiter in his wife rapidly mend.

Alcoholism is not, if I may put it so, a primary problem, but a secondary one, a flight, a compensation for secret distress. This is why it rarely gives way before moral exhortation. The organizations which have had some measure of success against it, such as Alcoholics Anonymous, the Salvation Army, the Good Templars, and others, aim at the restoration of the whole person and of his attitude to life.

One day a young lady came to see me. Right away she laid before me the problem of her life. As a governess in America, she had taken a doctor's advice to drink port "to pep her up" while convalescing from a slight illness. This inclination toward drinking had gone on growing until it had become a slavery from which she could not tear herself. What interested me was not the drink problem in itself, but the reason for which she had taken to drink. There are many people who take a little alcoholic drink during convalescence and yet do not become alcoholics as a result.

We had two long talks, but with no result. I was somewhat discouraged. I had the feeling that I ought to see her a third time, and I prepared for this final talk by devoting myself to a good hour's meditation. I was worried because I could not see what I ought to do. She came to my house, and after half an hour's conversation we were still in complete uncertainty. I then suggested that we should pray together in silence before God. In the silence an idea came very vividly into my mind: her mother. The subject had never been mentioned in our conversations. I said to her: "Your mother." She seemed most surprised, and said that her mother was a saintly woman, against whom she had no complaint at all. That was all: She went. I was disappointed.

But that same evening I had a telephone call from her. "That's it!" she said, and to my astonishment went on. "It was while I was going down the stairs from your apartment that suddenly the light broke in on me, as if a veil had been torn away. I saw that I have always borne a grudge against my mother for being a saintly woman, because her saintliness put me to shame. I saw that I had become a governess in order to have a chance to go abroad and get far away from her example, because it hurt me to have her near me. Over there in America the Atlantic Ocean was not enough to separate me from my mother, and unconsciously I dug a moral ditch between her and me by means of drink. . . . When I got home today I threw my arms around my mother's neck and asked her to forgive me for all this, and I have been set free from my passion for port."

What has just been said about alcohol could be applied to all other addictions. They are the visible symptoms of personal moral problems such as feelings of inferiority, shyness, idleness, sexual difficulties, and weak will. Thus one cannot help a person to free himself from his addiction without going back into its secret causes.

This is no easy task! Any doctor could tell of those gamblers who are the victims of an overindulgent and luxurious upbringing. Ill-prepared for life, incapable of getting down to regular work, they try to compensate for their feeling of inferiority by means of the popularity one wins by spending lavishly and elegantly following the fashion.

In this way they soon run through all their money, and experience hard times which are only made worse by their illusory attempts to make money by gambling.

They go on spending more and more on gambling, becoming more and more incapable of work, incurring debts, and hoping all the time that their luck will change. They isolate themselves morally, and this saps what little willpower they have left.

Mention must be made now of what may be called "noble flights." Addictions are not the only form of flight. Often some of the best things we do in this world are an escape.

I am thinking of art and of science. I know some scientists whose devotion to their work is wonderfully conscientious and fruitful. Nevertheless their work is a form of escape, compensation for a family life which is not a success. I am reminded of a man who told me that his life began when he went from his house to his artist's studio, and that it stopped again, in a sort of parenthesis, whenever he locked up his studio. How many studios and laboratories act in this way as an escape-world where we try to forget the reality outside which we do not know how to cope with?

The idea of flight may lie at the origin of the finest careers. An unaccepted disappointment in love may be the true cause of a vocation to devoted social work. But such a vocation will always carry a certain bitterness in it, because its origin lies less in a positive call than in an escape, an attempt to forget a failure.

I cannot close the list without referring to the most troublesome flight of all—flight into religion. The religious life itself can be an escape; an escape into a little mystic chapel which is like an island cut off from the world, where one can hide in order to escape the world and its wounds, to wallow in a passive enjoyment that is pointless and out of contact with reality. It is possible also to use the active and intellectual side of religion as an escape. I know myself how I have taken pleasure in theological arguments at which my mind was more flatteringly successful than it was in tackling the practical, concrete problems of my life.

Ariane is a nervous, agitated, voluble patient, who has filled several pages with notes so as to forget nothing of what she wants to ask me. She is constantly analyzing her own reactions, overtaxes her strength in all sorts of activities, and suffers from all kinds of indispositions.

She has been burdened since childhood with an inferiority complex, and this has made her moody, jealous, anxious, and willful. She lost her father before she was twenty, and had to cope with the consequent financial difficulties, taking upon her own shoulders the business he ran, although she had no experience whatever. A disappointment in love added further to the disquiet already set in motion by these various factors and a fair number of others as well.

A few years ago she underwent a religious conversion. It was real and profound, and helped her especially to solve certain sexual difficulties.

But into the Christian vocation which her conversion led to, she transferred her need to indulge in feverish activity, which is a form of psychological escape. To her already overloaded timetable she added a continuous round of church meetings and religious discussions which did nothing to bring her peace. Her mother chides her for overtiring herself, but she feels that her mother simply does not understand her Christian vocation. I am the last one to fail to recognize that she is doing devoted and useful work; she has really been used by God to help all sorts of people. Nevertheless her nervous instability is a handicap to her spiritual witness. She feels this, and it hurts her. It only makes her worry and analyze herself all the more.

Christianity, lived at its deepest level, is thoroughly realistic. In Ariane there is a trench dug between dream and reality, between her busy life and her immediate personal problems: her family and her work. When at last she introduces some order into the more material side of her life, when she finds through faith how to be disciplined in her work and to take a real interest in it, she has won a spiritual victory greater than any she achieved through the whole of her former religious activity.

I talked at length about her with her own doctor, a man of deep faith, who has gone on helping her through many crises and difficulties in this hard school of reality. She has given up many of the activities in which she thought herself indispensable; she has taken up studies aimed at equipping her better to carry on her special line of business; she has begun to take a quite new interest in her work; she has made friends with competitors; and she has seen her nervous health improving.

9

Overwork and Idleness

I have just been speaking of activity. This brings me to one of the most important personal problems in medicine, that of overwork. Everyone is aware of this, and the blame is put upon the development of the modern world, with its hectic succession of councils, committees, associations, assemblies, and enterprises. Problems are passed endlessly back and forth, no real solution being found because people are in too much of a hurry to do anything properly. Modern Western society is dominated and governed by noise, newspapers, radio, and speed, so that men have lost the sense of inner meditation, of mature reflection, and thoughtful action. But all this feverish activity is also a form of flight, by means of which men are trying to cover up the unease in their hearts, their spiritual emptiness, their defeats, and their rebellion.

A disciplined life in all spheres is one of the important conditions of physical and psychic health. Every day doctors have to deal with people who are worn out and unable to stand up to the life they lead. They generally assert that it is impossible to alter the way they live, and sincerely believe that their overwork is the product of circumstances, whereas it is bound up with their own intimate problems. It is ambition, fear of the future, love of money, jealousy, or social injustice that makes men strive and overwork, invent all sorts of unnecessary tasks, keep late hours, take too little sleep, take insufficient holidays, or use their holidays badly. Their minds are overtense, so that at night they cannot sleep and by day they doubly fatigue themselves at their work.

There seems to be a law of inertia in the psychological and physiological sphere, as there is in the realm of matter. On the one hand, a person who is run down may retain for a long time the appearance of health, while the balance of his strength is definitely in deficit. And on the other hand, when improvement in his condition begins he does not at first feel any amelioration. He retains a deceptive look of exhaustion which has to do largely with the destruction of his self-confidence. There is a sort of deferment of effect in both directions. It is as difficult to make a person who is overtaxing himself understand that the strength he thinks he has at his disposal is no longer anything but a facade as it is to make him realize, when he has cracked under the strain, that he could now take up some form of activity again, although he feels himself to be still in a state of exhaustion. This is doubtless one of the mechanisms of the cycloid conditions that are so frequent in neurotic subjects. Their alternations remind one of the discharge of a siphon which gives nothing during the long period while it is filling up, then suddenly empties itself as soon as it is full.

Francoise is a nervous, emotional patient. Her vitality is not great; she has an artistic temperament; and she suffers from periodical crises of depression. She imposes a strain of overwork on herself which her fragile constitution cannot stand. The doctors have advised her to lead a less tiring life, and sent her on rest cures, but without getting her to discipline her life—which is what she really needs.

She explains to me that this is not possible. Her responsibilities are considerable. She is the wife of a manager of a large hotel, and has to be always on tap, welcoming guests, supervising the staff, attending functions, going to bed late, and getting up early. She has to help her husband, of course, but when one looks further into the matter one finds that he does not actually require her to be as zealous as she is. In fact, she spends hours dashing between the kitchen and the linen room, the reception desk and the laundry, without method or real necessity, in short, "running round in circles."

Whence comes this irresistible urge to activity? I understood when she told me her life-story. She owes her nervous state, first, in part to the suffering she underwent in childhood because of the conflict between her parents and then their divorce. She was greatly attached to them both, and felt as if she were being torn in half between them. And then she had not received the affection her sensitive nature needed, for she claimed the affection of both of them at once. One small detail illustrates this clearly: The approach each year of Christmas and the New Year causes her acute distress. These festivities are painful to her, and she finds no pleasure in giving presents then, although at any other time she enjoys doing so. I ask her of course if this has anything to do with a protest against the passage of time, against the idea of growing old which these festivals suggest. She says not, adding: "I realize now that it is because it hurt me that other children should have family festivities, whereas I only felt my parents' separation more acutely at that time, when I should have liked to see them together."

But now we come, I think, to the chief cause of this patient's overwork. She became engaged when still quite young, doubtless a little in order to find at last the affective support which she had so much missed. During the period of her engagement her parents were ruined financially. It was terribly hard for this sensitive girl to have to tell her fiancé this. She was touched when her fiancé accepted the news generously and only loved her the more for it. But she had the feeling that in a way she had robbed him. A tremendous sense of inferiority toward him had taken possession of her since that day: she owed him everything. Even today she feels that she has nothing which she does not owe to her husband, and a need to repurchase the generosity of her husband by means of hard work, a life of labor, had dominated her whole existence. The more generous her husband was with her, and the more he urged her to take things easy, the more she tended to show her gratitude to him by her material activity. In her heart she had never yet really accepted the financial inequality between herself and her husband, and it had oriented her mental outlook toward a mainly material attachment to him. She was always trying to be a kind and zealous employee, not seeing that she could demonstrate her affection for him on a quite different level—that of spiritual collaboration with him.

The proof of this is to be seen in the fact that outside her work she found herself ill at ease with her husband, and that if they went traveling she would invite some relative or friend to come with them, when he would have liked nothing better than to be alone with her.

You can guess what I prescribed—a little "honeymoon" for the two of them, married couple of long standing though they were. In this way they would have a chance to talk to each other at leisure of the things hidden deep in their hearts, and say all the things they had not said to each other for twenty years. They would discover how much they really loved each other, and how they could show their love for each other quite simply, without Francoise needing to overwork to demonstrate her love for him.

Pride plays a large part in all these problems of overwork.

"When one wants a cow to give good milk," a doctor once said, "one does not make it do anything but eat and rest and watch the trains go by." There are many young mothers who do not know how to curtail in the slightest degree their feverish activity during the nursing period. They soon wean their children on the grounds that "they haven't enough milk," when God's purpose for them would no doubt be that they should dedicate themselves to this vocation of nursing. I am reminded of a young mother who was filled with happiness at having her first baby. When we talked together about the way she should organize her life, she very soon saw that it was her pride as a housewife, and not the demands she ascribed to her husband, that prompted the ardor with which she went about the job of keeping her house spick and span. To employ a domestic servant would have been too expensive, but it was her pride again which prevented her asking help from her mother, who would have been quite glad to assist her.

Equally well known is the intense mental overwork to which ambitious parents can submit their children, at the very age when some part of their energy ought to be reserved for physical exercises and for the mysterious and delicate work of growing up. Their pride makes them drive their children to pursue studies for which they are not fitted, or overload their timetables with music lessons for which they have no talent.

Many adolescents endanger their health by sacrificing hours that ought to be spent in sleep to their passion for television or aimless reading. And many people spend hours reading countless magazines and novels, or indulging in secret crazes, hours which could be better employed in activities that would build up the health of both body and mind.

There are more intellectual and spiritual gluttons than one might think—that is to say, people who make excessive and undisciplined use even of the best things. I am thinking at the moment of a friend with whom I had conversations over a period of several months. He was a Jew. He was seeking Christ. But our long discussions were getting us nowhere. One day he came back to see me and told me he had found Christ. He had met a Christian who had simply told him that he was an intellectual glutton. Examining his conscience, he had suddenly seen that his inexhaustible religious discussions, however interesting they might be, were nothing but a kind of intemperance, and that they were blocking the road to his conversion.

I have heard many educators, doctors, and parents denouncing the excessive indulgence of the young in sport. But if we are to judge by the results, their warnings do not seem to have much effect. The same applies here as to every other problem of indiscipline: Exhortation and advice given by others is of no avail. Real reforms will only be brought about by people who through their own personal victories reform their own lives.

I have seen many young people now who have put an end to excessive physical exertion in games, not because of pressure from parents or a doctor, but as a result of a personal religious experience. When a young man decides to put his life at the service of Jesus Christ, and to seek in prayer in God's presence to know all the changes he must make in his life, he perceives underlying motives that have been unconsciously inspiring his passions. He sees, for example, that his pursuit of success in sport has been hiding a longing to appear as a hero, which will find its true satisfaction in a dedicated and disciplined life.

Elisabeth is a young woman with a somewhat tainted heredity, and a sanguine-choleric temperament, who comes to consult me about arthritic pains. Together we find several points which ought to be corrected in her mode of life, her diet, her home too near the lake, and so on. But when we have a "quiet time" together she tells me that she has also known for a long time that she is overstraining herself in ski competitions. She sees too that the cause of this is a need not to be inferior to her brothers who are expert skiers and are always boasting of the fact in front of her. She sees that now that she has attained inner liberation she will no longer be afraid of this particular inferiority as regards her brothers, and will be able in the future to do just as much skiing as will be good for her health instead of doing so much that it is prejudicial to her.

Another example, from a medical student's letter to me:

Between the ages of twelve and sixteen I had pleurisy three times. As a result I felt myself to be inferior to my comrades. To compensate, I wanted to show, even where my health was concerned, that I was nevertheless quite strong. So, being good at games, I tried to demonstrate it in the field. That was what caused my last relapse, pleurisy with extravasation. . . . After several courses of treatment I learned a little more sense. But still I kept starting to overdo the sport again, and it was always as a compensation for my feelings of inferiority towards other people. Relapses due to indiscipline on my part have only disappeared since I gave my life to God. Since then it has been directed, not by ambition any more, but by God.

In the course of my work as a family doctor I have been struck by the number of women I have seen who make themselves the slaves of their families, either out of fear of blame or for sentimental reasons. Frequently husbands are unaware of what is involved in housework, and wives find it difficult to give them an account of how they have spent their day. When the husband comes in from his office, where the work is not always fatiguing, he does not think of helping his wife, and lets her serve him. It is as much her fault as his. She likes to feel indispensable. Up first, and last to bed, she has an ill-defined task which is never finished. Wives are sentimental enough also to spoil their sons, to make beds for daughters big enough to do it themselves, who later on will be embarrassed in life through not having learned to help those around them.

We shall give the name of Laura to a patient who, if I may put it so, is the victim of her own excellent health. Of sanguine temperament, very active, managing everything in her home and family, spending herself without reserve in good works, never sparing herself, and never tired, she has passed her sixtieth year, almost without having seen a doctor. She has never given a thought to her health, her diet, or to the passing years which might have made her shorten sail a little. Even now her family has the greatest difficulty in persuading her to come and see me. It is as if she felt it humiliating to have to have treatment.

A moral factor has broken in upon this easy, happy life: for the last two years she has been very worried about one of her sons.

She has had spasms of angor and paroxysmal tachycardia—a sort of alarm bell. I also find plethora, hypertrophy of the liver, and high blood pressure.

What she must do is to heed the warning, to reckon henceforward with her state of health, to regulate her diet, moderate her activity, and to fast periodically. These all demand a great inner change in a person full of vitality, who has been, in short, proud of her health. Prescriptions will not be sufficient if there is not a full commitment of the heart. And then only faith can bring to her maternal anxiety the relief she needs if she is to bear the distress caused by her son.

Fatigue does not come only from what one does, but also from the way in which one does it. If one does one's work in a state of feverish tension that betrays fear of the future, a feeling of inferiority or of rebellion, one expends ten times the energy in doing it. One of my patients, obliged for reasons of economy to give up her season ticket on the tram, consulted me because she found having to travel on foot so exhausting. Questioning her more closely I perceived that, with her worries and her fear of the world, she walked with bent head, straining, almost running, looking at nothing, taking no pleasure in nature, not knowing how to breathe, when these walks could have been a real relaxation between periods of work.

There are many other psychical causes of fatigue: the way so many people are ashamed of admitting that they are tired and should take a rest; a disappointment not accepted, a psychological complex not sorted out, a conflict poisoning a person's life and sapping his strength. And then all the physical causes that I have referred to: errors of diet, intoxication, constipation, or being a square peg in a round hole as regards one's occupation.

Of course iron must be given to a chlorotic, liver to a person suffering from pernicious anemia, adrenaline or thyroid extract in endocrine disorders, calcium in cases of mineral deficiency, and holidays in cases of overwork. But this ought not to excuse us from carefully seeking to discover the personal problems which almost always lie behind fatigue.

Too often we forget that life is like a great account book, with its "liabilities" and "assets," its receipts and expenditures. Fatigue represents the deficit on the balance sheet, resulting either from an insufficiency of receipts or from an excess of expenditure. No tonic could ever take the place of the essential task of ensuring that a person's strength-account is made to balance once more.

Delicate people, convalescents, chronic invalids, and old people must accept a reduction in their expenditure of strength in proportion to their slender receipts.

This is not to say that a life directed by God must be free from fatigue. Jesus himself knew fatigue, as did St. Paul, and many other men of the Bible. God may call us to perform tasks which are beyond our strength. This may be one of the aspects of the Cross. But a person who is fatigued must ask himself whether it is because he has obeyed God or because he has disobeyed him.

Christ was able, before the extreme fatigues of the Passion, to go and rest with his disciples in Caesarea Philippi. Knowing how to rest in time, and to rest properly, is one of the essential elements in the proper regulation of one's life.

One morning, after weeks of hard spiritual work, I felt tired. While my wife and I were having a quiet time together, the thought came to me that if God wanted me to rest, he would show me that this was so. A few moments later, I met an American colleague who told me that at the same moment the thought had come to him to advise me to go and have three days' rest. An hour later we were setting out in our car.

To rest under God's guidance, that is the first condition of really effective rest. Everyone knows the mistakes people make in this

sphere. There are those who tire themselves out more on holiday than
they do during all the rest of the year, dashing round museums,
visiting towns, climbing one mountain after another, devouring dis-
tances, sitting up till dawn in gaming rooms and dance halls, and
indulging in all sorts of gastronomical excesses!

In a recent article, Dr. Boigey of Vittel denounced "the pathological damage and disadvantages of the honeymoon . . . with its im-
promptu arrangements, put into effect by people already fatigued by
incessant sacrifices to Venus."[1]

Speaking of God's purpose for the normal life of man, Carton
formulates what he calls "the law of the three rests." First there is the
annual rest, the example of which is given us by Nature, which rests
during winter. It is possible that winter holidays are more beneficial
than those taken in summer. At the time when insolation is such that
we are deprived of part of the sun's energy, a few weeks in the
mountains—in the snow with its strong ultra-violet irradiations—
would without doubt be the best kind of holiday, and perhaps the day
will come when the educational authorities will realize this. As early
as the fifth century B.C. Hippocrates was recommending the reduction
of activity and of food during the winter—he even prescribed only
one meal a day!—in order to conform with the law of nature.

Next is the weekly rest, laid down in the Bible. Here again it is
scarcely necessary to point out the constant misuse of Sunday, a day
on which many people fatigue themselves even more than on week-
days.

Lastly there is the nocturnal rest, the importance of which was
understood by Christ himself, and which our civilization has so dras-
tically reduced with the perfecting of artificial lighting.

Many people who are sincerely seeking to follow the will of God,
feel that they must modify their habits as regards the hour at which
they go to bed and get up. Countless cases of insomnia are due to the
loss of the habit of sleep simply through the keeping of late hours
during years of overwork or self-indulgence. One of those vicious
circles that are so common in medicine comes into play in the matter
of sleep. Those who do not get enough sleep are fatigued, and those

[1] *Monde médical,* 1939, p. 622.

who are fatigued get to the point where sleep eludes them. The more tired they are, the less they sleep; and the less they sleep, the more tired they become. Sleep can come only through a process of re-education. The use of soporifics also sets up a vicious circle, one that is even more difficult to break. One gets so used to using them that one can no longer sleep without them.

I need not stress the part played by worry, interior and exterior conflicts, temptations to impurity, fear, and ambition in this question of sleep.

I can remember my astonishment and even my indignation as a doctor, on hearing a lady remark, a few years ago, that insomnia was a symptom of sin. My experience of these last few years has led me to realize how much truth there is in this assertion. Doubtless there are exceptions, nor is the relation always direct; and it would be wrong to suggest that a person who sleeps well is less sinful than one who suffers from insomnia. But I cannot keep count of the number of patients I have seen rediscover the habit of sleep as a result of the transformation of their lives brought about by submission to Jesus Christ.

It is the quality of sleep which is changed as much as anything. Here is what one such patient writes: "Sleeping less, I rest more, because my nights are absolutely calm now that my life belongs entirely to God. I sleep for about seven hours. Often less. I have learned to sleep in the afternoon when I have a moment's opportunity. My conviction is that God gives us complete directions for our physical life if we put ourselves entirely in his hands."

The alimentary canal also needs a daily rest. "Nighttime," Thooris writes, "ought at all ages to be a time of rest for the stomach as well as for the muscles."[2]

And then if one wishes to have an effective quiet time in the morning, it is important to prepare for it by going to bed in the right state of mind. How often, excited by the events of the day and the comradeship of the evening, we prolong futile conversations, stay up with some friend, engage in tasks which ought to be fitted into the

[2] *Médecine morphologique* (Paris: Doin, 1937), p. 248.

daytime, or immerse ourselves in unhealthy reading or selfish reveries?

Finally, whether it is taken at night, or in those brief moments with which many people, if they took thought, could break up their day, rest is one of the essential conditions for easing physical and moral tension. Few people know how to rest without doing anything, in real and complete muscular and mental relaxation. Few people, in particular, know how to shake off their cares and their secret worries. Some even seem to want to hold on to them, taking an unconscious pleasure in turning them over in their hearts.

It is surprising to note the extent to which merely once making a clean breast of all one's fears and feelings of guilt can bring unexpected calm and relaxation of tension.

The opposite of flight into overwork is flight into passivity, withdrawal, negativism, and idleness.

Laziness has considerable importance in medicine. Many people, even apparently very active people, are lazy in that they exert themselves only as much as they find agreeable. Thus, for example, while engaging in intense intellectual activity they neglect, from laziness, all forms of physical exercise.

It is laziness which prevents so many people from rising early so as to have enough time for prayer before the day's work and entering upon it zealously and joyfully. It is laziness which ties up so many people in unsociable, narrow, distant lives, deprived of the continual social exchange which is the law of human life.

Lack of exercise is one of the commonest physical shortcomings. Its consequences on the health of the body are well known: obesity and plethora of the sedentary.

This is all so obvious that I will not go further here into what can be found in any book by the naturists on the importance of physical exercise, respiration—which, properly practiced, is one of the best sources of energy for the weakened organism—swimming, sunbathing, and fresh air. I shall confine myself to repeating that walking and gardening provide the best physical exercise because they are the most natural and involve a measure of communion with nature. How

OVERWORK AND IDLENESS [121

many sick people need, more than any other treatment, to leave the town and go and live in the country, there to cultivate a little garden whose fruit and vegetables they will eat, and to do their shopping on foot!

There are those who suffer with their nerves because of overwork. Restless, incoherent, always tired, but always in motion, they both create and suffer from the atmosphere of feverish agitation which surrounds them. But there are others whose nerves suffer because of their inaction. Inhibited by some fear, crushed by an overbearing wife or husband, or prevented from following their vocation by their parents, they seem as if they were being slowly poisoned by the vitality they are unable to use up in useful activity. It is as if they were going round and round a closed circuit. What they need is to be shown some outlet on the world. It is not by making them rest that one can combat their nervousness, but by providing some meaning for their lives by means of useful work.

They remind me of the locomotives in a station, noisily letting off the steam they are not using. Their functional disorders are safety-valve reactions, a means of expending unused energy.

I have before me the record of a patient, full of vitality, who exhibited numerous functional disorders—dysmenorrhea, signs of anemia, acrocyanosis, and digestive troubles. Impulsive, undisciplined, and capricious, she undertook nothing methodically and persevered with nothing. She worked in an amateurish sort of way as far as her whims allowed, so that her life was practically useless, bearing no relation to the physical and moral strength she was endowed with.

The life led by our ancestors was a hard one. Civilization has made ours easy, and this has not been to the benefit of our health.

I shall give the name of Boris to a young man who exhibited functional disorders with anxiety, breathlessness, crises of acute asthenia, and slight catatonia. He was sent to me by a colleague who suspected that there was an underlying moral cause for all these nervous disorders. I found he had a LSM temperament, a state of neurovegetative unbalance with bradycardia of 58, and—paradoxically—slight exophthalmos, and Graefe's sign.

He had in general a passive nature, and had always avoided effort, in accordance with his temperament, An upbringing as a rich only child rather spoiled by his mother, had not, of course, corrected this tendency to indolence. He found schoolwork difficult, and did not need to be pressed to break off his studies and enter his father's business. But here too he was unenthusiastic about work, and he found it easy to look upon his tendency to day-dreaming as a sign of moral superiority. He despised commerce, although it had ensured an easy life for him. This contempt, moreover, was a projection of his negative attitude toward his father, who clearly represented the authority to which his uncommunicative, independent, and indolent nature was opposed. He felt uneasy about this life without real effort, and was dominated by feelings of inferiority which aggravated his moral separation from his parents.

In actual fact what brought a swift and wonderful improvement in his nervous state was a real discipline of religious practice, and a *rapprochement* with his father. He got up early in the morning to go to Mass, and to have a time of quiet afterward in church, preparing for the activities of the day in the sight of God.

But above all, Boris had realized that in breaking off his studies he had given way to his temperamental tendency to easy passivity, and that a real change in his life demanded a fresh effort in this respect. He had realized that his contempt for business was, at least in part, the projection of his dissatisfaction with himself and of the feeling of inferiority which he had as a result of having too readily abandoned his studies

An increasingly active life contributed to an improvement in his nervous state.

Order can of course be a personal problem, when it is so rigid and fussy that it is thought of as the most important thing in life. But disorder is also a problem, and one that is particularly harmful to the atmosphere of a person's life. I know something about this myself. I have a lot to do in this respect because I am untidy by nature. One day I saw that I had no right to suggest to others that they should put their lives in order when I myself had so many cupboards in disorder, letters unanswered, and unread medical journals piling up. When I said something of this to my son, he told me that he would pray that God would give me the strength and perseverance necessary for this great work. But on the following day he came back to talk to me about it. He had thought that he would help me even more by tidying up his own room to encourage me. Over a period of several months I gave up a number of other activities in order to get myself up to date, and it was a great liberation.

Closely related is the discipline of cleanliness, which is a problem for many young people, and which has great importance for physical and moral health. Every doctor has had those patients who refuse to allow themselves to be examined without admitting the reason, which is that they did not expect an examination, and have not been able to prepare for it by unaccustomed measures of personal hygiene. Lack of cleanliness is often symptomatic of moral disorder, and may be associated with an impure heart and immorality.

I want to say a word or two on silence. The effect on the nerves of modern man of immoderate use of the radio, of pneumatic drills, and of the noise of our big cities is well known. But modern man is afraid of silence, simply because of all the personal problems in his life which worry him and which he would like to forget. I know a theologian who had a serious secret problem and who always had his radio switched on when he was in his study, in order to avoid the silence in which the drama going on inside him became too acute.

Indiscipline is closely related to laziness and disorder. Charles was a man whom I got to know while he was unemployed. He had lost his job as a result of illness, and his heart was full of bitter resentment against social injustice. We had quite a lively discussion.

But three months later Charles, still unemployed, was in my consulting room again. He told me what had happened to him. During a walk in the mountains he had suddenly thought himself lost. At that moment the memory of the evening spent with me, and especially the memory of the serene joy of another unemployed man, had come to him. He had started to pray. His adventure ended without mishap, but as he came back down the mountain he had thought seriously over his own life. He was dissatisfied with himself and wanted to live the clear, confident life of which we had spoken. But he did not know how to go about it.

I told him what my own experience had been. Then he started to tell me of all the moral indiscipline to which the distress of unemployment had opened the door. I had a new man in front of me: no longer the victim blaming society, but the sinner acknowledging his own guilt. While he laid his faults before me one by one, I considered how great a moral danger the idleness of unemployment is for those who are lacking in culture and in depth of spiritual life. His wife, a militant Communist, had a job. And he, in his long empty day, could no longer even summon up enough energy to light the fire for dinner. His wife was threatening him with divorce, and their home was nothing but an arena for violent quarrels.

When he left me he said that he intended to get up early, begin his day with a period of meditation, and then take some exercise and do the housework.

His wife was astonished when, the next day at noon, she found the flat tidied up and the lunch ready.

He came back to see me and a friendship was formed between us. A few weeks later he was a quite different man, tidily dressed, disciplined, cheerful, and friendly. His home was happy and he soon found work.

At Christmastime I made the acquaintance of his wife. It was the first Christian festival she had taken part in since her childhood. She burst into tears when she heard her husband saying what God had done in his life and in his home. She made friends with my wife, and in her turn she unburdened herself to her. As she was a Catholic, my wife suggested that she should go to confession so that, in accordance with the practice of her church, she could there confess all she had just told her, and seek absolution.

One day two years later Charles came to me, very upset. He told me at once that he had been backsliding: that for some time he had given up meditation and prayer. And then temptations had come, and he had spent money which had been entrusted to him, and which he had now to pay back. He needed some money in order to get himself out of trouble. It was obvious what he had come for.

But I knew that what he really needed was a fresh experience of God's grace, rather than to get off lightly. I told him calmly: "You are going to see your employer, Charles, and to tell him what you have done."

"But that means prison!"he exclaimed.

I chanced to meet him in the street next day. He was beaming. He came toward me eagerly. He had spent a terrible night, but he had finally been able to pray. His employer had received him quite differently from what he expected, and had proposed that he should pay the money back in monthly installments. Now he really was determined to be disciplined.

10

Synthesis in Medicine

William James "imagines several Americans on the same European tour. Each will relate his memories accurately, but differently, for each will have noticed what interests him." Dalbiez, who quotes him, points out that this is a case of the "conditioning of cognitive processes by the subject's needs and affective states."[1] All thought involves choice. If, in a room, I observe an object, it seems to me that it is this object which is attracting my attention. Wishing to be scientifically objective, I try to observe it exactly. But why have I chosen this object rather than any other? It is because I am unconsciously guided by personal determining factors which are affective in kind, and in this I am necessarily being subjective.

So, as I have shown in Chapter 5, despite all his desire for scientific objectivity, the doctor examining a patient is determined more than he realizes by his own philosophy of life. Since Descartes, the philosophical concepts which hold sway in medicine have rested on a fundamental distinction between the material causes and the psychic and spiritual causes of biological phenomena. Material causes lend themselves to analytical study, to mathematical notation, and to scientific experiment. So the doctor tends to put them down as the only

[1] R. Dalbiez, *Psychoanalytical Method and the Doctrine of Freud*, trans. T. F. Lindsay (London and New York: Longmans, Green & Co., 1941), Vol. 1, pp. 97-98.

certain source of knowledge. The psychic and spiritual causes pertain to the art and the intuition of the doctor and to his personal interpretation of the case. In the cases to which I refer here, I note the concurrence of psychological and spiritual facts (personal problems) and material facts (pathological symptoms) and from this concurrence I infer a causal relationship between them. I am unable to demonstrate this relationship with the same precision with which a symptom may be related to a material cause, as for instance in the case of an anatomical change. But it is equally impossible to demonstrate that as a source of knowledge intuition is less sure than reason.

It is only a philosophical axiom—the Cartesian hypothesis—that material causality, demonstrable to reason, susceptible of experimental control in the laboratory, is the only sure source of knowledge. This hypothesis has made possible the prodigious advance of modern science. In medicine it has ensured the triumph of organicist concepts, and the systematic study of the anatomopathological lesions corresponding to each symptom and each disease. It is not necessary for me to emphasize the outstanding service that this method has rendered to medicine. Almost all progress over the last few centuries is ascribable to it. But it also has its limits: It is true in what it affirms, but false in what it denies. When, for example, it shows that the symptoms of locomotor ataxia are always accompanied by anatomical lesions of the posterior columns of the spinal cord, it is revealing a true causal relationship. But if it illegitimately goes on from there to deny that a spiritual fact, such as rebellion against God, can have any material anatomical or physiological consequences on the body, it is denying another causal relationship which is no less true.

The trouble with the anatomical method is that it does not take all the facts into account. It does not explain, for example, what the connection is between patients suffering from different diseases arising from the same cause. "Thus," Carton says, "out of a number of alcoholics subjected to the same type of intoxication—brandy, for example, taken in broadly equal quantities—one will end up with dropsy and cirrhosis of the liver, another will go mad after one or more attacks of delirium tremens, and a third will succumb to pulmonary tuberculosis. It is not unusual to find in such cases that the first patient had parents with a weakness in the liver, that the second came of neuropathic parents, and that the parents of the third were asthmatic."[2]

"The anatomical diagnosis," says De Giovanni, "is incapable of showing us why it is that a cardiac defect is manifested sometimes by the predominance of digestive disorders, sometimes by the sudden or periodical appearance of respiratory disorders, or again by that frightening irregularity in the functioning of the heart which follows upon a spasmodic or paralytic crisis, or else, finally, by those slight but continual disturbances which steadily wear the patient down."[3]

One day in the same family the mother suffers a uterine spasm, the father has diarrhea, and the maid suffers from vomiting. The doctor who concentrates exclusively on the anatomical diagnosis will stress the diversity of locale—dysmenorrhea, enteritis, gastritis. But on learning that on that day the children had left on a journey, he will intuitively make a synthesis of the cases, which are not cases of local disorders, one gynecological, another intestinal, and the third gastric, but all three emotional.

While it is readily admitted that spiritual and moral factors play a part in psychological and functional affections, which are *sine materia*, it is less willingly conceded that they can bring about anatomical and physiological modifications. What I maintain is that in the name of scientific objectivity itself we must take every factor into account, the spiritual and psychological as well as the material, in order to relate them to the symptoms which the patient is suffering.

A girl whom I shall call Isabella had suffered from serious dysmenorrhea since puberty. An operation, advice on hygiene, organotherapy, and antispasmodics had brought about a noticeable improvement. But in spite of this her menstrual periods remained so painful that she was continually preoccupied by the thought of them, and this had far-reaching repercussions on her nervous state. This no doubt hindered the cure of the dysmenorrhea.

Under the influence of her doctor she had already made real prog-

[2]Paul Carton, *Traité de médecine, d'alimentation et d'hygiène naturistes* (Brévannes, 1931), p. 126.
[3]L. Mac-Auliffe, *Les tempéraments* (Paris: Vigot, 1922), p. 29.

ress in the spiritual life. Opening her heart to Jesus Christ had enabled her to effect a reconciliation with her divorced mother with whom she had hitherto been in conflict. A friend advised her to consult me in order to see whether her spiritual life might not have an even more decisive influence on her health. For a long time she resisted the suggestion. I have seen a fair number of such patients over these last few years who have hesitated for a long time to come to see me precisely because they know my conception of medicine to be what it is. And when they do make up their minds to come, it is a sign that an important change has already come about in their attitude of life, and that they are ready to try sincerely to find out what effect their personal problems are having on their health. This development in their own attitude is without doubt more important for them than all I have to say to them.

When Isabella had put her story before me, I asked her to ask herself during her "quiet time" whether her menstrual troubles could possibly be the physiological expression of a spiritual rebellion against her lot. For God made her a woman, and revolt against her sex is a revolt against the lot God has decreed for her, and it could be a cause of dysmenorrhea. Menstruation is, in fact, a veritable symbol of the sufferings of the female sex. When a woman does not marry, the periodical pains of menstruation seem to her to be even more unjust, and her rebellion against her sex and her pain is colored by her rebellion against her enforced celibacy. So a vicious circle is set up: It is because she suffers every month that the woman is outraged against her unjust woman's lot. And it is because she has a negative attitude toward her sex and toward her periods, which are one of its attributes, that the spasmodic troubles to which they give rise are made worse.

Isabella seemed at first greatly surprised at the line I was taking.

But suddenly she exclaimed: "Of course! I *have* always rebelled against the fact that I am a woman! In every walk of life women come off worse than men! It's always the men who are right when there are family quarrels or arguments in the office, and it's always the women who suffer and have to give way. If they show any initiative they get blamed for it, whereas a man would be praised. Even in the Bible, the responsibility for the original sin is laid at their door! That's typical of the unfairness of men—they are always making excuses for themselves and putting the blame on the women. And then why must our bodies be continually making us women suffer, not only month after month, but also in order to bring children into the world, while men's bodies get off scot free, with nothing but pleasure?

"I am never so pleased as when people tell me that I ought to have been a boy. They used to say it when I was just little, and somebody said it again only yesterday at the office. It really does give me a feeling of pride and satisfaction."

Isabella was gradually becoming more thoughtful, surveying her whole life and recognizing the extent to which this rebellion against her sex had warped it. She told me how most of her gestures and actions were calculated so as to merit the compliment that she "ought to have been a boy." She had made her voice sound deeper, and adopted a brusque, tough manner; she assumed all the responsibility for running the household, and scornfully accused her brother of having a woman's character, lacking initiative and energy.

And then her self-examination went still further: her father had been a hard man, who had caused his gentle, unselfish wife much suffering. This gentleness on her mother's part irritated Isabella. She was proud of the fact that in looks she took after her father, and did all she could to accentuate the resemblance. She had always identified herself with her father, and had, so to speak, taken his place when divorce had separated him from her mother. Suddenly she saw where lay the origin of the conflict which had for so long existed between her and her mother. Her conversion had put an end to the conflict, without yet touching its essential cause. And then it was the same barrier which separated her from her sister, whom she could not stand because she had all her mother's gentleness of character. At work, too, she was in constant conflict with the most feminine of her fellow workers.

When Isabella left me that day she was determined to examine herself profoundly in her prayers to seek to discover the full extent to which this rebellion against her sex might really be rebellion against

God, and to prepare herself for a true acceptance of her sex, so that she could become herself again—a woman.

If medicine is inspired by the desire to know and obey God's will, it will aim at making women real women, and men really men.

I saw her a week later. She had spent long hours in prayer and meditation, day after day. She produced for me a whole sheaf of memories that had come back into her conscious mind. She had recalled the triumphant joy she had felt when, while still a little girl, she had won the victory in a tough fight with the most pugnacious boy in the class, and even the joy she had experienced at being severely scolded by the teacher, whom she boldly defied. There were many other details—the vigorous way she shook hands, the manner in which she mounted her bicycle, the mannish way she walked and talked, and so on.

Then she told me that a quite new desire had already been born in her heart, a longing to live at last the way God meant her to, as a woman, to act like a woman and acquire a woman's gentleness and feminine qualities. That day we prayed together, and Isabella was able to bring to God this new resolve to accept her sex.

The results on the physiological side were far-reaching. For the first time in eighteen years Isabella had a completely painless period, in spite of a sixty-mile cycle ride the day before—just the sort of thing she would formerly have avoided owing to worrying about her period being due!

Her whole attitude was transformed, to the astonishment of her workmates in the office, who asked her what had happened to her. She was now a close friend of the girls she disliked before. On the telephone she had been mistaken for one of her comrades whose voice was soft and feminine!

The physiological result has proved to be lasting. I saw her more than a year later: There had been no recurrence of the menstrual disorder.

It was quite proper that in the first place organotherapeutic preparations were prescribed for this young woman. She showed clinical signs of endocrine malfunctioning. She manifested numerous masculine morphological signs. Authors who have studied the relationship between temperament and endocrinology have stressed the significance of the secondary sexual characteristics—voice, hair, morphological ratios, skin, etc. This case confirms their views. But it shows also that these secondary sexual characteristics were the consequence of a moral attitude of opposition to her sex at least as much as they were its cause. And that is the point I wish to make here.

Endocrinology has rendered the greatest services to us. It has revealed the connection that exists between psychic tendencies and the secretions of the ductless glands. But it would be wrong to think of this connection as working in one direction only, that is to say, to look upon the glandular disorder as the organic cause, and the disorder in the character as the psychic consequence. It is in this way that many people draw from science the reassuring thought that they cannot help this or that fault of character, since it originates in a defect of the thyroid or ovary. What science establishes is the frequency of the coincidence of particular facts, for example, a sour and pessimistic outlook and hyperchlorhydria, or again, an irritable character and nervous symptoms, trembling, tachycardia, exophthalmia, increase in basal metabolism, and anatomopathological modifications of the thyroid. What science does not establish is the direction of the causal relationship between these various facts. It is an unscientific assumption of materialist philosophy which supposes that the material facts—anatomical and physiological—are the cause, and that the moral (psychological and spiritual) facts are the consequence, and not the other way about. "In every nervous disorder there is endocrinosis," wrote Léopold Lévi. But Lambert rightly adds: "Reciprocally, the psychic make-up, through the emotions, influences the functioning of the sympathetic and vagus nerves. . . . The effect of the emotions on endocrines and the autonomic nervous system explains the influence of the moral on the physical which has mystified us for so long."[4]

What, then, seems to me to be a fact is that in the biological unity we call man the anatomical, physiological, psychological, and spiritual aspects are all interdependent. What the scientific study of man ought to establish is the simultaneity of these facts, without arbitrarily

[4] Lambert, "Aux horizons de la médecine," *L'Avenir médical*, 1939, p. 39.

excluding those which belong to the realm of the spiritual, and without prejudging the direction of their causal relationship. This causal relationship seems to me to be always reciprocal, that is to say that the material facts are as much the cause as the consequence of the spiritual facts, and vice versa.

Materialist science is always seeking absolute causalities. The fact is that in biology such absolute causalities do not exist, because the living organism is a unity, all of whose elements influence each other reciprocally. In biology one cannot say, as in mathematics, "other things being equal," because the interdependence of the aspects of a living organism is such that one thing cannot change without the "other things" ceasing at the same time "being equal."

Thus, once the clinical picture has been built up, everything in it may be explained, in accordance with one's own particular philosophical standpoint, in terms of anatomy, of physiology, of psychology, or in terms of the spiritual life. All these explanations are equally true, but each is incomplete. A synthesized conception of medicine, it seems to me, must consider all the various aspects of man in regard to their reciprocal causality, in the same way as the equation of a law of equilibrium (Boyle's law is a simple example) expresses the constant relationship that exists between several variables.

"The whole consisting of body and consciousness is modifiable by organic as well as by mental factors," writes Carrel.[5]

He says, further:

The error of Descartes was to believe in the reality of these abstractions [body and soul, matter and mind] and to consider the material and the mental as heterogeneous, as two different things. This dualism has weighed heavily upon the entire history of our knowledge of man. For it has engendered the false problem of the relations of the soul and the body. There are no such relations. Neither the soul nor the body can be investigated separately. We observe merely a complex being whose activities have been arbitrarily divided into physiological and mental.[6]

I believe that the cultural crisis the world is experiencing in our day is the closing crisis of the age of materialism which was opened

[5] *Man, the Unknown* (Penguin Books, 1948).
[6] *Ibid.*, p. 118.

with that error by Descartes. A creative error, it helped make possible the prodigious growth of science and technology. But life is beyond its scope. The peoples of the world are weary of a rationalist culture, which analyzes endlessly but does not give them life and happiness. They follow men who turn intuitively to the meaning of life, to supra-rational values, to mysticism and the creative imagination.

The need of medicine is similar. It is to come back once more to an understanding of man as a living unity, complementing his conquests in the technical field with similar progress in the realm of the spirit. Much water has flowed under the bridge since Virchow could say that although he had spent his life dissecting bodies he had never found a piece of soul on his knife, and since Cabanis could say that the brain digested, as it were, the impressions it received, and organically secreted thought![7] Materialist science and materialist medicine have merely denied the fact of the soul, and they are largely responsible for the moral and spiritual regression that has taken place in the world. The present crisis is but the inevitable liquidation of the age of positivism.

I believe that the true answer to this crisis is to be found in a return to Christianity. Christ himself was constantly identifying the spiritual and the material, constantly passing from one standpoint to the other without a break, expressing the spiritual in terms of the carnal, and seeing the spiritual significance of the carnal, associating the healing of bodies with that of the soul. And even in the sacrament he instituted at the Last Supper he united the supreme spiritual reality of his sacrifice with a most carnal act—eating. He never set the soul over against the body, just as he never denied the existence of the one in favor of the other.

The Christian conception of man is thus neither a spiritualist nor a materialist monism, nor again is it a dualism. It is the concept of incarnation. In his excellent book *Le corps et l'âme*, Dr. Biot quotes the notable passage in which St. Thomas defines this doctrine, and then he quotes Péguy's remark: "The spiritual itself is carnal."[8]

I cannot omit to emphasize that there is no contradiction between

[7]E. Boinet, *Les doctrines médicales* (Paris: Flammarion, 1920), p. 94.
[8]Paris: Plon, 1938, p. 1.

this Christian conception of man and scientific determinism. To claim that the mind, the soul, and the body are but one entity is to claim that the spiritual has carnal effects and that the carnal has spiritual effects, which is quite different from saying that there are effects without causes. Where we do differ from physiological materialism is where the latter maintains that there are only material causes. We are not arguing about the fact of determinism.

For want of admitting the Christian concept of incarnation, all vitalist medical doctrines, from the naturism of Hippocrates to the archeism of Van Helmont, the animism of Stahl, and the dynamism of Barthez, have found themselves up against the insoluble problem of the relationship between soul and body. They have tried to avoid the problem by making subtle and difficult distinctions between various kinds of soul, the *pneuma* and the *psyche,* the "intelligent cause or inner direction and the experimental cause or principle of life," the soul proper and the archeus, which is its "minister," and so on.[9] Bleuler's conception, with its "psychoids," approaches these attempts to describe an intermediary between the soul and the body.

On the other hand, Christian doctrine gives us the key to a synthesis in medicine, a "medicine of the person." Man is a personal unity, in which there is a necessary and absolute interdependence between the physical, the psychical, and the spiritual.

Medicine, then, cannot arbitrarily ignore the spiritual, any more than it can ignore the psychical or the physical. The purpose of medicine is healing. Everything, therefore, that contributes to healing is proper to medicine. It cannot be denied that factors of a spiritual order may contribute to healing. They cannot in that case be dismissed by the doctor from his purview. Just as he may use radio waves without being a physicist, or inject morphine without being a chemist, so he may practice soul-healing without being a theologian. Soul-healing consists essentially in bringing souls into personal contact with Christ. From that contact come experiences which have psychic and physical consequences, and which are thus the domain of medicine.

Maeder writes: "The physician's ideal is not essentially to cure the

[9]E. Boinet, *op. cit.*, p. 24.

patient of insomnia, neuralgia, or phobias, but rather to act as the stimulator of consciences, and a trainer of men, as an animator, with a place beside the educator, the politician, the priest, the artist, and the philosopher, in the true, live meaning of the word."[10] Dalbiez, quoting him, answers him in accordance with the limitative tendencies of modern medicine: "The clinician who sets himself up as a stimulator of consciences and a trainer of men is trespassing on the domain of the educator and the moralist."[11]

Man, however, is a unity: body, mind, and spirit, which correspond to somatic medicine, psychological medicine, and soul-healing. Medicine, as I understand it, includes all three, and it is only doctrinaire prejudice which draws a line at any point through this unity.

To treat a man is to treat him, therefore, in his entirety. It no more involves neglect of his physical and psychic needs in favor of his spiritual needs, than neglect of his spiritual needs. I must emphasize this as I conclude this first part of my book. In the second part I intend to concentrate somewhat on demonstrating the physical and psychic effects of spiritual experiences, because modern medicine has been too prone to neglect them. But I do not mean to suggest in so doing that a synthesized medicine can therefore dispense with treatment on the physical and psychological side. The reciprocal causality of which I have been speaking is such that the physical and the psychological exert their influence also on the spiritual state of the patient.

Rose was a patient who came to me about acute attacks of dyspnea, the occurrence, duration, and character of which were irregular. There was no sign of bronchial disease, and no sign of cardiac insufficiency. There were, however, numerous signs of a nervous character.

As soon as she told her story, the genesis of the neurotic tendency was easy to understand. She had five brothers and sisters, all with the same marked nervous imbalance. Her father was an alcoholic and violent. Throughout childhood she had been terrified by the incessant quarreling of her parents, in which her sympathies were on the side of

[10]"De la psychoanalyse à la psychosynthèse," *L'Encéphale 1926*, p. 584.
[11]Dalbiez, *op. cit.*, Vol. II, p. 259.

her downtrodden mother. The mother died in childbirth, and it is not improper to suppose that the wear and tear of the life she led, with its hopelessness and frequent childbearing, was in part responsible for this premature death.

The father married again, and there followed a series of serious conflicts between her and her stepmother. These conflicts are not difficult to understand: Still faithful in her heart to the memory of her mother—a victim so promptly replaced—Rose must have adopted an attitude of silent hostility.

Thrown while still quite young into the rough-and-tumble of factory life, with no emotional support, she was exposed to many difficulties. She became involved in fresh conflicts, which even included a lawsuit against a female relative.

The Salvation Army, however, found this soul in distress, and held out to her the love of Jesus Christ. Rose became converted, and found a true piety which enabled her to forgive. But in spite of the inner peace she had found, the attacks of dyspnea continued, and the nervous symptoms remained in evidence.

There was still another physical obstacle. She showed signs of hypertrophy of the liver and hepatic insufficiency. The genesis of the liver disorders is doubtless very complex: hereditary factors, wrong diet, and the moral anxieties of her past life had all played their part.

Treatment for the liver condition, and a proper diet, combined with moral and spiritual action, brought about a rapid improvement.

I record this rather ordinary case in order to illustrate my assertion that a synthesized medicine will aim at treating the body, the mind, and the soul simultaneously, without omitting any one of these three aspects of man.

MEDICINE AND THE PERSON

CHAPTER

11

Suffering

I propose to show now that the spiritual message of the Holy Scriptures is the only true answer to the problems of men's lives. It is so rich and profound a message that I do not imagine I can cover all its aspects. I shall confine myself to bringing out a few points at which it impinges on my daily experience as a doctor.

The Bible tells us of the history, the acts and words, of men who were great because they listened to God and obeyed him. So God's will for men was revealed to them. This will of God the Creator is the law of man's normal life. To depart from it is to transgress the law of life. To recognize this transgression, to repent and turn away from it, is to come back to God's purpose. As we read the stories in the Bible, as we enter into communion with the men whose life stories it tells, as we meditate on their experiences and their teaching, as we follow their example and turn to prayer in order to seek, face to face with God, to know what is his will for us, each of us can recognize for himself where his manner of life is wrong, can repent and turn again. The Bible, you will note, makes no distinction between the material faults, the psychological faults, and the spiritual faults in men's lives. On the contrary, it shows their interdependence. The precepts, also, which it lays before us concern the physical regulation of man's life— food, rest, work—quite as much as his psychological and social behavior or his spiritual attitude, his personal relationship with God.

But in spite of all their efforts, men's hearts remain divided. Even if God's law is revealed to them, they do not succeed in keeping it without backsliding. Every new act of obedience brings them closer to God's purpose and normalizes their lives, but with endless cunning they keep on discovering new ways of disobeying.

And so, supremely, the Bible records the life and death of Jesus Christ, the God-man, who knew all our physical, psychic, and spiritual difficulties, and who alone, through his perfect obedience, resolved them all. He is the true Revelation; living in personal fellowship with him we see what our personal problems are, and above all we find the supernatural strength we need to supplement our own poor efforts to resolve them. Finally, through his sacrifice on the Cross, he brings us supreme deliverance, taking upon himself all the wrongs that our efforts have failed to put right, and granting us God's forgiveness.

Thus we find in the Bible, and through the Bible, in prayer and meditation, in personal fellowship with the risen Christ, in the teachings of his church, the surest indications of God's purpose for our lives, the strength that will enable us to conform our lives to that purpose insofar as our divided hearts will permit, and forgiveness for all the things that are still wrong in our lives.

The Bible alone gives a true answer to the incomprehensible mystery of suffering. The doctor's life is devoted to the relief of men's sufferings. In this he feels himself to be a fellow worker with Christ, who healed so many sick people, raised up so many who were in despair, loved those who were suffering physically and morally, and showed, in the parables of the Good Samaritan and of the Last Judgment, that this tireless devotion to the service of those who suffer is the supreme law of God. To fight against suffering is to be on God's side.

On the other hand, as I have shown in Part One, suffering is often bound up with our disobedience and our wrong modes of life, so that in order to strive effectively against suffering we must bring souls to Christ, who delivers them from their faults, who in order to heal the paralytic said to him: "Your sins are forgiven" (Matt. 9:2).

Despite his best efforts, however, the doctor does not cure all suffering. Despite the most telling spiritual experiences, there subsist in every man's life sufferings which God does not relieve. So to St. Paul, who thrice asked God to remove his "thorn in the flesh," God answered: "My grace is sufficient for you" (II Cor. 12:9). And Christ himself, without sin as he was, was not spared suffering. In the Garden of Gethsemane he accepted the supreme suffering when he said to his Father: "Not my will, but thine, be done" (Luke 22:42).

So the Christian answer to suffering is acceptance. Through acceptance, suffering bears spiritual fruit—and even psychic and physical fruit as well. Resignation is passive. Acceptance is active. Resignation abandons the struggle against suffering. Acceptance strives without backsliding, but also without rebellion. There is no greater testimony to the power of Christ than that which shines from the bed of a sick person who miraculously accepts suffering. There is no attitude more impossible for man—without the miraculous intervention of Christ—than the acceptance of suffering.

There is no life exempt from suffering. There is no life which, from birth, does not already have to carry the weight of hereditary weaknesses, which does not suffer emotional shocks in childhood, which does not suffer daily injustices, hindrances, injuries, and disappointments. To all this pain must be added infirmity, material difficulties, bereavement, old age, worry about loved ones, and accidents. In the lives even of the most privileged there is something that is hard to accept. I am reminded of a remark made by my son: "Life's always O.K., except for something."

There is no nobler task the physician can undertake than to help his patient to accept his life and his suffering. But the doctor whose training has been entirely aimed at rational understanding must remain embarrassed in face of the incomprehensible mystery of suffering.

Here is the story of the greatest despair I think I have ever met in my career as a doctor. Answering an urgent call to a little villa, I could hear the patient's cries as soon as I opened the garden gate. I shall call her Emma. She was a young woman of humble extraction.

Thirteen years before, against her family's advice, she had married an expatriate Swiss, for love.

The couple, who were very happy at first, had a little girl the following year. But it was not long before difficulties arose between them, coming as they did from such very different educational and cultural backgrounds. Material difficulties were soon added to the moral ones, of which they were to some extent the consequence, and which they tended to aggravate. The husband lost all his money as well as his job.

Emma's sole consolation was her daughter, whom she surrounded with a jealous and possessive love. She had come to Switzerland at the invitation of a relative who felt sorry for her in her moral and material distress.

Not without a struggle, Emma had allowed her daughter to go off with her relative's children into the mountains. Then, one day when the little girl was playing with the other children near a mountain stream, she had tripped and disappeared into the raging waters.

Exhaustive searches were made, but in vain—the torrent kept its secret. The local people were right when they said from the start that the body would never be found.

They had to go back and tell Emma the terrible news. Her despair was frightening. I found her in the grip of an agitation that nothing could calm. She was rushing about her room, deaf to the world, rolling on her bed, throwing herself to the floor, shouting, uttering curses and threats, and striking herself.

When I managed to tell her that I was a doctor, she planted herself in front of me, shouting: "I don't need a doctor! I'm not ill! Give me back my daughter! My only daughter! My dear little girl! Go away, all of you! Leave me alone!"

I stayed alone with Emma for a long time, saying nothing, not having a chance to put a word in.

What, in any case, could I have said? I was filled with a poignant emotion, and all the words that came into my mind seemed quite inadequate to the situation.

Then at last I said I agreed with her: It was true, she was not ill; my sedatives would remain in my bag. God alone could provide the answer to her grief.

As it happened, Emma's relative had herself come to have faith through great family difficulties. As I left I spoke to her of the great task that lay before her—that of bringing Emma to God.

During the first few days she came up against Emma's aggressive hostility, blaming God for the tragedy. But love and faith gradually won her confidence, and before long they were able to pray together. Emma opened her heart to her friend, little by little. She went back from her present grief to all the other sufferings that she had gone through before. She accepted the affection that was being shown to her. She accepted that her friend should talk to her about God.

Soon, she realized that total consecration of her life to God was the only possible response to her grief and to the void in her heart.

She acted on this realization without delay. One month after the accident I heard her say in front of several people that she was happy, despite her grief, because she had found God.

For several months she stayed there, helping in the house, quick to spend herself in service to all, making many friends and in her turn helping them to begin to mend their lives.

She asked a pastor to give her the religious instruction she had never received.

A few weeks later I learned that her husband, still abroad, was living with a woman who was seriously ill. He had formed a liaison with her some years previously, and had had a child by her.

This had to be told to Emma. I went and fetched her to my home. I shall never forget the hours my wife and I spent with her on that occasion.

At first she did not understand, and then her eyes were gradually opened to the harsh reality: While she had been weeping over the tragic death of her only child, her husband was cherishing another woman and another child.

But her grief was in marked contrast with that which I had witnessed six months earlier. Now there was no rebellion, no agitation, not a single bitter word.

Suddenly she said to me: "What I have to do now is to renew—much more deeply—the consecration of my life to Jesus Christ. I've got to be ready to go back to my husband, to tell him I forgive him, and to see the woman he loves and tell her before she dies that I

forgive her. I'll look after her and her child. I'll adopt him if necessary, and give him the toys that belonged to my little lost daughter.

"I wronged my husband quite a lot as well," she went on. "I'll have
to ask him to forgive me." And she knelt down to confess her faults
in front of me. A few days later my wife and I went with Emma on
her journey. She saw her husband and forgave him. She visited the
woman he loved, gave her her hand and forgave her. She looked after
her, tidied up the house, and made friends with her, and witnessed to
her concerning God's love. She offered her services to take care of the
child, and effaced herself when this offer was refused.

A few weeks later she wrote to tell us that the sick woman had died
in peace. She suggested to her husband that they should come together again so as to provide a home for the child. But he preferred
divorce, and this she accepted in order to allow him to devote himself entirely to the child, while she devoted herself to helping other
broken lives.

I have heard from her now and then. Several years have gone by.
She who was once so unpolished and almost without education, has
grown in heart and mind, becoming more and more cultivated,
refined, and thoughtful.

Recently I have heard that she has organized, and directed in the
absence of the person who was to have done so, a religious retreat
which has borne fruit in a number of people's lives.

I am reminded of a girl of sixteen. The doctor who devotedly
tended her knew that I was a great friend of her father's, and was
kind enough to call me several times to her bedside.

A week before her death, her parents came to see my wife and me.
They understood the gravity of the situation, and felt that they must
prepare to give up their child into God's hands. They wanted to pray
with us in order to say to God: "Thy will be done."

The mother went back to her post at her daughter's side, and filled
that hospital room with gentle serenity and unfailing solicitude.

On the last day my colleague called me back again. The girl had
sat up in bed, raised her eyes and said: "How lovely!" Then she had
fallen back, dead.

We went through into the next room, and there the parents and we two doctors prayed together. In memory of their daughter the parents renewed their promise to devote their lives to the service of Christ, sensing that that was the only victorious answer to the grief that had struck them.

When a patient of mine is approaching death I often find out what church he belongs to, in order myself to call, or advise the relatives to call, the priest to administer the Sacrament, or the pastor to assist the dying person, before it is too late. Collaboration of this kind between the doctor and the minister of religion, accompanied by deep mutual understanding, has a beneficent spiritual influence.

It does not mean, however, that the doctor is not called upon to exercise his own spiritual mission. I am reminded of one of my patients, whom I shall call Marcel. I had been treating him for a number of years, and there had grown up between us one of those quiet friendships that are slowly forged between people of few words. He was an old man, suffering from heart disease. His attacks had at first been widely spaced. After several days of acute distress he would improve, and some months would pass before he called me in again.

The attacks became gradually more frequent, and that winter they had followed one another without any real respite. For a number of weeks now he had been unable to lie down in bed, and spent his nights in an armchair in the sitting room. During the last few days the situation had become rapidly worse, and without my needing to speak of it overtly, both of us realized that there was no hope of recovery.

I had already called several times one day, when in the evening I was called by telephone. I told myself as I went that this would be my last visit. The patient was in an armchair in the dining room, his arms resting on the table, on which some cushions had been placed. He was already unconscious, his body racked by the difficulty he had in breathing. One more injection, though without much hope of any result. Then I sat down at his side, my fingers on his pulse.

My part as a physician of the body was ended. I felt that the family gathered around us realized this.

What I could do, now that my medicines could do no more, was to be there, to unite my presence with that of the waiting family. We spoke very little; less and less, in fact. Half-hours went by without a word in the silence of the night. But what I felt was that the later it got, and the less we said, the truer our words became. They were no longer words. There was growing between us that which words are always trying to express, though they ordinarily manage so badly.

We all had the same thought in our minds: "He is not really suffering; it is only his life resisting now."

I had never spoken seriously in that family about my views on life. I do not think I had ever spoken about God. But in those slow-moving hours I could not go on waiting for death to come and keep my faith to myself. It was the very silence, a silence that was exempt now from fear, that was turning our minds toward God.

But that was not enough, and I thought to myself: "I must talk to them about God. They are all thinking about him at this moment." But how? A little while later I felt that I did not have to talk about God, but just to pray. A few more minutes went by, and I had a feeling that the prayer was going to come without my having to suggest it myself. The long silence continued, and then the wife said gently: "We ought to pray." After a moment I said, simply: "Would you like me to?"

What followed was a real and profound meditation. I stammered out a few words to my God who was there with the dying man, his family, and his doctor.

There came once to consult me an elderly lady who had lost her husband some months previously. We shall call her Madeleine.

It was, moreover, her second marriage, and it had been a very happy one, compensating to some extent for the suffering occasioned by a former unhappy union, which had ended in divorce.

The man who was to become her second husband had been called in to give advice in certain financial matters after her divorce. He had taken pity on her, become attached to her, and had eventually married her. Such was the basis of the second marriage—a full measure of affection and tenderness. And so, with the death of this husband who lived only for her, Madeleine's world had come tumbling down about her ears. Her rather self-centered life had made her scarcely any friends. She was completely isolated spiritually, despite the efforts of a number of charitable people who tried in vain to console her.

The memory of her lost husband became more and more of a cult, which filled her mind without procuring her any peace.

I examined her. She presented a clinical picture of slight cardiac insufficiency, and dissolved into tears when she spoke of her bereavement. Her grief seemed to me to be the chief cause of her ills. I remarked at once: "I shall not try to console you, because I have never had any misfortune like yours, so that anything I could say to you would be ineffective."

She registered acute surprise and told me that I was the first person who had not tried to comfort her. Manifestly, her astonishment was raising in her all sorts of new questions. We talked together for a long time. I explained to her that those who are without faith always think that human words can bring comfort, whereas believers have the courage to confess their powerlessness, simply because they know that true consolation can come only from God.

Contact was established between us. She questioned me about the problem of suffering.

At last I said, gently but firmly: "Madame, you think you are weeping for your husband, but really it is rather over yourself that you are weeping. You are bewailing your own unjust fate, which you refuse to accept. Rebellion against our lot always separates us from God, and thus deprives us of his help, which is the only thing that can accomplish the miracle of making us accept our suffering."

This idea was a great surprise to her, but our conversation was the start of a long spiritual development in her. She sought to make contact with other Christians and asked them questions. She found some who had undergone the spiritual experience of being enabled to accept bereavement. She came out of her self-imposed isolation, made contact again with her family, apologized for the attitude she had adopted, and found once more a joy that she had thought gone forever. It was not long before she gave her life to Jesus Christ, and from then on she was able to help other souls to find the solution to their revolts and difficulties. This was an occasion of astonishment to all who had known her a few months previously, tearful and embittered.

True, her grief did not vanish entirely. The gospel does not promise us exemption from all woe. But in spite of her grief she was leading an increasingly active, fruitful, and even joyous life.

I shall not record here the details of her previous medical history. As she has aged, she has often been ill, and her physical condition imposes limits on her activity. But she is better now than when I first saw her. There is no doubt that had it not been for her conversion she would have been but a useless castaway, self-centered and sour. As it is, her life is one of Christian service, dedicated to bringing God's answer to the torments of injured souls.

It was to her that I once sent a young widow whom we shall call Irene. She too seemed inconsolable. She too was surprised by the message of acceptance. The sudden and premature death of the husband with whom she had been very happy had made her rebellious.

Her widowhood had also brought financial difficulties where she had formerly been in comfortable circumstances. As she suffered from an infirmity she did not find it easy to obtain employment.

But gradually our conversations became more profound. In the end Irene told me what it was that weighed most heavily on her mind: She had committed a sin, and she could not rid herself of the idea that her husband's death was a punishment for it. I told her then of the certainty, which I myself had found, of the forgiveness of sins in the Cross of Jesus Christ. And I entrusted her to Madeleine.

It was not long before Irene herself experienced this forgiveness. Giving her life to God, she started to work again, and was able to strive courageously and to smile once more.

The doctor daily meets people who will not accept illness, the dependence on others which it forces upon them, and the limitations it imposes on their lives. Mme. France Pastorelli, herself a sufferer from illness, has written a profound and true book[1] on this subject, full of the spiritual treasures which flourish in suffering. In it she describes the "drama with oneself" and the "drama with others," and shows at the same time how difficult and yet how fruitful true acceptance can be.

[1] *Servitude et grandeur de la maladie* (Paris: Plon, 1933).

Being ill? Apart from the pain, the weakness, and the disease that have to be put up with, being ill means living contrary to one's tendencies and tastes, it means foregoing everything one likes, renouncing the thing one feels one is in this world for. . . . No longer to be able to make music! Of all the sacrifices that have been imposed on me, this is one of the most agonizing. . . . illness brings spiritual benefit—as does normal life—only to those who know how to use it. . . . The most important thing in life is what one does in it with one's soul.

A doctor's words on this subject can be found in Carton's book— "Blessed are those who suffer."[2] There are perhaps no lives more radiant than the lives of those who have totally accepted disease. I am reminded of Adèle Kamm,[3] of Froidevaux.[4] I am also reminded of several of my own patients who have showed me great spiritual treasures. One of them, kept by illness from all social life for many years, taught me that one of the most difficult things to accept is the loss of time—to accept that when health returns it will not be possible to relive in health the lost years of youth which have gone forever.

Here is what one patient writes in a letter to me:

We often talk about the sufferings that Christ endured for us. But is the idea of those sufferings anything more than an intellectual proposition to any of us?

This remark made by the pastor of my parish one evening at Bible class struck me very forcibly. I went home deeply stirred by it, wondering how far I could imagine the pains Christ suffered for me.

That night sincerely and naïvely, I added to my prayers this question: "Is it possible, Father, to feel just for one minute what Christ suffered for me?"

Two days went by. I had forgotten about my prayer, when I was knocked down in a stupid accident. As I fell I felt as if a knife had been thrust into my back.

The doctors found that I had broken my back, and I was at once encased in plaster. I was reduced to a state of immobility which was to last for several months.

I felt as if I was on a cross, but one in which the center of crucifixion was low down. I did not know what to do with my arms and legs, and I

[2]Paul Carton, *Bienheureux ceux qui souffrent* (Paris: Maloine).
[3]P. Seippel, *A Living Witness: The Life of Adèle Kamm*, trans. Olive Wyon (London: Hodder & Stoughton, 1914).
[4]See Benjamin Vallotton, *Patience* (Paris: Payot, 1922).

could change my position only with assistance. I felt full of self-pity. I groaned and grumbled inwardly.

Suddenly a voice that was as gentle as a rustling breeze spoke to me:

"But all you've got is a broken vertebra! And your feet and hands are free; your feet aren't nailed together, and your hands pierced with nails, and all the weight of your body hanging on those three nails!"

"I am thirsty," I sighed.

"But all you have to do is to reach out to the orangeade at your side. And if you can't reach it you only need to ring. It is better than vinegar in the sponge the executioners wiped their hands on."

Then I came out of my pain, and all I could say was: "Forgive me, Lord, forgive me."

After a while I sighed again.

"How uncomfortable I am in this bed! Where can I put my head?"

"But you have a pillow, you are comfortably tucked up, you haven't a crown of thorns on your head, and you aren't exposed naked to the mockery of the crowd; no one has spat in your face yet."

Then I was ashamed. And every time the pain came back these words were the only ones that came to my lips: "Forgive me, Lord, forgive me!"

Night came, and with it anxiety, discomfort, and sweat streaming down my face.

"But still, they aren't tears of blood!" said the voice.

"Forgive me, Lord, forgive me!"

The more I saw what Christ's pain was like, the less my own became. Then I saw a huge cross raised up against the white wall of my room, with Christ on it. His head was especially clear, and his face bore a look of deep sorrow and intense pain.

My prayer had been granted; of course, I had not been able to experience the sufferings of Christ; but I had understood that all the pains which we think the worst pale into insignificance beside those which he suffered.

In a lecture delivered to the German Philosophical Society, the surgeon Sauerbruch declared: "Faith deep-rooted in the soul has more efficacy than all philosophical knowledge. Pain and suffering find their liberating meaning only in the Christian faith. Christians see suffering as a means used by God to lead man along the holy road of affliction. An instrument for the purification and edifying of the Christian character."[5]

The doctor daily witnesses rebellion against disease, or grudging resignation, each of which is a handicap to his patients not only in

[5] *Berner Tagblatt*, Sept. 5, 1940.

their spiritual development, but also in the process of healing, both physical and psychic. I have pointed this out in connection with tuberculosis (see Chapter 2). I could give many more examples. It is especially true of all chronic diseases, such as cardiac insufficiency, paralysis, etc., which give to the patient the feeling that his activity has to be so limited that his life is useless.

A generally incurable condition, Parkinson's disease, for example, with its slow, inexorable progress, is a terrible moral ordeal. There was the case of Charlotte, nearly eighty years old. She greeted me by telling me how much she longed to be delivered by death. She was alone in a nursing home, almost without visitors, separated from her family, who lived abroad. Faced with her disease, of the diagnosis of which there was no doubt, I was as powerless as all the other doctors who had already attended her.

I talked with her about the Christian message: the acceptance of her disease. I spoke to her about other incurables whose lives had been illuminated as they drew to a close with spiritual victory. Then little by little she told me about her past. For some years she had been looked after by a faithful friend. But, embittered by illness, she had quarreled with her. Now she was even more isolated and bitter. Then she decided to write to her, to ask her forgiveness, and to try to become reconciled with her before she died.

And then she went further back into her life. There were wrongs she had never admitted to anybody. She ought to make her confession. At her request I sent a priest to see her.

A psychiatrist told me that he had once been summoned by an old friend whom he had not seen for a number of years, and who also had Parkinson's disease. The sick man had added to the message he sent: "Only come if you have some new remedy to bring. I've had enough of doctors who say they cannot cure me."

As he went into the bedroom the psychiatrist said to his friend: "I've brought you a new remedy—Jesus Christ."

His remark was not at all well received: The patient bitterly reproached his friend for mocking him. But when the psychiatrist had talked of the change brought about in his own life since he had encountered Jesus Christ, the tone of the conversation altered, and the patient opened his heart as well. This was the first of many conversations. The spiritual life of this patient was nonexistent. Up to then there had been no room in his mind for anything but rebellion against his illness. His friends, wearied by his complaining, came less and less often to see him. But now a real transformation was taking place. In spite of the drawn look which disease imparts to a face, his expression brightened and he looked years younger. Soon he found such peace that people came to him to share the mysterious strength they found in him.

I have sometimes wondered if what the medical books call the "character of the epileptic" is anything other than the projection in his behavior of his inner rebellion against a disease that is singularly hard to accept.

I am reminded of a young epileptic girl, whom we shall call Henriette. She had had a pious upbringing, but latterly her disease had made her moody and unsociable. She had drawn further and further away, morally speaking, from her parents. One felt that she suffered acute mental anguish.

She continually demanded affection, but those who took an interest in her were put off by her moodiness. After much mental suffering, she had come under the influence of a Christian doctor, and had made great resolutions. But she would get lost in intellectual arguments, in objections to the Christian faith, so that her attempts to reform her character were stormy and erratic.

When I saw her she began to argue fiercely with me. But our conversations gradually left this type of discussion behind, and turned toward the consideration of her real difficulties. She was profoundly rebellious. She might have accepted her disease, she told me, but what she could not accept was that it prevented her getting married. Every other girl of her age had a right to look forward to finding happiness in marriage and motherhood, while her own life was cursed with sterility.

I reminded her of Christ's words in the Gospel: "He who believes in me . . . , out of his heart shall flow rivers of living water" (John 7:38). She began to see that at the cost of total abdication she could, despite her disability, live a useful life.

On the following Sunday she went to church, and the pastor preached on that same text! She was greatly impressed, and asked to come and see me again.

It was a very difficult interview. The battle raged furiously within her. But it ended in victory. In the profound calm that followed, she offered her life to Christ. That very day she wrote to her parents to ask their forgiveness for having allowed herself to drift away from them, and to tell them all about her troubles, her mistakes, and her new-found joy. She began to help other sufferers to travel along the hard road of acceptance.

Accepting suffering, bereavement, and disease does not mean taking pleasure in them, steeling oneself against them, or hoping that distractions or the passage of time will make us forget them. It means offering them to God so that he can make them bring forth fruit. One does not arrive at this through reasoning, nor is it to be understood through logic; it is the experience of the grace of God.

I had an old and dear friend, one of the men I have esteemed most highly. For some weeks his health had been deteriorating. It was on Christmas Day that the doctor who tended him asked me to go with him on what must be his last visit.

The patient could speak only with difficulty. Medicine could afford little relief; we concentrated on surrounding the sick man with our affection. I was left alone with him for a moment. He spoke painfully to me: "There's something I don't understand . . ." He did not succeed in saying what it was he did not understand. This struck me particularly in a man who all his life had been devoted to intellectual clarity. Faith had always had the last word with him, but it was allied to a most lively intelligence. One felt that he was still troubled by whatever it was he did not understand. But he was too weak now to put his problem into words. And I realized that it would have been useless to ask him any questions, or to start a discussion.

After a moment's silence, I bent over him and said quietly: "You know that the most important thing in this world is not to understand, but to accept." With a happy smile he stammered: "Yes . . . it's true . . . I do accept . . . everything." It was almost the last thing he said. After my visit he fell asleep. During the night he suddenly awoke, sat up, and said aloud: "I am going to heaven," and died.

Accepting Life

The Christian message of acceptance is not an answer only to exceptional suffering. It applies to hundreds of different aspects of daily life. I propose to show by means of further examples the considerable part it plays in medicine.

First, there is the acceptance of life itself. I am reminded of the old people who say: "Every day I ask God to take me, because I'm doing no more good here." If God leaves us in this world, it is because he still has something for us to do. His estimate of our usefulness is different from ours. But it is not only old people who wish for death. There are few people who have not at some time in the secrecy of their hearts desired to escape from life.

Moreover, acceptance of living is one of the most important factors in healing. I attended an old lady whose grandson was sitting for his medical finals. She was keenly interested, and said to me: "I should like to live to see my grandson a doctor." When he had passed his last examination she told me: "Now, I can die." And in fact from that moment she rapidly grew weaker, and three days later she died.

In telling the story of one of my patients, I emphasized the necessity of simply accepting one's sex. I also said that in women rebellion against their sex is often colored with revolt against enforced spinsterhood. Every doctor is aware of the large number of cases in which this particular kind of rebellion plays a part. How many maiden ladies there are who suffer from all sorts of physical and psychological ills, the real cause of which lies in rebellion against their celibate state! Celibacy is harder for a woman to accept because of the power of the maternal instinct.

If God directs us toward marriage, that is well; let us accept it from him. But if his purpose for us is celibacy, that does not mean that life need be any less rich for us. The richest life of all is that which God has prepared for us, if we will accept it whatever it may be.

It is particularly at the time of the menopause that the troubles due to rebellion against celibacy make their appearance. I could give many examples. A young woman who does not accept spinsterhood nourishes in her heart a secret romantic dream of marriage, in which she takes refuge more and more as the years pass and the chances of realizing her dream slip away. There is within her an increasing divorce between her secret dream and her real life. This inner divorce, with its psychological and physical consequences, is itself a factor contributing to the lessening of her chances of marriage. When the moment of the menopause comes upon her, she receives a terrible psychological shock as she is awakened to reality. The hope of motherhood, which she has secretly nurtured, has gone forever. All she has left is her life as a spinster, which seems to her to be a spoiled life because she had put her heart in her dream. And in fact her life really is spoiled, because it is full of "escapes," unreal emotional compensations, fads, artificial principles, criticisms of married women, and bitterness. Of course the doctor must bring some relief to such people by means of tonic medicines and organotherapy. But this cannot absolve him from his profounder task—that of helping them toward a true acceptance of spinsterhood.

It is only by faith that a young woman—and a young man, too— can accept enforced celibacy; by the faith that God has a plan for each person, which will be realized through obedience; by the faith which alone will allow him or her to live a full life, whether married or single.

True spiritual acceptance of her celibate state brings such liberation to a young woman that she will be enabled, even within the framework of her spinsterhood, fully to cultivate all her specifically feminine qualities.

Here, for example, is the case of a healthy young woman, whom we shall call Valerie. She is the maternal feminine type: the Italian school of morphology distinguishes two types of femininity, the *feminilità erotica* and the *feminilità materna*.

To say to an unmarried woman, no longer in the first flush of youth, that she is the "maternal" type, would once have struck me as likely to set up the worst kind of psychological complexes in her. But Valerie is a Christian. She has come to see me in order to understand more clearly what is God's purpose for her life. Her parents are no longer living, and she has no job. Her life, too, is lacking in unity. I show her that her temperament predisposes her to be the mother of a family. If God has not granted her to be so in actual fact, she can be so in a figurative sense.

This is what she has done. She has gathered together a group of young people who have given their lives to God, has made a home for them, and become their mother.

So, by the double acceptance of her temperament and her lot— which, being opposed to each other, could have led her into psychological conflict—she has found greater fulfillment.

I have just been speaking of the part played by rebellion against one's sex and against enforced celibacy in the physical and psychical disorders that sometimes accompany the menopause. But they are also tied up with another kind of rebellion: against the passage of time, and the loss of youth.

The psychiatrist Carl G. Jung[1] comes back again and again to the theme of the psychological shock inherent in the realization—especially in the case of a woman—that one's life has turned downward toward its end.

The fact that a woman is married, or even that she has a large number of children, does not mean that she is spared the moral shock

---

[1] *Two Essays on Analytical Psychology*, trans. H. G. and C. F. Baynes (London: Baillière, Tindall & Cox, 1928), pp. 77-78.

inherent in the menopause. One may say that if man is naturally polygamous, woman is naturally polygoneutic—insatiably maternal.

Diane was a widow who came to consult me for disorders connected with the menopause, which treatment by means of medicine had not reduced.

She was a Christian. She had a fine spiritual life which had kept her young in spirit. I might even say that it had kept her young in body, for the thing that all the beauty salons in the world forget is that a pure heart and a liberated mind are the most important prerequisites for the preservation of the youth of the body. It is always striking to see the physical change that comes over a woman who finds God. Nothing is more difficult to define than beauty and youth. Aesthetic surgery may approach it in a material way, but it lacks the indefinable charm which only a change of heart can give. I have heard many women—and men as well—say, after some great spiritual experience: "I feel ten years younger!"

Kretschmer speaks of the face as the "visiting-card of the individual's general constitution."[2] It is quite as much the visiting card of the mind. Are not wrinkles the traces left by the physiognomical expression of our fears, our cares, and our resentments?

Diane had found in her spiritual life the strength to accept her widowhood, and had become more youthful, in spite of her affliction. But what had happened was that a new reef had insidiously made its appearance on her course, in the shape of a refusal to accept the idea of growing old. In a sense she was the sister of her children. She took hardly any notice of her age, and lived as if she belonged to a different generation from her own. She turned to good account the tendency, which women almost always have, to make herself look younger than she was; but this tendency was in the last analysis only a rebellion against her age. My proof of this is the confession Diane made to me of her embarrassment in the presence of certain gentlemen who were very much younger than she. In fact, she was still behaving like a young woman, and yet Diane has a number of children and grandchildren. She is a grandmother.

[2]*Physique and Character*, trans. W. H. Sprott, 2nd edition revised (London: Kegan Paul & Co., 1936), p. 41.

Acceptance of growing old, of the "change of life," means that a woman must find a quite new outlet for her maternal instinct. It means discovering "the art of being a grandmother," if God grants her to have grandchildren. It means finding an even more sublimated form of maternity if he does not.

I therefore asked Diane if she had accepted her age. When she prayed about this, she became aware of her unconscious problem. And at the same time she experienced a spiritual renewal, and the disorders from which she was suffering disappeared.

Humorists have often made fun of the naïve subterfuges to which women resort in the perpetual effort to make themselves look younger than they really are; but little account is taken of the psychological struggle of which this is the expression, of the spiritual rebellion it conceals, of all the physical misery it brings in its wake.

Moreover, knowing how to grow older, and accepting it, can be as great a problem at twenty as it is at fifty or eighty.

Who can compute the harm that can be done to health by all the beauty care that so many women martyr themselves with?

How many old people accept the limitations called for by their age? I have mentioned this in connection with cases of high blood pressure. I have before me the details of such a case, a very old woman who is too active for her age, who rushes about, eats too quickly and too much, and is always chafing under restraint. Of course, God's purpose is not the same for all old people. There are some whom the enforced inaction of retirement brings to an early grave. But there are many, many more who do not know how to shorten sail. They do not know the serenity proper to their age. They eat like young folk, and still take great pride in excessive physical exertion. They refuse to recognize that their metabolism is less intense, their internal combustion attenuated, that they must protect themselves from cold and heat, and ought to be taking the precautions they reject under the pretext that they have always enjoyed robust health!

And then, accepting that one is growing older means also accepting that time passes, that customs change, that younger people behave differently. "In my time," old people are always saying, as if the present were no longer their time. How many lives end amid bitterness and endless criticism of the young! They are lives filled with negative thoughts and forces, which diminish them and undermine their physical and mental energies.

Lastly, acceptance of growing old means living in the present, at any age, even if the past has been rich in beautiful experiences. During a visit to one of my patients I admired the flowers on her balcony. But there were some faded flowers among them, and I said to her: "You must cut off the faded flowers so that the plant will grow new ones." I realized at once that this was a parable of life. The flowers were beautiful once, but time passes; and if we try to preserve the flowers of the past we have only faded flowers on our plant, and prevent it from producing new ones.

One must also accept one's parents.

Here is the story of a patient whom I shall call Josephine.

The first thing she did was to declare flatly: "I may as well tell you straight away that I am not my father's daughter. I am absolutely certain of it. I lost my mother when I was quite young. She was a fine, gentle soul, and like me she had a lot to put up with from *that man*. If he were my father he wouldn't treat me the way he does."

She was trembling as she told me this. The expression "that man," which she used of her father, held a world of meaning. When she wrote to me she used a visiting card so that her printed name served as a signature and avoided her having to write it by hand.

In answer to my questions she explained that when quite small she had read a children's book about a little girl who had been stolen and brought up by gipsies, who maltreated her. This had been, so she said, like a shaft of light in her mind. She had by then already suffered seriously from the brutality of her father, against whom she had rebelled, and the idea had occurred to her that as in the story of the little gipsy girl, she was not his daughter.

From then on this idea had taken possession of her mind, and had been continually reinforced by all sorts of details she had gleaned from her memories and from her perpetual conflicts with her father.

The obsession had brought her several times to a state of mental confusion which had rendered necessary her entering a mental institution. The idea that she was being treated as mentally ill because she was attempting to establish the truth made her still more rebellious, and she tried all the harder to find evidence to confirm her belief. A systematic delirium. Doctors whom she pestered with her questions would occasionally give evasive replies, so as to avoid a head-on clash with her. She fastened on these ambiguous remarks, seeing them as admissions that there was some mystery about her birth.

I suggested to Josephine that she should examine her conscience to see if there were any wrongs she might have done her father. She protested hotly. She could hardly have anything on her conscience in regard to a man who had behaved as badly to her as he had.

The following week she announced that she had come back unwillingly, that her attempt at an examination of conscience had produced no results, and that she was outraged by my method of treatment.

I suggested then that she should examine her conscience in prayer with me. She was frank enough to mention certain faults that she had committed in regard to her father. But she was extremely upset, and kept protesting that she would never be able to eat humble pie to a man like that. One felt that in her soul the battle was on.

I felt a tremendous pity for that poor distressed soul, and as gently as I possibly could I insisted that she should persevere in the practice of self-examination.

But the following week she produced only insignificant results.

I decided then to show her clearly how her whole life had been warped by her revolt against her father. It is true that all her doctors had considered that there was nothing in her obsession but a figment of her own imagination, and that it was only a projection of her revolt. If I could say this to her without ambiguity, this was because I knew that before God she could find the courage to face the truth, to accept her father, to forgive him, and to ask his forgiveness for herself.

I came up against fierce resistance. She became very upset, and left me. A few days later I had a brief note telling me that she was canceling her next appointment.

I thought the game was lost. But a month later I received a letter—

signed this time in her own hand. In it she said she would come and see me, adding quite simply that after a great battle with herself she had accepted what I had said and my explanation of her psychological error. She had felt a tremendous sense of freedom, and found fellowship with God, and an unlooked-for joy. She had had the strength to go humbly to her father and become reconciled with him.

She was a different person when she came to see me, relaxed and smiling. The fact that she was cured was plain to be seen. Now she was able to see many more faults that had weighed down on her life, and was beginning to make reparation for the wrongs done to other people.

I have seen her several times since then. At each interview she had taken a new step forward, found a more lively fellowship with God, and established more normal relationships with those around her.

She said to me: "I always looked upon myself as a Christian. Now I know what it is to be a Christian!"

We do not choose our parents. God gives us them. They are often other than what we might have liked. They have their failings, their psychological make-up, their illnesses, their social class. It often happens that the son who rebels most against his father is the one who resembles him most. His implacable criticism seems to be the projection of his own impotent struggle against the same faults in himself. One cannot be happy so long as one refuses to accept one's parents, so long as one dreams of a different life, with different parents.

Furthermore, accepting our parents means accepting the heredity they have passed on to us. One of my patients once said to me: "The reason why it is so difficult to straighten out my life is because it is not only my own life that has to be straightend out, but also, in a way, the chain by which the personal problems of my ancestors for generations back have been transmitted to me."

Another was obsessed by the fear of madness, because her family had a history of mental illness. She was afraid of the social stigma attaching to mental disease, and the financial burden involved in the illness of several of her relations. Worrying over these things was undermining her moral stamina. When I tried to show her that her trouble was very largely rebellion against her lot, and self-pity, she took offense. But a few days later she told me about the unlooked-for relaxation of tension and the spiritual peace she had found as a result of complete acceptance.

Parents, too, must accept their children. There are many parents who are disappointed in their children because the children do not fit into the fine pattern they had dreamed of. There are many children who feel vaguely oppressed by this undefined parental disapproval. Accepting one's children means accepting their temperaments, their failings, their character, and also their sex.

Richard was a man who suffered from a serious inferiority complex. He had had a difficult life, owing no doubt to this feeling of inferiority; and his difficulties, in their turn, had aggravated his inferiority complex. He occupied an administrative post in the intellectual world, and was highly esteemed, but in spite of this he doubted his own social usefulness. He openly said that he had "spoiled his life." His home was on the verge of breaking up when it was saved by the Christian faith. From then on he gradually regained confidence in himself. But he still has grand ideas which he does not dare to put into words—and yet he blames himself for letting them lie idle and sterile. He excuses himself by calling them fantasies.

I will not go into the details of all the complex factors which lie behind Richard's feeling of inferiority. One I will mention: His parents wanted a daughter so badly that when he came into the world they treated him as a daughter. They even dressed him in girls' clothes until he was eight. One can easily guess the effect of this on a child's mind!

This rebellion by parents against the nature of their children, this refusal to accept them for what they are, lies behind innumerable cases of infantile complex. It is not surprising that Freud found that many men bear a grudge against their fathers.

There is no need to invoke the Oedipus complex to explain it!

How many parents there are who ought to ask forgiveness of their children! How often I have had to ask forgiveness of mine! How many children feel that their brothers and sisters, whose achievements are more flattering to their parents, are preferred to them? How many parents correct their children in anger rather than in love?

It is not circumstances that make us happy or unhappy, but our own hearts. We cannot help others to find the strength to accept their lives if we have not found it ourselves. Only God gives it. Accepting one's life means accepting all that one considers to be unfair victimization, the injustices of fate as well as those of men. We sometimes say that we would be willing to accept the injustices provided that at least we were asked to forgive them. But the Christian is required to forgive even those who do not ask for forgiveness.

We are also required, of course, to accept reverses of fortune, and even utter ruin. I have a friend who lost everything in the Russian Revolution, and who is as merry as a cricket. He imparts his joy to many others who have long faces because they have lost some small part of their fortune.

I have before me my notes on several of my patients, too long to give in detail here, which show that the principal source of many physical and psychic ills is this constant revolt against injustice. They are men and women whose lives are sterile and clouded; they fight tirelessly, and load themselves with crushing responsibilities; they are always giving others advice—without ever succeeding in correcting their faults. All they get is an angry retort, and then they find themselves ostracized. They denounce evil at every opportunity, and seem to suffer more than most people from bad luck and injustice. They seem to call down upon themselves the storms that feed their rebelliousness. They say that they are fighting for principles, for truth and justice, and that acceptance would be connivance at injustice. They are determined to champion the oppressed, to stand up to those who have power, and to express their indignation without let or hindrance. But no one thanks them for it. Everywhere they go there is strife, conflict, and argument. They wear themselves out. This sort of bitterness in the soul adversely affects not only the nerves, but also the digestion, the heart, and the general vitality of such persons.

One day I met a man against whom I had often fought, though there was no animosity between us. It was our convictions which had found us so often in opposing camps as honest adversaries. He was suffering from a serious malady, and suspected that it might well be fatal. He had come now for my help as a physician. We shall call him

Jacques. All at once we were in a new relationship with each other, each of us feeling that a quite new trust and friendship must now be established between us, as man to man. As we prayed together I remembered several particular occasions on which in the heat of battle I had been unfair toward him. I talked with him about these incidents, and asked him to forgive me.

The next day he told me how he had spent the night. He had had to get out of bed. Walking was already extremely difficult, and in a moment of dizziness he had fallen, and dragged the tablecloth with him. There was a vase of flowers on the table, and it fell to the floor and broke. Jacques remained there for a long time, incapable of getting to his feet. And suddenly he had seen this as a picture of his life: The vase was broken now. He was going toward death, and must admit the defeat of all his struggles and campaigns for truth. But the flowers were still there. . . . He must pick them up. Slowly he had gathered them, one by one. And in his heart a voice spoke: "Love surpasses injustice." He had seen the error of his life, he said, the vanity of this great struggle for justice and truth, which did not bring forth as much fruit as the least gesture of love.

Listening to him, I too heard God's voice speaking in my heart. I realized that he and I had often found ourselves ranged against one another in a conflict of ideas, because we resembled one another. Each thought he was serving God in fighting for the truth, against error. Only our ideas of truth differed, and the zeal of both of us had worn itself out in a battle of ideas. I saw now that I too must admit to myself that all the effort was sterile, and that henceforth I must put into loving all the fervor I had put into fighting. There and then we knelt down together to ask God to transform us and to give us love.

Jacques lived for another few months, months which saw his physical condition growing relentlessly worse, and his spiritual life growing stronger. I had several long talks with him. Beneath his outward appearance of being a fighter he was shy and retiring. Now he willingly talked about himself and reviewed his life. In his mind he went one by one over the many men he had fought against. He wrote letters of apology to them. His death was peaceful and calm. His children were with him at the end, and when he had drawn his last breath I spoke to them of all that God had taught me through that sick man.

We have no right to expect that those around us should be perfect. Accepting one's life means also accepting the sin of others which causes us suffering, accepting their nerves, their reactions, their enthusiasms, and even the talents and qualities by means of which they outshine us. It means accepting our families, our clients, our fellow workers, our place in society, the country in which we live. How many wives there are who have not really accepted the nationality they have acquired by marriage! How many Swiss there are who have moved from Italian- or French-Swiss districts, and never come to terms with the German-Swiss canton in which they now live!

I meet few people who are satisified with their job in life, and few who devote themselves wholeheartedly to it. No doubt God does sometimes bring a person to see that he has made a mistake in his choice of career, and calls on him to change it. But this happens only to those who have first accepted what they are doing, and not to those who hanker after a change in order to escape from work which they have not accepted.

Unless one has accepted one's work, one does it half-heartedly, and remains dissatisfied with the result. It is also much more tiring. I am reminded of a young woman who lost weight while at work, and put it on again during holidays, with astonishing rapidity. When we looked more closely into the situation we realized that what was damaging her health was not so much the work itself as the wearing effect of a constant revolt against that particular work.

Many people will not accept their own bodies. No one knows the secret torment, often childish, but capable of turning into a regular obsession, that can be caused by a nose that is too long, legs that are too thick, by being too tall or too short, by a tendency to plumpness, or an unharmonious voice—in short, by revolt against not being as handsome or as beautiful as one would like. What fixes these preoccupations, and makes them worse, is the very fact that they are secret; for very often if such worries were openly voiced, reassurance would be forthcoming from the person's friends, and he might be quite astonished to learn that his little physical defects are hardly noticed, and that his friends know how to appreciate his other and more important qualities. Untold harm is done in this respect by literature, films, and women's magazines which concentrate on advice and publicity about the qualities necessary to impress people. Worry and dissatisfaction of this sort is widely maintained and exploited by the manufacturers of beauty products and by quacks. How many women have ruined their health by dosing themselves with slimming preparations which have actually resulted in iodism?

I remember a young woman whom I shall call Helen, and whom I attended for a patch of pleurisy. It was only after a number of visits that she dared to admit to me what was the cause of her illness. For years she had been obsessed with the size of her breasts (which, in fact, were not abnormal at all). Then she had read somewhere that streams of cold water on the chest could reduce their size. For weeks she had secretly and regularly practiced this treatment, until the onset of the disease brought her to me. Furthermore, she continued the cold applications at the same time as she followed the treatment I prescribed! It was only as the result of a spiritual experience that I was able to help her to accept her body as it was.

Aline was a young woman who arrived at my consulting room one day in tears of despair about her condition. She was slightly built, small in stature, her arm span short—three inches less than her height —and underweight.

At school she had always been called "the little 'un," a nickname which had caused her acute humiliation. This was a case of an extremely sensitive nature, a keen sense of inferiority having resulted from her rebellion against her small stature.

She had therefore sought compensations, and had been hungry for demonstrations of affection and esteem. Her family, irritated by her need for affection, grumbled at her about it, and this only made matters worse.

At work she encountered the same difficulties. As a child she had been happy and spontaneous. As a probationer in her first job she was so desperate to win the appreciation of an exacting chief that she behaved quite unnaturally.

Her doctor communicated his observations to me. Strange, imprecise, unexpected illnesses followed one after another, involving quite different organs, often difficult to diagnose, and disconcerting in their development. The feeling that she was being constantly held back by bad health made her even more rebellious, and drove her to further overwork to compensate for it. Radiography had revealed a congenital malformation of the duodenum, a discovery which had made a deep impression on the patient and had contributed to the setting up of serious functional digestive disorders. Merely being able to unburden herself to me about her feelings of inferiority, and about all the little humiliations which, unaccepted, had grown into great injuries, brought about an improvement in her condition and an easing of her relations with the people with whom she came into contact.

It was only after a long spiritual development that Aline was able to act naturally once more, to be less touchy, to put up with reproof, and be happy once again. Organotherapy and dieting helped. But the heart of the problem lay in the acceptance of her physical smallness. My wife's friendship with her helped to win the last spiritual victory.

I think also that her constant concern to put on weight was an unconscious cause of her digestive disorders. It is a paradox often met with in medicine that the more one wants to do the right thing, the less one succeeds—the more one wants to put on weight, the less one does so; the more one wants to calm down one's heart, the more one gets palpitations. Our vegetative functions, to be normal, must be unconscious and automatic. Any concentration by the mind on their working interferes with it. On the other hand, their malfunctioning tends in its turn to concentrate attention on them. Acceptance of a small stature is sometimes particularly difficult for those who, in appearance, enjoy perfect health. Take, for example, the case of a woman who shows both physical and nervous signs of being run-down. She has the shape which MacAuliffe classifies as "uniform round"—plump, full-blooded, fresh-complexioned. She is the type commonly described as enjoying "radiant health." She is a victim of the common misconception that plumpness implies health. In reality her weight is due to fat rather than to firm flesh. She thinks herself physically rich, whereas she is in fact poor. Her friends and relations do not realize that she has to husband her strength. She spends herself without reckoning the cost, and so the budget of her strength becomes unbalanced, with a consequent unbalance also in her neurovegetative system.

Delicate people ought to live a life in miniature, space out their activities, rest frequently, eat little and often. We live in an age obsessed with the idea of quantity. A person's output ought to be measured by the quality and not the quantity of what he does. Darwin, whose health was very delicate, worked only three hours a day,[3] and yet he left behind him one of the most important scientific works of all time.

Accepting one's physical make-up means that one will stop comparing oneself with others. My wife is delicate, while I am a man of action. One day during her meditation she came to see that God's purpose for her was different from his purpose for me. What he required from her was an account of her own talent, and not of mine. That was the beginning of a great development in her as a person.

Finally, experience has taught me to use differing methods in guiding people as to how they should live in accordance with their own individual make-up. With strong, independent types, one has to use the method of the challenge. The delicate ones, on the other hand, require a gentler and more understanding approach.

I often think that life is like a great staircase. The strong can cope with high steps. Throw out a challenge to them, and they can summon up the strength required for a veritable spiritual rock face. The weak, on the contrary, tend to get discouraged if faced with an obstacle that is too high, and to doubt their own capacity to tackle it. One must hew out little steps for them to climb one at a time. They take fresh courage when, eventually, they have been able to climb as high as the others.

I have several times alluded to the notion of vitality. "Weak," "lacking in vitality"—such expressions need more precise definition.

[3] Paul Carton, *Traité de médecine, d'alimentation et d'hygiène naturistes* (Brévannes, 1931), p. 775.

Vitality is not synonymous with strength of character. I have referred to several cases in which a strong mind wears out a weak body, as the blade wears the scabbard, to use Carton's simile. Carton set out to discover what were the objective signs of vitality. Following him I have made systematic researches into them, and can say that, on the whole, my observations confirm his. The clinical signs of vitality, therefore, seem to me to offer very useful indications as to the regulation of the lives of individuals.

First among the signs of vitality Carton puts the presence and development—much more frequent among men than among women—of the xiphoid appendage.[4] The importance of the presence and development of this process lies in the evidence it affords of the intensity of the process of ossification during childhood, and consequently of the intensity of the general metabolism of the physical build-up of the body at the age when its physiological capital is being constituted. I am surprised that Carton himself never to my knowledge ventured to formulate this explanation of his clinical sign, since it seems to me to be the only likely one. Similarly, he refrained from giving the explanation of another of the clinical signs he pointed out—namely, that of the number of lunules on the nails. This is, to use his expression, the sign of the "disposable revenue."[5] It seems clear to me that this sign, too, is connected with the intensity of the individual's regenerative metabolism, since it is evidence of the generative activity of the matrix of the nail. Carton, on the other hand, says that the numerousness and clarity of the lunules is a sign of an S temperament, whereas I have found it equally frequent in pure L types, in whom it would appear to be related to the catabolic tendencies of their digestive temperament.

However that may be, to count the number of lunules on the nails and to form an appreciation of their development, is a very simple piece of clinical research, and one whose practical value seems to me to be considerable. One constantly finds a great development of the lunules among active, positive, even restless subjects with a large appetite, who accumulate digestive resources. One finds up to two

[4]Paul Carton, *L'Art médical* (Brévannes, 1930), p. 76.
[5]*Ibid.*, p. 77.

lunules in subjects who are run-down, whose vitality is either weak or is exhausted as a result of overwork, or whose organic balance-sheet shows an adverse tendency.

On the other hand, Carton seems to me to have ventured into arbitrary and overrigid classifications in the scheme which he outlines of types of character divided according to the number of lunules combined with the absence or presence of his sign of the independence of the line of life and the line of the head on the radial edge of the hand.[6] All these signs require to be interpreted critically, and compared with all that one knows about an individual, including his reactions to his environment, and not to be catalogued like mathematical co-ordinates of vitality.

Happiness, inner harmony, acceptance of our lives, the solving of conflicts with others, satisfaction in work, victory over sin, over idleness, and over selfishness have doubtless more influence on our vitality than all the other physical factors of diet, heredity, constitution, or rest. They constitute a sort of coefficient which multiplies the basic figure of physical vitality.

Lastly, Carton gives another sign, that of the "depilation of the calves of the legs," which he describes as a "vital mortgage." All those who are overworked, or run down, all those whose reactions are no longer equal to the causes of weakening, show this fall, this nonreplacement of the hairs of the calves and the outer faces of the legs. It is a surer sign than that of the hair of the head, which depends more on autotoxic causes. Pyknic types lose their hair prematurely, but retain the hair on the calves unless they suffer from an organic deficit.

Of course, the classic signs of demineralization, decalcification, dental caries, and phosphaturia of the neurotic must also be taken into consideration when assessing vitality.

Sigaud based his classification of "the strong and the weak"[7] on extremely original studies of abdominal tonicity and sonority, and my own experience would seem to confirm his views.

---

[6]Paul Carton, *Les clefs du diagnostic de l'individualité* (Paris: Le François), p. 36.
[7]L. Mac–Auliffe, *Les tempéraments* (Paris: Vigot, 1922), p. 33.

13

Questions of Sex

In the preceding chapter I did not touch upon acceptance of one's marriage partner, because it deserves a place to itself, and brings us to the subject of sex.

Acceptance of one's wife, as she is.

Acceptance of one's husband, as he is.

True, there is no finer task for a married couple than to help each other to overcome their faults. But no one can undertake that task successfully without first accepting the marriage partner as he or she is, faults included. It is only then that help can be given disinterestedly, free from irritation, criticism, and bitterness. The husband who complains about his wife's faults and wants to put them right merely for his own sake will only end up by digging a trench between himself and her, provoking defensive reactions on her part, or giving her a sense of inferiority. Conjugal fellowship is not to be built on a basis of mutual moralizing. The best thing a husband can do to help his wife is to correct his own faults.

Further, accepting one's marriage partner involves real acceptance of marriage itself. There are more married people than one would think who are not totally married, without any mental or emotional reservation, who do not accept the restrictions which marriage imposes on their liberty, their independence, their wish to go their own way and enjoy their own amusements and pleasures, and to spend their money as they like.

I pointed out in Chapter 7 some aspects of these marital conflicts which the doctor encounters daily, and which have such a far-reaching effect on physical and psychical health. What I want to emphasize now is that marriage has been instituted by God, and that it can achieve full realization only within the framework of the laws which he has laid down for it.

The first prerequisite of Christian marriage is that the man and the woman should have been brought together by God. I know a man who during his quiet time was guided to marry a girl who at the time meant nothing to him. His first reaction was negative. The idea seemed absurd: He did not even know what language she spoke. But about the same time the girl had a similar call, although she did not know that the man had had a similar experience. Their lives were soon united in love.

Next in importance is that the engagement should be in conformity with God's purpose. The happiness of many a marriage is spoiled by unchastity and selfishness during the period of the engagement.

Lastly, it is vital that the union should be submitted to the authority of God. Both partners must seek to establish spiritual communion. The dictates of the Scriptures should govern their attitude to each other, every difficulty being resolved through prayer. The home must find its meaning in service together of God.

There was the case of a woman whom we shall call Martha. She made a long journey to come and consult me because she knew that I was a Christian doctor, and she expected that I would say something to reinforce the line she was taking in a disagreement with her husband.

She explained to me that she had always had an instinctive distaste for the idea of sex, and had always avoided going into such matters very deeply, and that she had been even more disappointed and disgusted by her experience of marriage.

Now that she had been converted and had dedicated her life to

God, therefore, she had announced to her husband that thenceforth she wished to live a life of purity—that is to say, to have nothing more to do with the sex life, which she considered to be incompatible with her new high-minded outlook. From what she said I could see that she despised her husband, who had little time for this sort of talk and such a conception of Christianity.

I talked first to Martha about the divine meaning of sex. Marriage as a physical, psychical, and spiritual whole has been instituted by God. It is obvious that God gave us the sex instinct with marriage in view. The fact that men often use the instinct outside the purpose of God is no reason for supposing that it was not he who gave it to us. If the New Testament in many places sets the flesh over against the spirit, this is in order to stress the necessity of the submission of the flesh to the spirit, certainly not to repudiate the flesh. On the contrary, one of the essential doctrines of Christianity is that of incarnation. Unlike the Oriental religions, Christianity never separates the spiritual from the carnal: It wants the spirit to be glorified in the flesh. A person who thinks he is coming closer to God by cultivating a discarnate spiritual life has not yet understood the extraordinary message of Christ, who claims the submission of the whole world, physical as well as spiritual, to the authority of God.

And then I showed Martha that contrary to her belief she was making no sacrifices at all in giving up a sexual life which she had never accepted. Her claim to have gone up in the world of the spirit was only a way of increasing the distance which separated her from her husband, whereas God demanded the unity of husband and wife. It would not make her more pure, but only less loving.

Was there not a certain self-complacency in the way she boasted of her spiritual superiority over her husband and her view of him as "bestial"? She, in fact, had never accepted the integrated marriage to which God had called her. She had not yet begun to love her husband in the way God was calling her to love him.

Martha seemed at first to be dismayed by what I had said. It ran counter to the theories she had invented to justify her marital frigidity. I spoke to her then of the married life to which God had led my wife and me—subordinated to his commandments in every sphere, including the sex life as well as the spiritual life. This view of marriage leads to true conjugal bliss.

Martha admitted to me then that her home was not a success, and recognized that her spiritual aspirations were a compensation for her dissatisfaction with her married life. Little by little she was opening her mind to quite new horizons.

She left me, having recognized what it was that God expected of her. She was going back to her husband to ask him to forgive her for not having fulfilled the promises she had made before God on her wedding day.

It must be frankly stated that the prejudices of religious conventionalism are the cause of untold marital unhappiness. People with these views have the greatest difficulty in welding together sexuality and affectivity, because of the feeling of guilt they have about the former. There is nothing wrong with the sex instinct: God made it. What is sinful is its use outside what God meant it to be. But it is precisely in this welding that God's purpose for sex is accomplished. It is easier to turn one's back on sex than to accept the lordship of God over the whole of one's life.

I was perhaps never more moved myself by the doctrine of total acceptance than when I was faced once with a young woman whom we shall call Josette. She came to see me because she was worn out by the life her husband forced her to live. An alcoholic and bad-tempered, his sensuality was such that he demanded that she submit to him a large number of times every day, uttering the direst threats if she refused. The poor girl had, as a result, come to look on sex with horror and disgust.

All I could do was to remind her that the love demanded by Christ accepts all things, forgives all things, endures all things. Such a love could win the husband better than any resistance or reproof.

I hesitated to give such an answer to Josette, and yet I could see no other.

She prayed to God to give her the courage to accept joyfully.

I learned later of the quite new love for her husband that was born in her that day, and the spiritual heights to which this extraordinary victory of the spirit over the flesh led her!

It is one of the aspects of the Christian faith that one should recognize the God-givenness of instinct. In the physical world—in the universal gravitation of the heavenly bodies, for example—God's law is irrevocably kept. In the biological world, instinct ensures that it is kept. In man, free will makes its appearance, freedom to disobey the law of God, to use instinct as a means to personal enjoyment rather than for the accomplishment of God's will. When he puts himself face to face with God, a man learns to see clearly into his own heart. He is enabled to see the impurity and lust there is in his temptation to use his instinct outside God's purpose, and the equally serious disobedience of not trusting to instinct in the conduct of his normal sex life.

Take, for example, the case of a man of a rather intellectual type, well versed in sexual psychology, who, with the best of intentions, tried to guard against possible subsequent marital difficulties by not rushing things at the start of his married life. He allowed himself to be guided by his knowledge and his intellect rather than by his instinct. His calculated prudence killed the necessary spontaneity of the sex instinct and resulted in life-long impotence. It was a case of "striving to better, oft we mar what's well." In such a case the true problem is not sexual, but intellectual. It is a failure to recognize the fact that the will of God can be fulfilled in the instinct of sex so long as it is not spoiled by impurity. The objections of the psychoanalysts to religion stem largely from the error of religious people in opposing spirit to flesh, and failing to recognize the God-given nature of the instinct of sex.

That is why so many children of religious families have been brought up to have a fear of normal sexuality. For them the subject of sex is wrapped in a cloak of unhealthy mystery. And this is the source of great psychological troubles.

But those doctors who, while not sharing the Christian view of sex, have tried to liberate such people from the conventionalist prejudices which weigh on them, have brought a new catastrophe on humanity, one worse than the first! This is the frightening decline in moral standards of our time, with its laxity, its misery, its psychical troubles shown in marital conflicts and divorce, and its falling birth rate. In formulating their notorious "principle of pleasure" they have opened the door to all the new complexes that are set up by the claim to enjoy untrammeled sexual satisfaction. The married couples whom they have reconciled by showing them that what was wrong with them was that they were sexually unsatisfied, are indeed momentarily cured through their sense of sexual fulfillment. But when the time comes when the husband takes notice of the fact that his wife is growing old, that she is less desirable, that he would find fuller sexual satisfaction with some other woman he has met, or worse, when the day comes when he is left a widower, he will be haunted by the fear of falling ill again if he cannot find complete sexual satisfaction.

Thus these medical doctrines based on the "principle of pleasure," and the ideas that they have fostered among the public, promote rebellion against their lot in all those whom it has not been God's will to lead to sexual fulfillment—those who have never married, those who have been widowed, those who have been physically disappointed in their marriage partners, or whose partners are less highly sexed than they are, even those whose sex life is harmonious but has to be limited, those who, whether married or not, are called to chastity, and lastly those who suffer from impotence or sexual inversion either in themselves or in their marriage partners.

Whereas many impotent men suffer from secondary complexes arising from their infirmity, such as an inferiority complex, or self-pity, the man I referred to above was with God's help able to accept (as did his wife) complete chastity. In this way he achieved real psychological balance, and has been enabled to live a happy, harmonious, and useful life.

Problems of incompatibility between differing sexual temperaments are problems of selfishness rather than of impurity. A husband who finds that his wife does not give him the sexual satisfaction to which he imagines he is entitled, adopts in his heart an attitude of silent accusation against her. It is this accusation, and not his sexual dissatisfaction, which creates trouble between them. When a husband and wife take their sexual life in prayer to God and together submit it to him, all the accusations vanish away. Harmony is reborn between them, and even sexual felicity.

Without God, sex is either an obscure taboo, the source of repressions and compensatory psychological troubles, or else it is an insatiable divinity, a god of pleasure holding man in bondage without making him happy.

Without God, the regulation of the sex life in marriage is either a compromise in which each partner hides his real thoughts from the other, or else tyranny by one over the other, or it may be an artificial and rigid edifice of formal principles. No moral or psychological system can regulate by principles a domain which belongs to daily obedience to God, to the free submission to him of the conscience enlightened by the Scriptures and the teaching of the church. When God directs the sex life of a married couple, they can practice it divinely, if I may use the word—in a full mutual communion that is carnal, moral, and spiritual all at once. It is the crowning symbol of their total giving of themselves to each other. Ard when God leads them to abstinence they can practice renunciation without rebellion, without repressions, and without mutual reproaches.

One form of disobedience is for the husband to deprive his wife of the feeling of being desired, which is part of the divine law of marriage. Again, a man may impurely lust after his own wife at the time when this is not in accord with God's will. One may say that the more vigilant people are, and the stricter they are with themselves in regard to the absolute demand for purity in the law of Christ, then the more that which is divine in sex will grow and blossom in them and ensure their physical and spiritual well-being.

It is also on this level, that of seeking together to do God's will, that a married couple will be able to find the answer to the question of birth control. Here again I must be careful not to attempt to formulate theoretical principles in regard to a problem which is a matter of individual obedience. Only under God, and enlightened by the Holy Scriptures, will a couple be able to see whether their actions in this matter are dictated by selfish considerations or by motives in harmony with the will of God.

We have come here to a problem of first importance in medicine. It is that of the physical, psychological, and spiritual state of parents at the moment of conception. An entire life may be marked with debility, infirmity, and with all the consequent physical and moral sufferings, because it was conceived when the parents were in a state of sickness or of acute or chronic alcoholic intoxication. And later on when their friends commiserate with them on having a sickly child, they will not dare to admit to the secret remorse that haunts them and turns these marks of sympathy into burning accusations.

Many parents and educators who generally have not themselves succeeded in resolving their own sex problems think they are helping young people by parading before them the specter of the supposedly terrible results of masturbation. These young people then get bogged down in a negative and obsessive struggle. They come to isolate this problem from all their other personal problems, such as that of having a frank and loving relationship with their parents. The reader must understand that I am not advocating here anything but a high ideal of purity in young people. But what I maintain is that the struggle for this ideal is effective only when it takes its place in the framework of a total consecration of one's life to Jesus Christ, and when obedience to him in all other respects concerns the young person quite as much as his sexual continence.

A negative struggle leads to continual defeats, to psychical disorders and to religious doubt, which in their turn make the struggle harder. A positive struggle counts on the supernatural strength which Christ gives to those who dedicate the whole of their lives to him. I know a young man who when he was tempted, instead of bracing himself stiffly in a negative effort, used to get down on his knees and thank God for having placed in him such a life-force, and ask him how he ought to be using it.

The following case will show the reader how far removed this Christian view is from some ideas still current among psychiatrists.

A young lad, whom we shall call Dominic, goes to consult a specialist about his serious inferiority complex. Retarded in his mental development, he was backward at school, and since then has had several different jobs but has been unable to hold any of them. The fact that his parents worry so much about him does not help to create around him the calm and confident atmosphere he needs. Finally they send him to see a psychiatrist.

The psychiatrist has a long talk with him, and concludes by saying something like this: "What you need is to find a girl friend—it will give you courage and self-confidence. At your age a girl is just the thing a young fellow needs, to help him grow up and relax his nerves."

And so, when Dominic is out on a cycle ride and meets a not very coy young girl, he thinks that the moment has come to follow his doctor's advice. She is not difficult to persuade, and allows herself to be taken into the woods.

Dominic is quite surprised when a few days later he is summoned for abducting a minor, a complaint having been lodged by the girl's parents, to whom she has confessed her adventure.

The magistrates entrust Dominic to the expert care of another psychiatrist, who gravely concludes that he was not entirely to blame, and recommends treatment in a clinic. What the expert does not mention is the responsibility of a psychological medicine which, having lost all idea of the law of God and of men, can openly give to a receptive person advice which, if followed, exposes him to criminal prosecution.

I hardly need add that the "little girl friend" does not cure Dominic of his inferiority complex.

I have of course been consulted by a large number of men and women whose lives have been completely ruined by the deviation of instinct known as homosexuality, and its repercussions.

In talking to them, one perceives that they suffer much more from the moral and social consequences of their infirmity than from the infirmity itself. In all homosexuals, because of the social prejudices of which they are the object, and also because of the rigid formalism of current religious ideas, which casts the first stone at the sick instead of loving them as Christ did, there are feelings of inferiority, of moral isolation, and of being under a curse, which are much worse than those felt by a one-eyed person or one who is lame.

They feel themselves to be excluded from human society, that everybody guesses their trouble and despises them. This feeling stops their acting naturally and spontaneously. In its turn, lack of naturalness and of human society aggravates the psychological difficulty.

They can experience sexual happiness in liaisons in which they give way to their instinct. But it is a happiness haunted by malaise and guilt, so that they are prevented from fully developing their personalities, for this carnal happiness is not part of God's purpose. So they break off the association, but are no happier in an emotional separation which they do not really accept.

They are full of self-pity, of rebellion against the fate which forbids their knowing true happiness. Furthermore, they are afraid of their emotions; they can have no normal social relationships, either with the other sex, which is a constant reminder, because of the revulsion it inspires in them, of their infirmity, or with individuals of their own sex, to whom they are afraid of becoming too attached.

The results are a complete inability to behave naturally and aggressive reactions against their families and their colleagues at work, the cause of which they cannot confess, and which are put down to their having an unpleasant nature. All of which increases their moral isolation still further.

They cannot be happy and spontaneous, either in giving way to the impulses of their misdirected instinct or in resisting them.

The following is, I think, the Christian answer to this problem:

1. Homosexuality is an infirmity. But whereas all other infirmities call forth sympathy, this one is looked upon as a social reproach, because of the conventionalism of society. Christ, who condemned conventionalism with the utmost severity, is always nearest to those who suffer.

2. Acceptance of one's nature as it is, with its infirmities and the difficulties they entail, acceptance of them without rebellion, is one of the demands Christianity makes. Christ does not promise us a life exempt from infirmities and difficulties, but he gives us true happiness in the acceptance of them. This particular infirmity is to be regarded in the same way as all the others, which are compatible with happiness insofar as they are not rebelled against.

3. But the person who gives way to his or her homosexual tendency, even if it be only in thought, commits a sin. For sin is disobedience of God, that is to say, the use of any instinct outside God's purpose, for one's own pleasure.

This is why homosexuals are not beings apart in humanity. They have no sex problem essentially different from that of other people, from that of the unmarried, the widowed, or the married. For all, it is the same problem, namely, that of absolute obedience to God's will, in sex as in all other domains of life. A man who by a look "commits adultery in his heart," to use Christ's words, or a man who uses his wife otherwise than as God wills, is as disobedient, as sinful, as a homosexual who gives free play to his abnormal impulses. It can be quite as difficult for a married heterosexual really to obey God's will for his sexual life and to be absolutely pure in marriage as it is for a bachelor or a homosexual to observe an absolute sexual discipline.

Sexual life guided by God means absolute obedience to God, it means the employment of the prodigious strength of the creative instinct in accordance with his purpose, whether it be in the accomplishment of the normal sex act within the marriage bond, or in the direction of the creative urge to other spheres of the life of the mind, in social life, or in spiritual life.

This is the Christian view of what the psychologists call sublimation, which, for unbelievers, is merely a second-best substitute for sex, whereas for us it is a different incarnation of the creative urge which God has implanted in man's heart. Through the instinct of sex God has associated man with his creative work. But God's creative work is not only carnal : It embraces every aspect of life. Heat energy can be converted into mechanical energy. We do not therefore say that the second is really a form of the first, but rather that they are different manifestations of ultraphenomenal energy.

In the same way we must look upon sublimation not as a disguised form of sexual energy, but as a different phenomenal manifestation of the divine creative force.

From the Christian point of view, the homosexual who is prosecuted by law ought to be declared to have absolutely no legal responsibility for his condition, since an infirmity can hardly be looked upon as a crime. On the other hand, he will be cured only if he feels—on the same grounds as the heterosexual—entirely responsible before God for using his instinct in accordance with God's will, abandoning to God the direction of his sexual life.

I am reminded here of a teacher who came a long way to see me one day. We shall call him Peter. I could not say, in his case, whether it was the aberrant tendency of his sexual instinct which had unconsciously influenced him in his choice of teaching as a career, or whether it was this career which had arrested his sexual evolution at the infantile stage of homosexuality. It was, however, the case that for him his professional life was one long martyrdom. A prey to terrible temptations, he was wearing himself out in struggles with himself. His spiritual life, which had been awakened, was blocked by this unresolved problem.

He was able to abandon his sexuality to God, and find at once a relief which none of his inner struggles had ever been able to procure for him. A negative struggle only concentrates the mind obsessively on the thing one is fighting against, and makes liberation from it more difficult. But Christianity is a message of good news, of miraculous and freely given liberation accorded by faith to those who are willing really to obey Jesus Christ.

One year later I saw Peter again. He was happily engaged to be married. He had been able to make a full and frank confession to his fiancée of the difficulties he had had, and he was looking forward to his marriage with complete confidence.

Positive Health

The biblical message of acceptance is the only possible answer to the great problem of suffering.

From the miracles that are wrought through acceptance, it can be seen that spiritual strength is the greatest strength in the world. It can transform both peoples and individuals. It alone can ensure victory over the negative forces of selfishness, hate, fear, and disorder, which destroy peoples and undermine the health of individuals. It alone gives them the joy, energy, and zeal needed in the daily battle for life and for the defense of health.

There are three suicides a day in Switzerland.

Putting men's lives in order, helping them to win victories over themselves, to control their passions, to refresh their strength through daily contact with God—all this does not only mean reducing the risk of their falling ill, it also means helping them to find the source of "positive health."

Health is not the mere absence of disease. It is a quality of life, a physical, psychical, and spiritual unfolding, an exaltation of personal dynamism.

Many Swiss physicians are troubled at the almost exclusively negative character of their professional activity. They spend their lives rushing from emergency to emergency, repairing the breaches, like a ship's

crew rushing to stop up one leak after another. Such a crew would
soon be insisting that the shipbuilder should undertake, once and for
all, the systematic reconstruction of the ship, so that it could with-
stand the sea with a new solidity.

The liberal atmosphere in which we have been brought up in Switzerland, and the spiritual neutrality of the state, have up to now prevented us from thinking of such a national reconstruction.

When we consider the activities of the Swiss Federal Public Health
Service, or those of our cantonal services, we can see the incompar-
able service they render to public health; but we must recognize also
that the program of work with which they are charged by the state is
still only that of a vigilant sentry posted to watch for the leaks in
order to stop them up as quickly as possible. With wonderful care
and organization they devote themselves to tracking down epidemics,
warning doctors of the dangers of them, so as to prevent their spreading.

But the re-education of our people, showing them how to rediscover what was once the source of their physical as well as their
moral strength, is a task they scarcely dare to undertake.

I must be careful not to exaggerate. My remarks imply no sort of
criticism of Swiss public health services.

I do not underestimate the measures they adopt for the prevention
of disease, the effort they put into the encouragement of positive
prophylactic activities, the school medical services, the education of
the public in notions of hygiene, the labors of district nurses, the
development of preventoria, holiday camps, antituberculosis campaigns, and societies for gymnastics and sport.

What I should like to show is that a spiritual renewal of our people
would be the complement of all this effort, would increase its effec-
tiveness, and ensure its lasting success.

What made our forefathers strong both physically and morally was
the spirit that animated them, the austerity of their lives, their endurance of hardship, the solidity of their family life, and the ardor of
their dedication to God.

Out of our best national traditions a complete constructive program could be drawn up.

The spirit that presided over the organization of Switzerland's National Exhibition in 1939 marks a clear watershed in this respect. Whereas formerly our exhibitions were no more than a forceful panegyric of technical progress, glorifying the comfort and luxury it affords, or a romantic and sentimental tableau of "picturesque Switzerland," the Zurich exhibition expressed first and foremost the desire of our people to go back to the deep springs of national inspiration. To lead a nation, more is needed than a perfect system of law and technical education. A people must rediscover its soul if it is to enjoy good health as well as to attain true prosperity. It must rediscover its vocation. Our nation received its vocation from God, when on the plain of Grütli those robust highlanders, healthy both in soul and in body, swore their oath before him; when the Confederates at the Diet of Stans bowed to the spiritual authority of Nicholas of Flüe and put an end to their selfish quarrels; and when all the citizens of Geneva, meeting together in General Council, swore their unanimous oath to "live in accordance with the Holy Gospel."

So my aim in this book is not to write a treatise on psychology, nosology, philosophy, or theology, but to help our nation to discover a new physical, psychical, and spiritual health, through submitting itself afresh to the sovereignty of God.

We must take an entirely new view of the prevention of disease. The scientific method is to extirpate the primary cause. Malnutrition, a falling birthrate, the use of narcotics, venereal disease, etc. . . . are all symptoms of a primary cause in the nation, namely, moral deficiency.

The health of a nation depends on the discipline and altruism of all its citizens. Moral health, spiritual health, and physical health form one indivisible whole. . . . [1]

The medico-social organization of our nation during the last hundred years has chiefly consisted of "societies." One needs only to glance at the yearbook of one of these charitable societies to appreciate the tremendous amount of work done at this level. One only needs, for example, to look through the Federal Antituberculosis *Bulletin* to marvel at the enormous sacrifices and the huge expense

[1]Manifesto of the doctors meeting at Interlaken in the first rally for the moral and spiritual rearmament of the nations, Sept., 1938.

this program entails. I ought also to mention the temperance societies, poor persons' dispensaries, the societies for rehabilitation, and
for the re-education of juvenile delinquents, and so on.

Let us not underestimate all this effort, which is admirable. But the
nation can no longer be content with this, and feels an evident need
for medico-social action aimed more at securing "positive health"
than at repairing the breaches and coming to the aid of the unfortunate. The idea of the "charitable society" always implies an attitude
somewhat humiliating to the object of its attentions. What a doctor
such as Vincent complains of in these societies is the "lady bountiful"
spirit, and all the petty egoism, pride, and favoritism that slips inevitably into even the best undertaking if the heart of man is not
changed.[2]

A national "positive health" program must seek to discover the
underlying causes of the psychical confusion and the signs of physical
degeneration among our people.

The physical conditions of life have been more profoundly modified
in the course of the last hundred years than in the preceding twenty
centuries. This last century has seen the growth of great conurbations,
the extreme development of the restlessness, the speed, and the intensity of human affairs, as well as a great increase in the nervous
excitement due to the sensationalism of entertainment and of the
presentation of news. This century too has seen an alarming increase
in the consumption of exotic foods, of tea, coffee, industrial sugar,
and meats, and the invention of preserved foods and of forced vegetables, which make it possible to eat all kinds of produce in and out
of season, thus destroying the normal alimentary rhythms of nature.
It has seen, too, the development of artificial light, and the general
habit of night life which that makes possible. It is obvious that such
far-reaching revolutions in habits of eating and living, taking place
in such a short space of time, must necessarily have had repercussions on public health.

It is no good, however, expecting to be able to turn back the course

[2]A. Vincent, *Vers une médecine humaine,* collection "Espirit" (Paris: Éditions
Montaigne), p. 75.

of human development, suddenly to deprive it of all the fruits of progress and reverse the new trends in dietary habits. The idea, therefore, of a completely natural life, as envisaged in the extremist doctrines of nudism and vegetarianism, cannot form the basis of a constructive plan for public health.

God is more than nature. His purpose for men fits in with the laws he has imposed on nature, but takes account of the particular and present needs of man.

A country whose citizens rediscovered personal discipline through obedience to God—self-mastery, the solution of their psychical and social conflicts, moderation in all their appetites, the exaltation of their vitality through a positive attitude of mind—such a country would achieve a quite new level of health.

For since God created man and gave the universe its laws, obeying him must mean that man puts himself in the conditions most favorable to health. I am not trying to deny that there are sick people among those who are most obedient to God's will. That would be to deny the solidarity of the human race. But the spiritual decline in the world in general, and in medicine in particular, has had a deleterious effect on the health of the nations.

Obeying God does not mean solely avoiding wrong modes of living; it means also coming back into fellowship with him, and thus finding the spiritual strength necessary to life.

The real problems of men are always, in the last analysis, religious; so that if we spoke only of reforming lives and of concrete discipline, we should be doing no more than proposing a tedious moralism or a cult of discipline. This would be tackling people from outside. The only true source of discipline in this world is fellowship with Christ. The moment Jesus Christ really comes into a person's life, he finds a new discipline, one which is no longer rigid, formalist, or heavy, but joyous, supple, and spontaneous. Discipline is not the goal of life, nor even a means of coming to Christ. It is a consequence of the change in outlook which takes place when Christ breaks into a person's life.

When medicine pays due regard to the spiritual struggle in men's hearts, when it realizes once more that men cannot be treated without

God being taken into account, it will experience the great renewal it needs today.

When one thinks of the physiological materialism which held sway over medicine at the beginning of this century, one is thankful to recognize that the renewal has already begun. On all sides books are appearing which express this universal need to break out of the materialist impasse. I should like to mention that of my Genevan colleague Georges Regard, *Étude biologique et scientifique des grands problèmes religieux,* which points out the mistake our predecessors made in considering science and religion as contradictory. I could mention many other books. Coming to the fore now are many doctors who from their personal experience of Jesus Christ are deriving a quite new vision of their profession. Dr. Jack Brock, occupying a chair of medicine in the University of Capetown, declared in a speech: "My task as I see it is to train a new generation of medical students in South Africa. . . . We want men who will give themselves completely to medicine, with a sense of responsibility for their vocation. Only a new generation of doctors, whose work is based first and foremost on their personal contact with God, can really respond to the needs of the nation."[3]

Dr. Alexis Carrel said:

The spiritual activities of man are no less real than the physical and chemical phenomena of his body, and their importance is much greater.

Emancipation from the dogma of materialism will usher in a new era, in which life will be completely understood in all three of its basic constituents. We talk of peace, but we must not forget that life loves strength, and peace demands strength. The strength of nations, like that of a man, is composed of spiritual as well as material elements. That is why the call of the present hour must be a call to moral and physical virility. And the spiritual rearmament of men and nations must open the way to it.[4]

The great German surgeon Sauerbruch, in a lecture delivered before the Medical Society of the Hague in March, 1940, said: "The problem which dominates our economic, technical, and cultural life, is that of the relation between man and technology. . . . The doctor

[3]*Church of England Newspaper*, March 11, 1938.
[4]Message to the national rally for moral rearmament in Washington, D. C., June 8, 1939. Proceedings of the United States Congress.

knows at the present time that one cannot do everything by means of technology. He uses both his medical techniques and his personality as a doctor, bending both together toward his true aim, which is to fulfill his duty and his mission of healing. He knows that technology will not penetrate to the core of the mysterious being called man."

In answer to a journalist's question he declared: "The world needs a directing idea. . . . Technique without such an idea is the most dangerous thing there is."

"What, in your opinion, sir, ought this directing idea to be?"

"One man calls it God, another fate, a third something else. The important thing is to renounce selfishness and the pursuit of profit. We must learn once again that we are all men. . . . We must have done with materialism."[5]

In a lecture on "The Doctor and Soul-healing," Sauerbruch said again: "There is no true medical art in the absence of an attitude of submission to God. From this attitude of submission springs a strength which we need in order to practice our profession and to shoulder our responsibility for each of our patients as an individual, as well as for the whole nation."[6]

Spiritual renewal will bring to medicine a renewal of authority.

When the people of Zurich voted in favor of a law permitting palmists to practice their art, shrewd doctors frankly recognized that the modern trend in medicine was not entirely without responsibility for the popular misgivings evinced in regard to it by this vote.[7]

It is the attempt to preserve spiritual and moral neutrality which has rendered doctors powerless to fulfill their role as guides. And now ordinary people blame them for thus betraying their responsibility. Doctors have reduced themselves to the role of indifferent and even cynical spectators. They watch the sad human comedy play itself out; they see all the faults of mankind. But they want to remain objective, avoiding value judgments and any affirmation of faith.

Through spiritual renewal also doctors will come back to aware-

[5]*De Telegraaf*, March 16, 1940.
[6]*Berner Tagblatt*, Sept. 5, 1940.
[7]Dr. L. B., "La brèche dans la citadelle," *La vie médicale*, Cahiers protestants, March, 1939.

ness of their mission and confidence in the part they have to play. How many doctors today are secretly discouraged, and have less faith in their art than their patients have? Such success as they have is partial or superficial. They heal men's diseases but not their lives. They have a vague feeling that they are not coming to grips with the essential problem of man. The ideal of respect for liberty of conscience has closed to them the field of radical action. They have been unwilling to constrain men and direct them. They have respected a man's right to make mistakes. But the people, as in Christ's day, are like sheep without a shepherd. They have had enough of having no leaders, of finding among the intellectuals only knowledgeable and objective observers.

The moral authority of the doctor is the key to all psychotherapy, whatever technique is used; and this authority can hardly depend only on his knowledge and his will. It must depend also upon his attitude to life, upon the solution he himself has found to the difficulties in his own life, upon concordance between the principles he professes to hold and his actual behavior, upon his personal faith and upon the fruits of conscientiousness, disinterestedness, love, and honesty which that faith brings forth in his work.

How is a patient's morale to be treated?

Many doctors think of a patient's morale only in terms of optimism. It follows that all they think they can do to sustain and improve a patient's morale is to reassure him about his condition, by every possible means. They will remain silent, give evasive answers, or exaggerate the importance of some trifling sign of improvement—in order to preserve the patient's illusions.

I do not deny the beneficial effect of a positive suggestion made by an understanding and affectionate doctor, insofar as it is honestly made. Coué's advice to his patients that they should tell themselves over and over again that every day, in every way, they were getting better and better, undoubtedly worked wonders in minor psychopathic cases. But we fail to recognize the depth of the human drama and the power of the destructive forces at work in men's hearts if we think that they can be dealt with by such methods. When events give the lie to his hopes, and his secret failures are repeated despite all his good resolutions, the patient learns that therapy through optimism has its limits.

A morale capable of standing up to the worst vicissitudes of life, and of facing death itself, can have its source only in spiritual strength. To help his patient at this level the doctor's aim must be not to delude him, but to be as honest with him as he can.

I imagine that here the reader will want to ask: "Do you always tell a person with cancer what disease he has?"

I must point out first of all that the family is generally much more concerned than the doctor to hide the truth from the patient. It is often the family which urges—even demands—that the doctor should take part for sentimental reasons in an elaborate pretense of optimism which only puts a barrier between the patient and those about him as the solemn hour of death approaches.

The reader can have no idea of the naïve suggestions, the secret visits to the doctor, the subterfuges, and the playacting in which a family can indulge, even in cases where to reveal the truth would be quite simple and without real danger.

A relative of the patient follows the doctor downstairs and says: "Now, doctor, tell me the truth; but of course you mustn't say anything to the patient." The patient, however, knows quite well that secret conversations are going on, and the feeling that they are "keeping something from him" only sets him imagining all sorts of frightening but unlikely things—even in cases where the doctor has in fact been quite frank with him.

At this point it must be reiterated that Christianity is not a code of morals, but a religion. If honesty is applied as a "principle," without due consideration, one can of course do more harm than good—though this is more rarely the case than people think.

Christianity is a religion. That is to say, we are not called upon to practice honesty brutally, as a morality without love. What we must do is to bring to the patient, through personal fellowship with Christ, the spiritual climate in which he can bear to know the truth, in which the truth will bring him closer to God instead of plunging him into rebellion and despair.

The message of Jesus Christ is a whole. One cannot isolate one aspect of it, such as honesty, and leave out all the rest—love, for instance, and especially personal experience of God's grace. The doctor who cannot yet, without risk, tell the whole truth to a person who is seriously ill, is one who has not yet been able to help his patient attain the spiritual maturity which will enable him to look death in the face and continue his upward march.

I should not like it to be thought that I am indulging in facile criticism of families. I know well all the love, the pity, and the desire to save the patient unnecessary suffering that prompts them to hide the truth. I am not speaking lightly of a problem of conscience the complexity of which I know well from my own experience. But the fact is that I consider it absolutely insoluble on the ethical level; it finds its solution only through a spiritual miracle. I have not myself told the truth to all the dying people I have tended—far from it! And I am not claiming that their families stopped me. But I know that in every one of those cases the very fact of not having been able to be honest was a demonstration to me of the failure of my spiritual ministry: It was proof that I had not been able to lead my patient into communion with God.

My mother, for six years a widow, died in the prime of life, leaving two small children, after suffering for several years from an implacable disease whose course three operations had failed to arrest. I recall that during her last few months an architect often came to see her in order to discuss with her a building project which he was purposely proceeding with very slowly. Doubtless no one was taken in by this, and possibly my mother was not either. Everyone knew that she would never see the first brick laid.

It is impossible to blame families for maintaining such fictions, with the pious intention of making the patient think about the future rather than about his illness.

But I now know that there is a more profound and powerful means of sustaining a patient's morale: by helping him to become strong in the spirit. On the day she died my mother expressed regret that people had not had more confidence in her religious maturity, which no doubt would have made it possible for her to face reality. She would have liked, she said, to have been better prepared to meet death and to leave her children.

However profound and serious the problem of telling the truth about the diagnosis and the prognosis of a particular case, it is far from being the only form taken by the problem of honesty in medicine.

Quite as often in daily practice we must face difficulties of a more modest nature.

I have often had to admit to a patient that I have told him a lie—such as, for instance, saying that I had found nothing in an analysis when really I had forgotten to make it, or inventing an excuse to hide the fact that I had forgotten all about an appointment. Another difficulty encountered daily is that of confessing our ignorance in reply to some question asked by a patient. All these little admissions, which are so very important for the doctor who is desirous of applying his faith to his professional practice, are frequently harder to make than big ones. We feel that we are going to lose our patient's confidence. The truth is that we are more concerned with our reputation and our patient's good opinion of us. In all branches of social life, this fear of destroying confidence serves to justify manipulation of the truth, and all this falsification and dissimulation is the true cause of the crisis of confidence from which the world is suffering.

In recording now some features in the story of one of my patients I should like to touch upon another aspect—more subtle, but not less important—of the problem of honesty in medicine.

Edmée was a young woman suffering from functional paraplegia.

As soon as I took up her case, various people who knew her put me in possession of certain facts which threw doubts on her sincerity. Her nurse informed me of the difficult situation she had to face: ought she, in order to humor Edmée's susceptibilities, to pretend not to notice untruths she told, putting them down as due to her illness, or should she reprove her for them, at the risk of increasing her moral isolation?

196]   THE HEALING OF PERSONS

Edmée was caught in the vicious circle of neurosis which I described in Chapter 4. She was unable to act naturally. The neurotic adopts an artificial attitude in order to protect his sensitivity, and this artificiality awakens distrust in others. In the atmosphere of distrust the sensitivity of the patient is quickened, and he is driven to further subterfuge.

In my turn, I found myself caught in the toils of the problem. Everything I had been told about Edmée disposed me to mistrust of her, whereas only confidence could help her to be herself again. But one cannot forget what one knows about a patient and be trustful to order. This situation is commoner than is generally thought: A member of the family comes to us in secret and tells us things about a patient to put us on our guard. He says as he leaves: "Of course, doctor, not a word of this to ——!" But there is always a certain feeling of strain between our patient and ourselves if we are hiding from him what we know about him.

I have often had to refuse to listen to this sort of family gossip, so that there may be no danger of it forming a barrier between my patient and me. Such a barrier would make all my efforts barren. Or else I warn the family that I must be told nothing which I cannot repeat to the patient. Utter honesty on the part of the doctor in regard to the patient is the first prerequisite of Christian medicine, above all in nerve cases.

Without absolute honesty, no confidence is possible. The failure of so much of our work is certainly due to the fact that we are too apt to set more store by our skill than by the effects of honesty. We count more on our psychology, and psychology is very often a form of diplomacy, and diplomacy always involves something less than honesty.

I approached Edmée, therefore, determined to be frank. "I cannot help you," I said to her, "unless there is established between you and me a feeling of complete trust, and that means that I must be absolutely frank with you. So I want to tell you all that I have heard about you, and what I think about you myself. That will be the best possible proof that I do trust you." Calmly and at length I went on to tell her in detail all the things that had been reported to me.

I had no idea what was going to happen. Perhaps I would spark off some nervous crisis. On the contrary, the patient allowed me to speak without interruption, gradually became more relaxed, and looked at me with eyes wide with astonishment, but lit with quite a new light. She was visibly relieved to know where she was with me. When I finished, I started telling her about my own lies. I told her about one which I had been guilty of quite recently. I can still remember it. A few days previously I had had a coffee somewhere, and bought a packet of cigarettes. But in my accounts I had written "Snack, 1 franc 20," whereas I had spent 55 cents on the coffee and a tip, and the remaining 65 cents was cigarettes. The fact was, then, that I felt guilty about having spent a little too much on cigarettes, and I was not averse to reducing the total that would be shown on that account at the end of the month. It was a kind of forgery.

The next day I told Edmée that I wanted to go on being honest with her, and that the greatest mark of my confidence that I could give anyone was to reveal the thoughts that had come to me during my morning quiet time before God.

That morning, after reading a chapter from one of the Gospels, I had been shocked by the realization of how little faith I had. I realized, in fact, that Edmée was one of the kind of sick people whom Christ and his disciples healed with a single word, and that if I did not succeed in doing that myself, it was because I had not sufficient faith. I had written all this down, and much else besides, and I read it all out to Edmée.

When I visited her for the following day, I again read her what I had written in the morning. She told me then that she too had tried to have a quiet time, with her nurse, but God had not revealed anything to her.

I told her that I had had the same sort of difficulty when I was learning to use the quiet time. The first time nothing had happened to me either. When I had read some passage from the Bible, I kept imagining the sermon that might be preached on it, and that stopped me praying properly.

At last, on the fourth day, Edmée told me that the day before, after I had gone, she had had a quiet time in God's presence, and had written a whole page. And that morning she had done the same. She now wanted to read me what she had written. Naturally it is not for me to set down here the contents of the two pages, the details of which, in any case, I have forgotten. But I was astonished by what I heard. Edmée had learned to be really honest with herself once more. Several wrongs were confessed, and notes made of people whose forgiveness was to be asked for. There were lies to admit, fears to be abandoned, and reconciliations to be attempted. There was a clear insight into the underlying causes of her malady. There was, finally, the decision to dedicate her life to Jesus Christ, and thenceforth to seek to follow God's will instead of her own.

Our interview closed with prayer.

The same day I took her by the hand from the nurses who were supporting her by the shoulders, and for the first time for more than a year she made a few firm steps with this as her only support.

A few weeks later she was able to unburden herself to me competely, and confided to me the great injury which had always darkened her life.

Sickness may be the solemn occasion of God's intervention in a person's life.

Had it not been for her illness, Edmée would still have had her employment, but she would also still have had the immense void within, her psychological complexes, and her feverish compensatory activity, without anything really worthwhile to show for it.

I cannot bring to a close these few pages on honesty in medicine without alluding to social insurance. René Dumesnil, in his book *L'Âme du médecin*,[8] stresses, as many have done before him, the influence which the development of social insurance has had on the medical profession, and the seed of mistrust which this development has sown between doctor and patient. Sickness and accident insurance companies have increased precautions against fraud. Doctors, willy-nilly, have allowed themselves to be influenced, and have adopted an attitude of systematic distrust which has become one of the problems of contemporary medical practice. To all this Dumesnil

[8] Collection "Présences" (Paris: Plon, 1938).

has no answer, any more than he has to all the other moral problems raised by his book. The obvious answer is shown in the action of a woman who came to see me recently. I had previously examined her in accordance with the requirements of an insurance scheme in which she wished to take part. Shortly afterward, she had met some Christians who had helped her to find a living faith. Examining her conscience, and looking especially for what had not been honest in her life, she remembered that when I examined her she had deliberately concealed a previous illness. She recognized that to be consistent in her faith, she must come and admit it to me.

CHAPTER

15

The Laws of Life

The doctor's task is to teach men the physical and spiritual laws of normal life. This conception of medicine has its roots far back in the remotest tradition of our profession.

Pythagoras, in the sixth century B.C., declared that the noblest task one could undertake in this world was to teach men how to live.

As a philosopher he taught that man must seek to find the sources of normal life in contact with God. His disciples began the day with prayer, and then devoted themselves to meditation by taking a solitary walk "so as to prepare themselves for the day's work."[1]

In the evening they used to take a walk together, and pool the inspiration they had individually received.

As a statesman Pythagoras reformed customs, politics, and trade, and succeeded in ushering in a veritable Golden Age at Crotona.

Finally, as a physician he taught men to live in accordance with God's purpose for them. "He saw health as a harmony, and disease as a loss of equilibrium."[2] He desired that food should contribute as much to health as to the uplift of the mind, and to this end he instituted his vegetarian diet.

In these concepts he is the precursor of the Greek genius—of the

[1]Paul Carton, *La vie sage* (Paris: Le François), p. 13.
[2]E. Boinet, *Les doctrines médicales* (Paris: Flammarion, 1920).

greatest of its philosophers, such as Socrates and Plato, as well as of its greatest physician, Hippocrates. Trousseau and Pidoux, in the preface to their book, *Traité de thérapeutique*, write: "Science has changed again and again since the time of Hippocrates. Nevertheless, that great man founded medicine on fundamental truths so solid that they have become the common sense and the permanent rules of medical art." It is true that for Hippocrates medicine is an art rather than a science; an art founded on an understanding of man as an individual and not as a generalization. "Life is short," he wrote, "and the Art long; the occasion fleeting; experience fallacious, and judgment difficult."[3]

For Hippocrates, it is nature which heals, that is to say the vital force—*pneuma*—which God gives to man; and the chief function of medicine is to place man in conditions of life which will no longer run counter to nature. "When one has fallen ill," he writes, "one must change one's way of life. It is clear that the life one has been living is bad altogether, or in part, or in some respect."

I could go on giving quotations from Hippocrates which show him as the reformer of men's lives. "There are two rules for remaining healthy: to eat less than one might eat, and to work." Like Pythagoras, he underlines the importance of meditation, which our modern world has forgotten: "Meditation is for a man's spirit what walking is for his body." As Ambroise Paré was to say later: "I tended him, God healed him." He writes: "When medicine succeeds, it is to the divinity that the credit is due." And again: "One cannot love medicine without loving man."

Finally, if the physician wants to help men to reform their lives, he must reform his own: "I shall keep my life pure and undefiled, and my art also" (Hippocratic oath).

This spiritual view of medicine, which would heal men by bringing them back to obedience to God, has persisted through the ages, in spite of all the triumphs of materialist medicine. This is not the place to recall all the medical geniuses who have professed it. But I cannot refrain from mentioning the name of the great Sydenham.

[3]*The Genuine Works of Hippocrates*, trans. from the Greek by F. Adams (London: Baillière, Tindall & Cox, 1939), p. 299 (Aphorisms, I.1).

Tronchin, Voltaire's doctor, when he was summoned to Paris by Philip of Orleans to inoculate his two children against smallpox, took upon himself the task of reforming the habits of

high society, worn out by the pleasure-loving life of the century, and the "vaporish dames," enervated by excesses of all kinds.

To these neurasthenics, as we should call them nowadays, whose treatment consisted of bleeding, purgation, emetics, baths, and cinchona, Tronchin proposed to apply only moral remedies, his chief boast being that he healed the body through the soul. To dissipate these "nauseous vapors" by moderating the passions, by calming the emotions, by building up everyone's strength of mind—this was his doctrine. He set himself up at once as the man of Nature, the apostle of the healthy and frugal life, the enemy of the artificial existence of the city, making each patient his friend. . . . There was to be seen in Paris the strange spectacle of apartments turned upside down by the advice of the subtle Genevan, curtains that obstructed the air removed, windows thrown open to let the sunlight into the dark, dank rooms; eiderdowns, feather-beds and down pillows banished, and replaced with horsehair; and carpets discarded. In the streets, fine ladies with mincing steps, short-skirted, forsook their carriages and chairs and mixed with the passers-by. At home the lady of the house would be found bustling about, polishing the floors and the brasses, while Monsieur would take off his coat and chop wood or shift the furniture.[4]

Coming to our own day, I must mention Dr. Dubois, of Berne, who treated neurotics by reforming their attitude to life; Reymond, of Chexbres, who had them sawing wood; and above all Liengme, of Vaumarcus, who taught them what he called the rules of life.[5] Finding among them some that were undisciplined and in revolt against their environment and against themselves, he undertook a regular scheme of moral education. One of his favorite ideas was that the Bible was the most valuable book on psychology, and that all the good things discovered by that science had already been stated in the Holy Scriptures.

In German-speaking Switzerland one man has had a tremendous influence on the health of our people, namely Dr. Bircher-Benner.

[4]Jules Bertrand, in *Le Temps médical*, May 21, 1938.
[5]G. Liengme, *Pour apprendre à mieux vivre: Conseils pratiques aux "nerveux"* (Neuchâtel: V. Attinger).

His method consisted of the re-education of the mind, coupled with discipline, exercise, hygiene, and proper diet.

Fifty years ago it could be said that food in German Switzerland was much worse than in the French-speaking part of the country, where more vegetables and less pork were consumed. Today, thanks chiefly to Bircher's influence, German Switzerland has a much healthier diet than French Switzerland. Throughout the area people eat "Birchermüsli"—fruit and raw vegetables.

It is to this version of Hippocratic medicine that all the "naturistic" schools belong (Kneipp, Sigaud, etc.).

Paul Carton, of Paris, seems to me to have made clearer than others the philosophical and spiritual import of a medicine whose aim is the reformation of men's lives.

He insists always on the obedience, the renunciation, and the sacrifices which must be accepted by the person who wishes to conform to the laws of healthy living. A life that is too easy is dangerous, and illusory utopias must be cast aside.

There is first the belief in the possibility of controlling for our benefit the forces of Nature, even if this means flying in the face of the laws which govern human life and evolution. And then there is the idea that the riches of the earth can be extracted indefinitely from the ground and so distributed as to make possible unlimited indulgence in food and material comfort. Lastly, there is the search for maximum enjoyment in return for minimum effort. All these dreams of easy happiness are dangerous illusions, since human progress can be realized only through work and simple, natural living.[6]

He quotes Bouchard:

It is most important that doctors should know how to think, and that they should give themselves time to do so; they must look beyond the material expression of a disease, to the conditions which endanger and sustain it; they must frame a doctrine, and reach towards general ideas.[7]

It was one of Carton's pupils, Dr. Schlemmer, who set me thinking about the true meaning of medicine when he said to me one day: "Medicine is the art of giving advice on how to live."

[6] *Traité de médecine, d'alimentation et d'hygiène naturistes* (Brévannes, 1931), p. 117.
[7] Bouchard, *Introduction aux éléments de thérapeutique de Nothnagel et Rossbach*, p. xxiv.

There are, then, laws of life which cannot be infringed without danger to health. Civilization, however, in its search for material comfort, tends constantly to annul them. One cannot with impunity turn night into day, keep oneself too warm in winter, go everywhere in a car, eat whatever one wishes, or live in conflict with others.

Since it is God who created life, it is clear that it is from the Bible that we may most surely learn its laws. The Bible is a rich mine of medical counsel. The subject is so vast that I cannot hope to deal with it in detail here. I hope that it will be possible for me to devote a book to it some day.[8] I have already shown the importance of its answer to the problems of suffering and of sex. Everyone knows that it contains the rules for the spiritual, moral, and social life of mankind. I shall refer later to some aspects of its psychological teaching. But it also contains plenty of guidance for the conduct of man's physical life.

The Bible commands man to work: "Six days shall you labor" (Exod. 20:9). And work is one of the prerequisites of health. A country that is anxious to safeguard national health ought not to permit men to remain idle. The Bible also commands rest: "The seventh day is a sabbath to the Lord your God; in it you shall not do any work" (Exod. 20:10), and "Night comes, when no one can work" (John 9:4). Rest is also one of the essential laws of health.

The Bible gives plenty of guidance on the subject of food, beginning with this from Genesis: "God said, 'Behold, I have given you every plant yielding seed which is upon the face of all the earth, and every tree with seed in its fruit; you shall have them for food" (Gen. 1:29).

Fruit and vegetables are thus essential foods of mankind. The prejudices of a civilization founded on money have misled many people in regard to this. There are countless families in which the consumption of fruit by children is restricted on the grounds that it is a "dessert"—families in which they are even threatened with not being allowed to have it "if they do not behave themselves"! I once

---

[8]*Translator's Note*: The promised book has been written. The English translation, *A Doctor's Casebook in the Light of the Bible*, was published in 1954 by SCM Press Ltd., London, England.

treated a housemaid who was suffering from lack of fruit in her diet. Her employers gave her meat twice a day, but did not allow her to have anything from the fruit bowl, which was reserved for her masters' table.

While overeating is wrong, so also is undereating. God has planned our feeding, and if we deprive ourselves of any particular category of food which he has laid down for us, we shall find inevitably that our health suffers for it. Whether out of laziness, or from gluttony, or following the fashion or some sectarian theory, many people seriously restrict the variety of their diet.

The following case is instructive. It concerns a patient whom we shall call Marcelle. The constitutional situation was clear. She had an uncle and an aunt who were both asthmatic. Her illness had taken various forms, the kinship of which was attested by the way they succeeded one another. In infancy—the digestive age (see pp. 00-00) —she had severe enteritis, which gave place to repeated attacks of bronchitis and to recurrent adenoid growths at the respiratory age. Then, at the muscular age, a stubborn form of eczema made its appearance. Finally, this gave way to asthma, which was so bad that it made any activity impossible, and prevented any form of social life.

These successive morbid metamorphoses, well known to medicine, show how erroneous it would be to treat each manifestation as an individualized local malady. Clearly, each is the translation into visible form of a more deep-seated general disorder.

Mention should be made of the psychical factor in this case. Without insisting on the effect on her attitude of her poor state of health, and the way it tended to monopolize her thoughts, I specially noted that it was since the breaking-off for health reasons of her engagement to be married that her asthma had become so much worse. By nature strong-willed and decisive, she had repressed her disappointment rather than accepting it. In order to spare her family the backwash of her grief, she had pretended to bear it with equanimity.

This attempt to block the expression of emotions is so contrary to the human law of childlike spontaneity that it invariably has harmful repercussions on health. Coming as it did in this case on top of a general condition that was itself precarious, it had serious consequences.

But the most striking thing in Marcelle's case was the alimentary factor. From a very early age she had shown an aversion to sugar. The answer had been quite simple: She had abstained from sugar ever since. This abstention had only served to fix the idiosyncrasy. The mucous membrane of the mouth was overstimulated by contact with sugar, and swallowing it caused immediate vomiting.

The problem, however, had become even more serious. Her aversion to sugar had finally caused an intolerance of fruit, including even those that were least sugary. The result was that Marcelle had not absorbed any sugar at all, nor eaten a single fruit, for more than twenty years.

Was this idiosyncrasy a symptom of the condition, or was it the other way round—was the condition a result of the lack of sugar and fruit? There are grounds for thinking that both are true, and that what we have here is one more of those vicious circles which are so frequent in medicine.

The least one can say is that no treatment by "specialists" in bronchial diseases, in eczema, or in asthma, and no adrenaline injections (she had had two a day for several months) could lead by themselves to a satisfactory result so long as there persisted such a serious deficiency in the matter of a food as basic as fruit. She had been accustomed for so long to abstaining from fruit, that she had no longer thought it a point worth mentioning!

I explained to Marcelle that fruit was man's basic food. Cost what it might, she must accustom herself to eating it. The process would last as long as was necessary. She would start with a tiny portion of grated apple daily, very gradually increasing the dose. But victory over her aversion to fruit was the *sine qua non* of a real cure.

A few months later she wrote to tell me the point she had reached in her course of readaptation. She was already able to take half an apple a day without ill effects, and her general condition and her asthma were considerably improved. She was making do with a single adrenaline injection, and was feeling much better.

A course at the Mont Dore spa completed the cure.

Man's normal diet ought always to include, in judicious proportions, the following three categories of nutritive elements:

1. Body-building elements, in order to ensure the growth and continual replacement of our tissues. These are, on the one hand, the albumins, nitrogenous products to be found chiefly in meat, eggs, and cheese. The Bible does not forbid the eating of meat, as many people suppose. There are, on the other hand, the mineral salts, which are found chiefly in green vegetables and cereals. These foods are especially necessary to growing bodies and in convalescence.

2. Combustion elements, the purpose of which is to provide the body with the heat and energy it needs. These are the sugars, farinaceous foods, and fats. They are all the more necessary during periods of cold weather and when the body is making a big muscular effort.

3. Finally, living elements, containing vitamins, those fragile substances which modern chemistry has isolated, but the importance of which wise physicians had long suspected. These elements are to be found in fruits and in raw vegetables.

As a general rule, every meal should contain elements from each of these three categories.

A simple reform, and one which would have a considerable bearing on health, would be to eat some fruit at each meal, including breakfast, and particularly at the beginning of the meal. A fruit is a germ which contains in essence the life-force of a whole plant. By the same token untreated wheat is one of the most valuable tonics, and bread one of man's basic foods.

A raw food which is very easy to obtain is the radish, a vegetable which anyone can grow, even in a windowbox; it grows rapidly and for most of the year. One can thus go and pull a few radishes every morning, and eat them quite fresh.

Too many people must have things cooked, and instead of fruit they eat far too many concentrated sweetmeats, sweet dishes, preserves, and jams.

Another example: Luke was a timid, worried sort of man. In his youth he had had an inferiority complex in regard to his brother and sister, and now he had the same feeling toward his wife. But I do not wish to deal at length with his psychological problems.

He had a noticeable albugo, and on questioning him closely on his diet, I found that he had been put on an exaggeratedly vegeterian diet by his wife, a woman of decided views. The result was a definite nitrogen deficiency. I therefore corrected his diet by adding to it (in default of a small quantity of meat, which his wife on principle refused to have anything to do with) more cheese, mushrooms, cereals, walnuts—in short, vegetarian foods rich in nitrogen. This seemed to me to be quite as important as the spiritual and psychological counsel which I naturally did not fail to give.

There are a number of other possible moral causes for bad eating. Everyone knows the heroic restrictions of diet to which women can subject themselves in order to reduce. On the other hand, there are people who worry about the danger of contracting tuberculosis, and will stupidly overeat because they are naïve enough to think that plumpness is a protection against it.

Lastly, the Bible lays down a most important rule of health in regard to eating, namely, that of the periodical fast. Men have been greedy and clever enough—even those who submit themselves in principle to the rules of the Roman Catholic Church—to get round the rule so effectively that their health is endangered. Among Protestants, matters are even worse. The Swiss Federal Fast, religious in inspiration, has become a holiday on which banquets proliferate.

For thousands of years mankind has practiced days and longer periods of fasting, at first from necessity, in accordance with the hazards of primitive life, and then in accordance with religious prescriptions. It is only very recently that the custom of a real fast has practically disappeared for the great majority. Civilization tends to make the whole of our life uniform, and to procure foods for us out of season. Civilization is directed by the selfishness and pride of men. If, on the other hand, they turn to prayer and meditation, they rediscover God's plan for living, and accept the idea of fasting, with all its great spiritual and medical significance. The success obtained by doctors who, like Guelpa, have used the simple method of periodical fasting in nutritional diseases, shows clearly the error of a civilization which despises God's plan.

Inspiration

In the preceding chapter I have shown that the Bible is the surest source of information about God's plan for the lives of men. But it would be a serious misunderstanding of the wonderful message of Jesus Christ to see the Bible as no more than a collection of divine laws to which men ought to try to conform. This would be to fall into the error of legalism, formalism, or moralism. Moral effort of this kind has nothing whatever to do with the miraculous transformation brought about by Christ in the person who opens his heart to him. The gospel is not a call to effort, but to faith.

Psychologists have clearly shown the futility of the idea that one can get rid of an obsession, regain confidence, or recall a forgotten name simply by trying harder. The fact that one can go to bed with a problem and "sleep on it," and wake up in the morning with the solution, is evidence of the beneficial effect of a relaxation of tension on the mental processes.

The person who makes tremendous efforts to become better is like a man pushing on a door marked PULL. He must relax his efforts before the door will open and let him through. The story is told of how when Im Grund went up to Nicholas of Flüe, the Swiss national hero, to inform him of the serious dissensions that had broken out among the Confederates, and to get his advice, the saint took his girdle, made a knot in it, and handing it to Im Grund, asked him to untie it. This Im Grund easily did. "That," said Nicholas of Flüe, "is how the difficulties of men must be unknotted." When Im Grund protested that it was not so easy, Nicholas answered: "Nor would you be able to untie this knot, if we were each to pull on one end of the cord, and that is what men try to do."

The Christian experience is the irruption of Jesus Christ into a person's life, bringing relaxation of tension, confidence, and a quite new liberating force, and abruptly changing the course of its development. Legalism, on the other hand, means slavery to "principles," and continual efforts to satisfy the imperious demands of a moral code.

True liberation through Jesus Christ, however, is a very rare thing, because of the littleness of our faith. It is in order to hide from himself his lack of real experience that the religious person so often pretends to be freed from sins and passions from which he has not in fact been delivered. This lack of sincerity with himself sets up a conflict in him. The doctor sees plenty of these religious people, ravaged by inextricable inner conflicts. The man in the street does not need to be a psychologist to sense this fact, and he simply says that he has no desire to be like them.

It is possible to turn Christ's teaching into a new formal morality quite as tyrannous as the Judaic law, which St. Paul contrasted with the grace of Jesus Christ. Whether or not it is called "Christian," formal morality leads only to psychological disasters.

The "naturist" schools of thought do not escape this danger either. One sees their followers weighed down by a truly obsessive fear of the slightest disobedience of the laws of the natural life.

Being a "new man" means escaping from every kind of system: Nothing is good or bad in itself. Good and evil are in men's hearts, not in things. Christianity appeals to the impulses of men's hearts, and counts on miracles, whereas legalism calls for moral effort, counts on the will, and passes judgment on others.

Nothing is further from the spirit of Christ than exhorting a person sick in mind to make the effort of will of which he is incapable. On the other hand, to lead him into personal contact with Jesus Christ will be to help him to find the supernatural strength which will bring him victories his own efforts could never have won for him.

This may be illustrated by an analogy taken from mathematics, from analytical geometry, contrasting the equation of a curve with its derivative. The former establishes dimensions and co-ordinates, and deals with quantities, in the same way as formal morality sets out to reckon up the moral value of men. On the other hand, the derivative indicates the direction of a curve, whatever its cusp—that is to say, whatever co-ordinates it has. The experience of the grace of Christ may be likened to a change in the direction of the derivative from negative to positive, in a virtuous man as well as in anyone else.

If I seem to be insisting too much on the ill effects of religious formalism, this is because it has turned so many doctors away from the Christian view of man. They have seen so many religious people claiming to help others to solve their problems, who themselves have been struggling impotently against difficulties often greater than those of the unbeliever, experiencing the same failures, subject to the same passions and the same sufferings. This is why so very many doctors have shut their eyes to the spiritual tragedy which nevertheless is there, being played out in the heart of every man, and having enormous repercussions on his health. This tragedy in the heart of man is that of sin, the ultimate cause of all the personal problems of our lives. When doctors deny its existence, it is in protest against a formalistic conception of sin, whose baneful effects they observe, but which is not the view of sin taken by the Christian gospel.

It is no light matter to struggle against sin! It is not sufficient to urge people to mend their ways, to point out the price that has to be paid for men's faults, to denounce the modern decline in moral standards, or to write impressive articles on the thirst for personal gain which has overtaken so many of our doctors. We underestimate the power of sin if we imagine that a few pointed books will provide a solution. There is no power that will stem the power of sin, apart from that of Jesus Christ himself. This is why leading a person to a personal encounter with Jesus, in prayer and meditation, is the only certain road toward a real transformation of his life.

Lives are not to be transformed by means of regulations and advice only; this merely tends to turn the regulations into a new tyranny laid on the backs of those who try to keep them. It is, above all, a misunderstanding of the nature of the tragedy in the heart of man: his powerlessness to conform to his own principles. "Incapable ourselves of doing any good thing," as Calvin said. If we are to become obedient to the will of God for us, we need something other than laws and exhortations. We must go through a real inner transformation. The source of all reformation of life is in personal fellowship with Jesus Christ.

This is why I feel that the deepest meaning of medicine is still not in "counseling lives," but in leading the sick to this personal encounter with Jesus Christ, so that accepting it they may discover a new quality of life, discern God's will for them, and receive the supernatural strength they need in order to obey it.

In introducing to the readers of *L'Esprit médical* his excellent *Précis de médecine catholique*,[1] Dr. Henri Bon wrote:

Paradoxically, a negative observation may serve to demonstrate how doctors are predisposed in favour of theology. Do we not frequently read, from medical pens, such remarks as: "To go further would be to enter the field of metaphysics," or "Here we come to a domain which belongs properly to philosophy, or to religion"? This simple remark, this recognition of the perpetual encounter with the neighbouring domain, bears witness to the relatedness of medical and religious questions.

And is not this the reason why we see large numbers of doctors, over the ages, becoming priests or monks—beginning with Luke, "the beloved physician" as St. Paul called him, to whom we owe one of the Gospels, and continuing with Nicholas Stenon who became Bishop and apostle of North Germany, and, in our own day, the Rev. Fr. Gemelli, Rector of the Pontifical University of Milan? It ought not to be forgotten that the catalogue of the saints of the Catholic Church includes some sixty doctors. . . .

Indeed, the very aim of medicine—the preservation of life, the fight against death—is a metaphysical aim. What is this life that has to be maintained? What is this death that is to be warded off? Doctors have always been keenly interested in the nature of life. Barthez and the Montpellier School went so far as to construct their own theory on the subject. And in the case of death, we have the meditations of Bichat, Buisson, Dastre, and many more. . . .

[1]Paris: Alcan, 1936.

In short, medicine has broken away from the priesthood, but has not been able to cast off the spirit which united it with it in the past. Medicine cannot help being a priesthood; it has the duties and the dignity of a priesthood, and that is why theology holds, and must hold, such an important place in medical literature.[2]

What doctor, after all, has not felt the futility of most of the advice he gives, aimed at the reform of people's lives? I could give examples of this in regard to every one of the types of problem we have studied! Faced with an alcoholic, for instance, the doctor knows quite well that the wise advice he gives will be of no effect unless there takes place a profound transformation of the individual. The alcoholic has taken to drink not from preference or thirst, but in order to fill up the void in his life, to escape from the failures of his family life, defeated by conflicts or worn down by disappointments. In the artificial environment of the café his friends listen to him talking freely of all that needs to be put right in the world. But he lacks the strength to follow the advice of the doctor for his own life.

Advice acts from without. The spiritual revolution takes place within.

When a man encounters Jesus Christ, he feels all at once that he has been freed from some passion or some habit to which he has been enslaved, from some fear or rancor against which he has deployed his stoutest efforts in vain.

What sort of approach can we make to men to lead them to a decisive experience of grace, that will avoid moral exhortation and preaching, which is the business of the minister of religion, and not that of the doctor?

Spiritual renewal comes only from meeting God face to face. We know well that in spite of all our efforts and successes, in spite of all our principles and our good will, in spite of all our knowledge and experience, there are difficulties in our lives that cannot be overcome by an effort of the will, problems that cannot be solved by the exercise of reason, and faults that time cannot efface. Spiritual transformation of our lives will not come unless we can stop in our tracks and examine the hectic course of our thoughts and activities honestly in the

[2]*L'Esprit médical,* Feb. 29, 1940.

sight of God. People usually think that in order to get inside the problems of a person's life, it will be necessary to probe with all kinds of indiscreet and insistent questions. More often than not, however, all that is required is to be ready to listen patiently and trustingly. I am reminded of a patient whom I shall call Constant. He had persevered in asking for an appointment which had been postponed several times. It was at the time of the Abyssinian war. When he came, I said to him simply: "I imagine that since you have been so insistent on seeing me it isn't to talk about the war in Africa." I did not say another word. He sat down and began to talk to me about his life, his poor health, and then little by little he told me about his past errors, and the troubles which they had brought upon him. He talked for more than two hours without my interrupting him. When he had finished I merely suggested making a further appointment.

This time I responded to his confidence by talking to him in my turn about my own life. He let me speak as freely as I had done for him the first time.

My life was quite different from his, being much more privileged. I used to think that we could help only those who suffered from the same difficulties as we did. I would tactfully avoid mentioning my happy married life to a person who was in conflict with his wife, or my financial position to a person who had difficulty in making both ends meet. I have learned now that one helps those to whom one gives oneself freely. Giving oneself means speaking quite simply of one's experiences, one's sufferings, one's failings, and one's victories.

When Constant came to see me again, I said to him: "On your first visit, it was you who spoke. On the second, it was I. Today, we are going to let God speak." I handed him a sheet of paper and asked him to note down everything that came into his mind during this period of meditation.

When he handed me back the paper, he had written out, almost without realizing it, a complete program of amendment. There were lies to confess, articles to return to their owners, forgiveness to be sought, reconciliations to be attempted. It only remained for me to say: "Go and put all that into practice."

"The intellect," Bergson wrote, "is characterized by a natural inability to comprehend life."³ Science, on which our civilization is founded, proceeds by analysis only, and life always eludes analysis. A grave crisis has overtaken this civilization of ours, which has asserted the primacy of logic over intuition, of the scientist over the artist, of technology over human beings, of the logician over the believer, of the committee of experts over life. This crisis is a demonstration of the impotence of intelligence and technique when they are divorced from inspiration. The world has accumulated knowledge, but has lost its understanding of simple things. We have seen the League of Nations unable to define peace and war, law unable to define equity, and medicine to define health. Our modern world longs to rediscover the deep springs of life. It will succeed in finding them only by traveling along the road of the inner life which leads to the presence of God, the Creator of life.

In prayer and meditation we see quite simple things in our lives which our intelligence has failed to perceive. We are also inspired to act; for true life is made up of an alternation between meditation and action. They are complementary: meditation leads to action, and action is matured in meditation. This is the universal rhythm of involution and evolution, withdrawal and advance, the inner life and the outward. Action prepared in meditation is quite different in quality from the hectic, breathless activity which characterizes our age, filling it with noise, agitation, and frenzy, and which is one of the chief causes of the catastrophic increase in the incidence of nervous diseases. We blame the railways, the automobile, the telephone, the radio, and the economic complexities of modern life. This is fair enough, but it is man who is really to blame.

For a long time I myself indulged in a restless kind of life, always racing the clock, always in a hurry, incapable of finding the time I needed for my spiritual life. Since I began devoting to it an average of an hour a day, and often longer, I have had to give up activities which I used to think essential. But I have found more happiness in my work, and have been able to put more into it.

Benjamin was a hypochondriac who had for several years been

³Henri Bergson, *Creative Evolution*, trans. Arthur Mitchell (London: Macmillan and Company, 1911) p. 174.

dragging his hopes, his troubles, and his complaints from clinic to clinic. In one he had been given ultra-violet rays; in another they administered tranquilizers, and in a third he was given a course of multivalent organotherapy. Furthermore, he had submitted most unwillingly to all these treatments, always arguing, grumbling at the climate, refusing to conform to hospital regulations, dodging the physical exercises prescribed for him, and then leaving the doctor who he had hoped would work a cure in order to chase after fresh illusions elsewhere.

He was intelligent and well-traveled. He had a child whom his wife had taken overseas to visit grandparents.

Benjamin had insisted on his wife coming back alone, leaving the child with his grandparents. Two years later the child had died after a short illness.

Benjamin was deeply affected by this. He had suffered a nervous breakdown, and had had to go into a nursing home. Digestive disorders had followed, and had become an obsession with him. Various other disorders were added. He was a miserable creature, interested in nothing but his own troubles, his conversation nothing but complaints and requests for advice from all and sundry. He found it impossible to make decisions; his medicine bottles went everywhere with him; he had difficulty in finding things to eat that he had not been warned against by one or another of the succession of doctors he had consulted.

He had just spent some time under observation in the clinic of a famous neurologist who, in my presence, assured him that he had no organic lesion.

But this period of observation, with a nurse coming at all hours of the night to see if he were sleeping soundly, had revived Benjamin's fears and self-pity, despite all the reassurances of the specialist. He had got it into his head that only a prolonged stay in that clinic could cure him. In consequence he gave me a cold welcome.

It would have been useless to attempt to reassure him about all the ills he complained of. It would only have led to an interminable argument. But I should also have forfeited all his confidence if I had refused to listen to his complaints, or suggested that he should forget all about them: He said he wanted nothing better than to get well again and to forget all his troubles. It would also have been futile to preach religion at him: He took no interest in spiritual matters, which had long ceased to play any part in his life.

When I went to see him he was lying on his bed. "My dear friend," I said to him, more or less, "I have come to tell you frankly what is the matter with you. The cause of your trouble is the death of your child. And you would no doubt have been able to bear your grief were it not accompanied by a sense of guilt. You feel you are to blame for having sent your child away and entrusted him to his grandparents, where he contracted the disease which carried him off. Ever since then you have been running away from yourself in an effort to get away from your sense of guilt. All these troubles of yours are nothing but an unconscious attempt to escape, to avoid having to live a life which you no longer have the courage to face with all this weighing on your mind. I am certain that all the doctors who have treated you one after another have had basically the same view as I have as to the cause of your illness. Now, there is nothing that weighs on men's lives that cannot be removed by Jesus Christ.

"You have come to a crossroads. I have no doubt that God has brought you to this present moment so that you can make your choice. There are two roads in front of you. One goes on from clinic to clinic; it is full of suffering, but it is relatively easy to take. It is the road along which you expect healing to come from others, from doctors clever enough to discover some new remedy which will cure you.

"The other road is very much harder. It is the road to Jesus Christ, who has warned us that it is a narrow and difficult one. If you take it, you must accept what comes to you, carry your cross, put up with your troubles, have the courage to go back to work, and face up to life even though it hurts. It is a road which demands a change of heart. But you do not travel it alone; and even if it demands the greatest sacrifices, you will find joy in it, because as you go you will find that Christ is at your side, and sins are forgiven."

Benjamin looked at me thoughtfully when I had finished. Then he said, calmly: "I want to choose the harder road. But I need help, because I don't know what I ought to do."

Then I handed him my pad of prescription forms and a pencil. I took out a notebook myself. I simply said to him: "God will tell you what you must do. We are going to listen to him together, and you must write down what he says to you."

I began writing at length all the thoughts that occurred to me. When I had finished, I read them to him.

He then handed his sheet of paper to me, and I read what he had written on it: "I am ill because I think of nothing but myself. I must do some loving action."

"In regard to whom must you do some loving action?" I asked him.

" In regard to my wife."

"Is it a long time since you last wrote to her?"

"Three months at least."

"Do you want to write to her?"

"Yes."

"When?"

"Now."

"May I come back at six o'clock and see your letter?"

"Yes."

And I left him.

When I came back, his letter was on the table. In the most affectionate terms he asked his wife for news of herself. He went on to tell her quite simply that he had found God, and wanted to devote his life to his service, to listen to him day by day, in order to find out what he expected him to do, and to obey him. He was confident that with God's help he could face life and bear its burdens. She had been right, he added, when she told him that he would only get his health back if he found faith; and he asked her to forgive him for not having believed her. Then he asked her to forgive him for a host of other things. He was looking forward to being with her again, to making her happy, and to going back to work.

At the evening meal his friends were astonished at Benjamin's high spirits, his good appetite, and his lively conversation as he talked about his travels.

I cannot omit to mention here that the days that followed were still bad ones for Benjamin. I do not want to oversimplify the message of the gospel. Doubts assailed him, and with them his hypochondriac tendencies reappeared. But when he went back again to God he found in him the strength and confidence that freed him once again.

But the gospel affirms that there are decisive moments in a person's life, when under the guidance of the Holy Spirit there takes place a radical change in his basic attitude. Everything may not yet be in perfect order in his life, and the skeptical observer may find it easy to deny that any essential change has taken place. Nevertheless, in his heart a new life has been born. As the years go by its fruits will be seen, showing themselves gradually in concrete and visible changes.

One can spend one's whole life trying to obey God, conscientiously applying oneself, regularly and methodically, to the task; one can live a life of austerity and scrupulous uprightness, without ever knowing this explosion of joy, this quite new strength that bursts forth when one is face to face with God and says, Yes! to him with all one's heart.

The effect on one's health is considerable—directly, through the joy and the release of vitality which always accompany this decisive experience; and indirectly, through the solving of one's personal problems which it makes possible, and the harmonization of the whole personality.

There are certain functions in man's organism—the vegetative functions—which are not subject to his will. They are automatically subject, one might say, to the will of God, If, therefore, we disobey his will in the functions over which we have been given free control, discord results. It is as if in a beehive one section of the bees followed the divine purpose dictated to them by their instincts, while others departed from it. One might indeed describe such a hive as diseased.

This is why to seek in prayer the purpose of God for our lives, and to enjoy personal fellowship with Jesus Christ who delivers us from the things that stand in the way of that purpose, leads to that harmony of the whole person which is one of the prerequisites of health.

Christ himself compared this spiritual experience with the germinating seed. The seed contains potentially all the power which will develop as it grows, but the tree which will come from it is not yet manifested. There is a radical difference between the dry seed and the germinating seed in which a new life is born. But this birth is still hidden, and objective examination will show the two seeds to be exactly alike. The change is a qualitative one, not yet quantitatively measurable.

A man whose "life is changed" is like that. A supernatural, qualitative, absolute event has taken place within him. He knows it and proclaims it, but it will bear visible fruit only insofar as he understands what necessarily follows from it. Like a young plant he still needs care and attention, even though the power that will ensure his healing has already entered into his heart. That is why faith and vigilance are not incompatible.

One of my patients once told me that his spiritual director wished to see me. As I went into his study the priest challenged me with this question: "Doctor, what do you do to change a man? After every consultation your client comes to see me, and I realize that he is finding for himself what I have been trying for so long to make him see."

"Before my life was changed (last year)," a young man writes to me, "I was subject to constant attacks of migraine. They have completely ceased. If by any chance I feel one coming on, I pray and meditate, to see what it is that is not in order in me, because these attacks are the direct result of lapses (impure thoughts), of guilt, or of the tension that results from a lack of trust."

"For the first few years of my married life," a young woman writes, "I was under treatment by doctors, never free for long from attacks of enteritis and metritis. From the moment that I accepted that God should direct my life, these attacks ceased. I found I had reserves of strength and endurance I had never known before. God also delivered me from two bad habits—the habit of eating too much chocolate, and that of eating between meals anything that came to hand. I had been unable to rid myself of these habits, even though I knew them to be harmful."

And this is what her husband wrote: "As for me, up to the age of thirty-eight I had two bad habits of which I was unable to break myself despite all my efforts—smoking and masturbation. Both disappeared without effort when I surrendered them to God. During the last three years I have fallen into them again several times, but always at times when the 'I' had become once again the center of my life. Each time I have been freed from them again by a sincere surrender of my life into God's hands. Now I feel absolutely free on these two points."

"I was nervous and high-strung," a young woman writes, "going rapidly from a period of enthusiasm to one of depression, always having ups and downs—tiring both to myself and to those I was with, and finding lack of sleep very hard to bear. My digestion was bad; I used to eat too quickly and was easily and often sick. I suffered from skin eruptions. I was a terrible glutton, and though I fought against it, it was without much success. I had very little self-control, and used to give way to all my feelings—anger, enthusiasm, or despair—not without a certain violence, in a way which was painful to the people about me. I began to pray, to obey; and my life began to be centered on Jesus Christ. . . .

"There came a day when I realized that a new balance had been established in my body—an evenness of temper. I hardly know now what it is to feel despairing and depressed. I feel tremendously joyful sometimes, but it is a deeper, calmer sort of joy. . . . I used to be ashamed of my sexual desires, which I restrained or not, as I could, and that was terribly painful to me and helped to give me a feeling of unbalance. . . . I can rest better now, too. The skin eruption has almost completely disappeared. My digestion is improved, and the vomiting hardly ever happens now. As for my gluttony, it has disappeared without trace, and without any effort on my part. I appreciate good food even more than before, without being tempted to eat too much of it. My sex life has become more balanced and mature. I used to hold myself badly before, too, and used to get backaches. I realized one day that I ought to do exercises every morning, and I was given the perseverance to keep it up; it has been a great help. My health is a personal testimony. But it has happened all by itself, I might even say without my knowing it. This new state of mine depends on my regular quiet times and my surrender to God. It isn't something acquired once and for all, but it remains and lasts in the measure to which I obey God, confess to him, and am freed from my sins. The health of my body depends upon the health of my soul."

"I was exceedingly lazy about my personal hygiene," writes a young lady. "God guided me to confess this sin. It was very hard to do, and humiliating, but it was the beginning of a change of habit. . . . I have also been guided to drink much less wine and strong drink than before."

"My experience," an old man writes, "is that my physical health is in direct ratio with my moral and spiritual health."

I could, of course, quote many more such letters.

What I have tried to emphasize in this chapter is that it is not the application of the laws of life that leads to Christ, but the personal encounter with Christ which transforms men's lives and helps them to return to the laws of life. It does not always require religious discourses to bring souls to this personal encounter. I may say that I only rarely take the initiative in starting conversations on spiritual matters. It is almost always my patients who broach the subject with me, because it is the point to which the exploration of personal problems always leads.

I always think of a patient of mine whom I shall call Max, when I am tempted to resort to religious sentimentality.

I had already treated him over a number of years for minor ailments, when he suddenly suffered a heart attack. Naturally, I saw him at first several times a day, and then once a day over a number of weeks. Gradually my visits became more infrequent. I had a quite natural sympathy for him, and this long illness was the occasion of our becoming firm friends. When still young he had lost his wife, and since then he had devoted himself to the upbringing of his children, carrying on at the same time a tiring professional occupation. On the occasion of my brief but numerous visits we used to talk of his life and mine, but our conversation never turned to specifically spiritual matters. Quite simply, I was interested in him, and I was fond of him.

I recall my surprise when, one day, without any sort of preamble, he said to me: "You know, doctor, this illness has been a real turning point for me in my spiritual life. I have gone back to my Bible, which for years I have been too busy to read. I have meditated on it every day, spending longer and longer on it. I have found communion with God once more, and that has been a great support to me in the long trial of my illness. We haven't spoken about it together, but I know that you are a Christian, and I believe that you have helped me without realizing it, and without saying anything to me about God. Now, I want to thank you, because I have found an inner peace that I never had with all my hard work. I feel that when I go back to work I shall not be able to do without my daily meditation. I am grateful to this illness for having brought this new life to me."

Some time afterward he spoke to me of a woman colleague who faced great difficulties in her life, and whom he had been able to help by his witness to find in God the solution to her difficulties.

He lost his job, but remained absolutely confident and serene.

It was not long before he found other employment, without even having to look for it—a more secure post than the previous one. His work was so highly appreciated that a year later he was congratulated by his new chief.

Any Christian may at times be called upon to witness openly to his faith.

I am reminded of a woman of doubtful character whom I treated from time to time for various complaints. Let us call her Antoinette.

I was sometimes called out to go and see her for attacks of a neurotic nature. I naturally thought that the state of her nerves was due, at least in part, to the sort of life she led. When I went to her house I affected complete indifference to the suggestive pictures which covered the walls of her bedroom. But I knew quite well that my indifference was largely hypocritical. And it was doubtless this feeling of being a hypocrite that had always prevented me from bringing to that sick woman the message she needed to hear.

But once, in the middle of the night, there came another telephone call from her. While I was getting dressed I was all at once quite certain that that night I must talk to her about God.

As I expected, I found her suffering from acute nervous disorder. She had an intense and painful contracture of the leg. As usual I administered a sedative, as well as a few reassuring remarks about her condition. Then I questioned her about the events of the preceding day, about her worries and possible conflicts. She showed herself very disinclined to confide in me. The conversation was stiff and hollow. I was thinking all the time to myself about the definite command I had received from God while I was dressing.

Then I started clumsily trying to twist the conversation onto religious matters. I said something complicated and embarrassing about "the profounder side of life," and mentioned "spiritual values." I was thoroughly dissatisfied with myself, feeling that all this verbiage was getting nowhere. Then I was suddenly aware of a clear-cut call. I felt in my heart that God was chiding me for not obeying him. It was as if he were saying to me: "I did not tell you to talk about religion, but about Me."

So, all at once, I changed my tone. I laid aside all my abstractions, and spoke to my patient about God, about Jesus Christ, about my personal experience of Christ, and how I was convinced that he had an answer to all the problems of men and women.

In the silence of that night we talked completely frankly for more than two hours. Then Antoinette said: "I should like you to go through to the kitchen, where my friend is, and talk about all this to him as well." I went, and once more I experienced the same hesitation, the same difficulty in passing from abstractions to simple, straightforward witness.

A few days later Antoinette came to see me. It was an ordinary consultation, with neither of us making the slightest allusion to that conversation in the dead of night. But suddenly, as she was at the door, about to leave, Antoinette turned and said: "By the way, I have decided to follow the line you suggested. I have broken things off with my friend, the one who was leading me on in the sort of life I was living—you know. I have made things up with my husband, and he has come back home. And I am so happy!"

The next time I was at Antoinette's house I found it transformed— clean and tidy, with everything in the best possible taste.

CHAPTER

17

Confession

A friend of mine who was in great torment of mind went to see a certain young man. They spent almost the whole of the night talking together. My friend said: "I have so many problems to solve," and the young man answered: "There are no problems. There are only sins."

If I look honestly into my own heart, and into the tragic situation of humanity, which my vocation as a doctor allows me to do day after day, I see that behind all "personal problems" there lies, quite simply, sin.

It is in order to hide his own sin from himself that man has been so ready to welcome that positivist scientific outlook which denies sin. "People no longer want to know about good and evil. . . . In place of strict principles, we have psychological explanations. Sin is rejected as one of those outworn ideas which in a century of intelligence ought to be dead and buried."[1]

It is an odd state of affairs, that of our day, "which rushes head-long toward sin, feeling its power of attraction, and yet passionately denying its existence,"[2] which exploits it as an "affair,"[3] at the risk of causing more damage to public health than any other single factor.

Cartesian rationalism believed it had attained absolute objectivity

[1] *L'Homme et le péché*, p. 1.
[2] Jacques Chevalier, *Le sens du péché*, p. 107.
[3] P. H. Simon, *Le péché est une affaire*, p. 185.

by resolutely rejecting all value judgments, recognizing only facts, causes, and effects, and excluding *a priori* all moral judgments. But of course every *a priori* assumption involves a lack of objectivity. Man's moral drama so dominates the problem of man that if science is forbidden to have anything to do with it, science has no contact with life. It constructs systems which are satisfying to reason, but have nothing to say to the real anguish of man. They leave him to fight his inner battle alone, and he is always defeated.

Cartesianism has brought about a fundamental divorce between the spiritual and the material, and this is the disease from which our modern world is suffering. This is because in God's plan for the world spiritual and material are one.

Truth to tell, science had good reasons for denying sin. In describing as "sick" people whom the theologians called "sinners," science was trying to relieve them of the intolerable burden laid on them by a certain kind of social hypocrisy which gave to this word "sin" a color quite different from the sense in which it is used in the Bible.

Mauriac, in an interview on the subject of "medicine and life," has shown that when medicine denies the fact of sin, it is only in order to learn how to understand men, to have compassion on them, and to avoid condemning them—in other words, to go back to Christ's attitude when he was faced with sin. Mauriac goes on: "Yes, it would be a good thing if theologians were physicians. . . . What is much more important is that God is a physician." [4]

Christ's attitude to this problem of the connection between sin and disease is quite clear. First of all, he affirms that there is a connection when he says to the paralytic before healing him: "Your sins are forgiven" (Matt. 9.2). He indicates that his power to forgive sins and that of healing the sick are two different aspects of a single ministry. This unity between his spiritual action and his medical action strikes one all through the Gospel.

But on the other hand, when his disciples ask him about the man born blind (John 9:3) or the victims on whom the tower of Siloam fell (Luke 13:4), in an attempt to get him to formulate theologically,

[4]Mauriac, "La médecine et la vie," *Le Temps médical*, March, 1939.

so to speak, this link between sin and the suffering of mankind, he categorically refuses to do so. Very clearly he wants to avoid the connection between sin and disease (which the whole of his ministry affirms) being used hypocritically to condemn the sick as specially sinful.

But he at once adds: "Unless you repent you will all likewise perish." In this way he brings them back to the consideration of their own sin.

Thus Christ calls men to recognize more clearly their own sin when they see the evils from which mankind suffers, and not to use these ills as the occasion for passing judgment on other people.

The practice of a Christian ministry constantly affords confirmation of this double truth, which is contradictory only to our rationalistic outlook. On the one hand, as soon as there slips into our hearts the slightest spirit of condemnation in regard to one of our patients, we set up a barrier between him and us, and thereafter all our efforts and all our love will be powerless to help him. At the same time, if we have a theory of medicine which denies sin, so that we encourage the patient to blind himself to his sin and to use his illness as an excuse for it, we are preventing him finding liberation. For liberation comes only when we are humble enough to see ourselves as we really are.

The fact is that in denying the reality of sin, by giving people to understand that a fault of character is due to the malfunctioning of an endocrine gland, or by calling some impure temptation a "psychological complex," science destroys man's sense of moral responsibility. The present state of the world shows where that leads.

Here is a passage from a lecture delivered at the Lycée in Valence by Frank Abauzit. It seems to me to establish clearly the connection between a sense of moral responsibility and the rational explanation of facts:

I was charged with the task of taking a small child for a walk. We were going along quite a busy street. The little fellow trotted along in front of me, coming back every now and then to take my hand. Suddenly I heard a dog bark, then a piercing shriek, and then commotion. . . . At that precise moment my attention had been caught by a person whose presence there intrigued me, and so I did not look immediately towards where the child, frightened by the dog, had rushed blindly into the road where he was knocked down by a car. In forming an opinion about the event, two methods are available to me—the scientific and the moral. I can seek out all the causes of the accident—the sudden appearance of the dog, the nervousness of the child, the unexpected presence of that other person which had attracted my attention, lack of skill on the part of the driver, the speed of his vehicle, etc. . . . This is the scientific point of view. Or else I can simply say to myself that it was my fault; the child was injured through my negligence. This is the moral point of view.

The moral point of view involves feeling one's own responsibility and courageously accepting the burden, recognizing where one is to blame as soon as one is concerned in some unhappy event, and never trying to unload any of one's responsibility onto anyone else. The frivolous and immoral man (alas! the tendency is there in all of us) is the one who will say to himself: "The child's parents have brought him up badly. Why did he let go of my hand? Look how he ran away, how disobedient he was! The owner of that dog ought never to have let it wander loose in the street. That driver is a criminal: he has knocked a child down!" No, indeed! The sincere, moral man will say to himself quite simply: *"Ego adsum qui feci*—I am to blame." All the other causes will seem to him almost negligible, since they did not depend on him. In his own eyes he is the true cause of the unhappy event which has taken place.

There are thus two points of view from which each of life's problems may be seen, both of them true: that of the scientific explanation, and that of moral responsibility. It is our logic which sets them over against one another, when in fact moral responsibility does not rule out the scientific explanation any more than the latter rules out moral responsibility.

Now, this sense of moral responsibility is the road to all real religious experience. In practice we meet two attitudes in our patients. Some tell us the things they suffer from, all the misfortunes that have befallen them because of parents, neighbors, circumstances, or germs. The others spontaneously tell us the things for which they are to blame, and speak of their own responsibility for the ills they suffer from. That is the measure of the difference between confidences and confession. Only those who have a conviction of sin find a spiritual answer to their anguish, even if their life remains full of suffering.

I remember how in my youth I rebelled against Calvin's "confession of sins" in our liturgy: "Born in corruption. . . ." This arose simply from the fact that in spite of my genuine desire to live a Christian life, I had not yet experienced a true conviction of sin. I experienced it one day when I met some Christians who talked to me about their own sin, their own experience, and their own fellowship with Christ.

It is when in meditation and in the penetrating presence of Christ we face up to the moral demands of the gospel that we measure our sin and see the fundamental part it plays in our lives.

Soul-healing means bringing souls into contact with Christ. Outside that our efforts are incomplete, and our results indecisive. The conviction of sin is not a thing we acquire by being told about it.

The only possible foundation for a Christian ministry to one's fellows is this profound realization of one's own sinfulness, which comes when one is face to face with God. "You want to know why they all come to me?" wrote St. Francis of Assisi. "You want to know why the whole world runs after me? For I have learnt the reason, from Almighty God, whose eyes see all the good and evil in the world. Well! It is because those most holy eyes found nowhere a greater sinner than I, or any poorer or more pitiable. It is because on the whole earth God saw no creature more miserable, through which he might accomplish the work which it is his will to accomplish."

Scientific knowledge is acquired only through the intellect, and that is why N. J. Mathieu writes of this "feeling of guilt and sin" that it is the "superior form of knowledge."[5]

In denying sin and moral responsibility, science has lost the sense of man's inner drama. Freud's great merit, it seems to me, is that he called attention to it again.

At the time when Freud made public the results of his early researches, the very idea that psychical troubles might be due to an intrapsychic conflict was almost lost. The organicist view of psychiatry had led it into extraordinarily oversimplified conceptions of how the human mind works. Nevertheless the blame for the failure to recognize at that point the fundamental reality of intrapsychic con-

[5]"L'Appel de l'abîme," *L'Homme et le péché*, p. 294.

flicts, must be laid at the door of the Christians, for the Bible shows on every page examples of this drama of man in conflict with himself. In place of Pierre Janet's psychoasthenic theory, according to which the patient suffers inner conflicts because he is ill (a primary deficiency), Freud substituted his view that the patient is ill because of his inner conflict. This inner conflict of which Freud speaks is none other than what the Bible calls the conflict of sin, described by St. Paul in the Epistle to the Romans. This is what makes Freud, paradoxically enough, in many respects an ally of Christianity. For Janet, the fundamental fact is an insufficiency of strength, whereas for Freud it is a contrary force. And this contrary force, this power of evil, is known to Christianity, which calls it Satan. If we consider how seriously Christ took Satan, and measured his strength, we shall understand the true gravity of the human drama of sin.

I was interested enough to reread the details of the 260 clinical cases which Freud quotes in his book, *The Psychopathology of Everyday Life*. All, without exception, can be classified in one or other of the four categories of sin described in the Sermon on the Mount: 57 are concerned with dishonesty; 39 with impurity; 122 with self-centeredness; and 42 with lack of love. It will be noted that in this list, contrary to what one might have expected of Freud, the smallest number of cases concern impurity.

The reader will now understand why I claim that Freud confirms Christian teaching, since he shows that all the psychological conflicts suffered by men stem from violation of Christ's commands.

It is impossible to read through those cases without recognizing how we constantly dissemble our real thoughts behind our carefully composed speech. Freud gives a detailed demonstration of the basic dishonesty of man.

The psychiatrist's commonest fear is the fear he feels in the presence of the man who is not deceived by his little untruths. Psychoanalysis has thrown sufficient light on the workings of the human heart for us to be able to say that no man can spend one day without telling a lie—even if he does not utter a single word. One can see too the fatal determinism of sin, for one lie leads to another, and that must be covered up by yet another. So that the only answer is Christ's demand of absolute honesty.

Freud was sincere enough to recognize in himself the sins which he denounced in others. On page 100 of the work quoted, he speaks of a slip of the tongue which revealed to him, himself, the "little lie" which he confesses to having told. On page 221, after telling of how he admitted to one of his patients that he had told a lie in order to preserve his own authority, he goes on:

I now had to be fair; as I had so frequently confronted my patient with his own symptomatic acts I could only vindicate my authority in his eyes by being honest and showing him the motives (which I had kept secret) for my disapproval of his journey. It may, in general, seem astonishing that the urge to tell the truth is so much stronger than is usually supposed. Perhaps, however, my being scarcely able to tell lies any more is a consequence of my occupation with psychoanalysis.

This is exactly the experience of the Christian who, in the light of the gospel, discerns his own dishonesty with ever increasing acuity, and becomes more and more exacting toward himself in regard to it.

And what are we to say of Freud's revelation of the part played in our lives by sexual impurity? It must be admitted that the hostility with which his work was received in religious circles is in large part to be attributed to the perspicacity with which he revealed the immense impurity of heart hidden under the apparent morality of church people. But long before Freud, Jesus has spoken about "whited sepulchres" (Matt. 23:27).

"In the past," writes a young man who has given his life to Christ, "I could write off 30% of my thoughts as concerned with sex (especially the formulation of impure projects on seeing women). I was even pursued by it in my dreams, so that I found it impossible to get a good night's sleep. I used up a large part of my energy in fighting against these thoughts and in trying to remain pure in actions. But the effort was getting me down.

"With the change that has taken place in my life all that has gone, and now my mind is free. From the purely intellectual point of view I find I can work infinitely better. The most fundamental change has been the switching of all my sexual energies onto a different plane, which has increased the efficiency of my life enormously."

The reader will have noticed that in the list I gave of Freud's cases, the greatest number are concerned with failures in that absolute standard of selflessness which the gospel demands. Our hearts are full of all the self-centeredness, the fears, secret ambitions, jealousies, egotisms, and rebellions which the experienced observer of men can see constantly revealed in the way we behave. Particularly is this the case with our demand to be loved, and our sense of inferiority, the two things which are most apt to upset our relationships with those with whom we live.

Sin is everything that separates us from God and from each other. And if we stop talking vaguely about our "neighbor" in general, and think in particular of wife or husband, parents or children, employer or competitor, our best friend, or some specific politician or social rival, we can see how far we fall short of the absolute love required of us by the gospel.

So the practice of Christian soul-healing leads to the same discoveries as psychoanalytical investigation. The human personality as St. Paul saw it is indeed as Freud described it.

This is why it has been possible to say that it was necessary to invent psychoanalysis in order to make up for the failure of the church in the care of men's souls. This failure is especially serious in Protestant countries where the practice of private confession—contrary to Calvin's injunctions[6]—is extremely uncommon. Protestantism, with its intellectual, didactic tendency, has concentrated too exclusively on preaching and collective action. I think that in order to be true to its mission it ought to recover the sense of the individual cure of souls. Seed is sown broadcast, and this is how the Word of God is sown. But if the terrain is to be favorable it must be plowed. This preparation of the ground can only be done when two souls meet face to face.

On the other hand, however, I have often been surprised at how many Catholics, accustomed as they are to the practice of private

[6]John Calvin, *Institutes of the Christian Religion*, Book III, chap. iv, para. 12.

confession—too accustomed, perhaps, to a superficial practice of it— find in the soul-healing I have been taught to practice a liberation that is quite new to them. In meditation with me they have recognized secret faults which it has never occurred to them to confess to the priest. They have found also that confession to a layman is a "strait gate" requiring a humbling of themselves which they have never experienced in the confessional, any more than many Protestants have in secret and solitary confession to God.

One of my patients, whom we shall call Violaine, had been a missionary. On her return she had expected to be welcomed warmly by her family, who had been proud of the fact that she was working in the mission field. It was a shock to her to find that they were set in their ways, and that her return was in fact an inconvenience to them. Her brother, now married, preferred to be with his in-laws, and used to take his mother with him.

In her disappointment, Violaine adopted a completely critical attitude toward them, full of bitterness. She was sent to a psychotherapeutic clinic. After a few months, she made up her mind to undergo a course of psychoanalysis. The course, which lasted three years, enlightened her on the psychological mechanisms of her childhood, but brought no relief for her moral distress. A further course, in a foreign country, was scarcely more successful. Time passed, and she was able to take up some sort of work, but without finding happiness or nervous stability.

One day she was invited by a Christian group with which she had come into contact to carry out a sincere self-examination in meditation before God. During this meditation she suddenly saw that her life was being dammed up by a sin—namely, her self-centeredness and her claim for affection from her brother and her mother. She went and asked them to forgive her, and at once felt a new freedom.

I am not suggesting, of course, that psychoanalysis is not efficacious in many cases. I simply maintain that the "quiet time," when properly practiced, can give results in all respects comparable to those obtained by psychoanalysis, and can produce them more quickly. I have seen many other patients who have followed lengthy psychoanalytical courses uncover during their very first "quiet time" repressed memories of the greatest importance which had never come up into the conscious field during psychoanalysis.

Catherine was a patient who opened her heart to me with exceptional thoroughness.

She came to see me knowing nothing about me or my religious convictions. At first I refused to accept her, since she was already in the devoted care of a psychiatrist. But she persisted, and herself arranged things with her doctor.

I told her then that I was not a specialist like my colleague, but that if she wanted me to help her to set her spiritual life in order, I had some experience in that direction. "Perhaps if your spiritual life is put in order," I said, "your mind and body will be in better health."

The first condition to be fulfilled if order is to be brought into a person's spiritual life is that he must be absolutely honest with himself, and the only way to do it is to come into the presence of God.

So, from her first consultation onward, Catherine prepared in her daily meditation the things that she had to tell me.

I explained to her that in order to see clearly into our own hearts all that was necessary was to ask God to show us the things in our lives that were contrary to his commands; and then to write down during our meditation all that came to mind in this connection.

Anyone can easily try this for himself. I have never seen anyone sincerely attempt it without feeling a real conviction of sin and winning a spiritual victory. I have seen some people, the first time they attempted the experiment, bring me a notebook quite full of unconfessed sins: lying words or attitudes, customs frauds, tax frauds, falsifications of household accounts; impure thoughts, actions, or glances; irritability, jealousy, anger, fear, rancor, selfish ambitions, rivalry, hostility, and hate.

It was in this way that Catherine, being prepared to enter at once with me into the realm of Christian confession, unburdened herself in a quite concrete fashion. I wish to stress the importance of confession being detailed and concrete. It is the precise details which it costs us most to bring out into the open; but this is the only way to make sure that the confession will be effective.

There existed between Catherine and me a relationship of real sincerity, and this enabled her to explore the psychological jungle in which she found herself. It was not easy. She showed such a marked tendency to negativism that at first I had sometimes to wait as long as half an hour before she could utter a single word. She took refuge in hebephrenic attitudes, and became inhibited at the least sign of impatience or criticism. Her reactions had become quite unnatural, and she showed signs of functional disorders that were connected with her serious psychological complexes.

As far as Catherine was concerned I had always carefully avoided any psychoanalytical technique, properly so called. Meditation and confession brought up to the surface, one by one, all kinds of repressed memories. In short, we always remained within the ambit of Christian soul-healing.

Despite this, the analytical discoveries to which the method led were of such compelling psychological interest that I found the psychologist in me gradually taking precedence of the spiritual director. She has since pointed out my mistake, and recalled the period when she was there in front of me as one soul confronting another, and not as a "case" in front of the doctor. She felt the need to get back on to the spiritual level, so as to be able to make a still more searching confession without having in the back of her mind the fear that she was becoming an object of psychological rather than religious interest to me.

Every time we turned back into the path of true confession instead of losing ourselves in a maze of interesting but inexhaustible subtleties, we touched the vital points which were the key to real liberation. A complete change was taking place in her, involving her writing, her physiognomy, her walk, and the look in her eyes. Her meditations were increasingly successful, and she was ridding herself of her burden of negativism—all her sin, her fears and fantastic imaginings, and the ill-intentioned remarks which, it seemed, some other self used to utter in her, in order to block her progress. There is in all of us a sort of negative echo which at each uplifting thought insinuates an answering doubt, and it is only in God's presence that we can sort out which is our true self. Once Catherine wrote to me: "You must tear

this letter up, because all that is in it is the evil that is in my heart."
However, although our interviews were mostly filled with this discharge of the waste from her heart, in her life she was winning a
succession of victories. She was becoming more open and natural,
and was beginning to talk once more, overcoming her shyness, regaining confidence and consciousness of a spiritual vocation to help
others in similar difficulties.

Christian confession, then, leads to the same psychological liberation as do the best psychoanalytical techniques. As I write these lines,
I am going over in my mind an interview I had today with a Sister of
Charity whom I shall call Florence. She had been sent to me by her
superior.

Without any preamble she admitted that her difficulty was that she
did not know how to begin to tell me about the problems on her
mind. So we began with some small-talk about her work. She is
scrupulous, shy, gloomy, full of worries, especially about her work, at
which she is too slow. Her state of mind is a further worry to her,
because she feels she is being a bad witness to Christ by being so
lacking in joy. Then she has doubts about her vocation—doubts
which take away the last positive prop on which she might lean. This
vicious circle of thought has made her ill. Her superiors have already
transferred her once to other work, but without securing any improvement in her condition.

I say hardly anything. Her story goes, bit by bit, right back to the
sources of her vocation, then to her childhood memories, to the premature death of her mother, and the moral barriers which separated
her from her father. Then, all at once, she goes to a deeper level still.
While I pray in silence, she tells of terrible emotional shocks suffered
in childhood, which have weighed on her mind all her life. I cannot of
course recount them here, but what I want to point out is that they
are the sort of repressed memories which psychoanalytical technique
sometimes helps to bring out into the daylight, but never as quickly as
this.

When I thanked Florence for the trust she had shown in me by being so frank, she replied simply that what had made it possible was that she had come with me into the presence of God.

I then suggested to her that she should pray, to bring all these things from her past and lay them at the foot of the Cross. But she did not dare to pray aloud—and this too was a great obstacle to her in her service for Christ. After some minutes of silence, however, she found the courage to make this second decisive step. When she left my consulting room she was radiant, and had no further doubts about her vocation.

There are formidable psychological barriers in the way of true confession. One must be on one's guard when confession comes easily. An authentic confession is always a hard struggle—often as much for the confessor as for the person confessing. I can remember having been made ill by it. These barriers are what Freud termed "censorship."

In order to overcome the resistance of censorship, some analysts have been led to deny the reality of sin. In order to set the patient's mind at rest they assure him that he may recall any of his memories, actions, feelings, or associations of ideas without incurring any moral criticism in consequence.

In actual fact, along with this doctrinaire denial of sin there goes another imponderable factor, namely the attitude of patient understanding, free of any trace of conventionalism, which the analyst observes toward his patient, and which doubtless contributes much more to winning his confidence than this theoretical moral neutrality.

But Christianity has for twenty centuries declared that there is another method of overcoming the resistance of censorship and creating confidence. Far from denying the fact of sin, it calls it by its name. But it shows at the same time that while God abhors hidden sin, he is always ready to accept the confession of the repentant sinner. The latter is sure to find at the foot of the Cross that deliverance from all formalist judgment which the psychoanalyst is trying to achieve.

When one looks more closely into this, one sees that there are in reality two "censorships." One, which has been brought to light by the analysts, tries to prevent the return of a repressed memory to the field of consciousness; the other tries to prevent the confession of this memory in the presence of another person. Freud himself, moreover, seems to be alluding to this double censorship when he speaks of "unknown and unavowed motives."[7] To the first of these censorships are due the astonishing gaps we often observe in our patients' anamneses when in all sincerity they forget important facts in their own life histories. But true liberation comes only from victory over the second class of censorship, that on confession. Furthermore, there is a close connection between the two kinds of censorship. As soon as a person finds the courage to confess before another person everything that is in his field of consciousness, he sees other repressed memories returning to consciousness. It is in this way that the continued practice of meditation and of confession brings about a progressive extension of the field of consciousness. It is to be noted that this extension is exactly the treatment of neurosis advocated by Freud.

But how many pastors have come to dignify by the name of "cure of souls" vague visits, filled with random conversation, moral uplift, Bible teaching, or theology! How many pastors have admitted to me their embarrassment at the difficulty of passing from this superficial level to that of the true cure of souls, which always touches upon the subject of actual sin and leads to a decisive experience of liberation.

In order to overcome the resistances of censorship, an atmosphere of real trust is necessary; and nothing is more conducive to the creation of this atmosphere than the communion which is established between two people who come into the presence of God together.

Often a woman will say to me: "I cannot trust my husband any more, he has so often lied to me." The trust she is thinking of, a purely human trust which is made to depend on the sincerity of another person, is quite utopian. There is no one who does not lie every day, so that such a trust is bound to be disappointed. And the serious thing about it is that the moment we feel people do not trust us, we tend to prevaricate all the more. A psychological vicious circle is set in motion: The wife has lost confidence because the husband

[7]Freud, *The Psychopathology of Everyday Life*, trans. J. Strachey (London: The Hogarth Press, 1960), p. 154.

lies, and the husband tells more lies because he feels he is not trusted. This is a vicious circle which does untold damage in families, and in all kinds of business and social relationships. It is the source of the present crisis of confidence in the world. Everywhere distrust engenders dishonesty, and dishonesty maintains distrust.

But there is another quality of trust—that which comes from God —which breaks this vicious circle, and is given to others to help them.

I know an elderly maiden lady who has devoted her life to the work of a religious mission. For at least fifty years she has exercised a decisive influence on generation after generation of young people. She told me the following little story.

One day she was asked if she would be kind enough to take an interest in a certain young lad who had a serious failing: He was a thief. Everything had been tried to break him of the habit—punishment, bribes, and kindness as well. He had been put into the hands of distinguished educators. The help of moral welfare associations had been sought. Nothing had any effect: He went on stealing. The habit was too strong for him. The old lady said: "Send him to me; I shall do what I can." A few days later the small boy presented himself at the door and rang the bell. Our old lady came to the door herself, and greeted him with: "Oh! You've come at just the right moment. I need some change—I wonder if you would run round to the post office with this hundred-franc note and get it changed. I'd be most obliged." A quarter of an hour later the boy was back with all his change, but also with a shining face. He was transformed. For the first time someone had really trusted him. He became a Christian, and brought many other souls to Christ.

All men have an immense need to be trusted. The strongest among us would be hurt and daunted if we felt that those people whose confidence we most valued were withdrawing that confidence from us. In fact, we find that the main factor underlying the psychological disorders of a great number of our neurotic patients has been their feeling that their parents did not trust them.

The converse is also true, that nothing is more conducive to the creation of confidence than sincerity. If I climb down from the pedestal of scientific knowledge and moral authority on which my patient has placed me, if I present myself to him as man to man, and tell him honestly about my own difficulties, failures, and sin, I shall help him far more than by all my advice to him to overcome the resistances of censorship within himself and to show himself as he really is.

"I have been completely cured," an old lady writes to me, "of attacks of melancholia that were verging on the suicidal, which returned periodically and without any obvious cause. . . . Since I confessed in the proper quarter a serious wrong I had committed, I have had no more such attacks."

There is of course a certain sense of euphoria produced by the feeling of having won a spiritual victory. But religious experiences are not just a matter of euphoria. Once the original enthusiasm has passed, they continue to bear fruit to the benefit of a person's nervous balance, in concrete results in his life. When these results include the confession of a serious fault, reconciliation, and the ending of moral indiscipline, it would be childish to attribute their effects to a state of euphoria brought about by autosuggestion.

I have been laying stress on the vicious circle of mistrust. Earlier in this book I have referred to other vicious circles—those of lack of spontaneity, and of fear. The more I study man and medicine, the more important does this matter of the vicious circle seem to be for an understanding of the genesis of pathological conditions. I have insisted on the reciprocal links between the physical and the moral. Similar links play an even more important part in the evolution of neurotic conditions; for the nervous system is one which influences itself: Its state affects the way it functions, and the way it functions affects its condition. All nervous states, physical or psychical, good or bad, tend always to become more accentuated. So one meets few "average" characters among old people: Either they attain a sort of sublime serenity, or else they relapse into a bitter and tyrannical selfishness. The neurotic is to begin with only "a little nervous"—an ordinarily emotional type. But he is ashamed of his emotionalism and tries to cover it up, adopting a false attitude to those around him. This makes his emotionalism worse. Stage fright starts in the same way: Following one slip the fear of further slips takes hold. One acts less well because one has stage fright; and one has stage fright because one is acting less well.

This is also the way nervous tics and stammering get a hold. The fact that the stammer is worse when the stammerer is talking in front of a person who overawes him, or when certain subjects of conversation are touched upon, shows the part played by his inner preoccupations.

Many stubborn cases of insomnia result from a vicious circle. A person has slept less well than usual on one occasion, owing to some chance physical or moral cause. He has taken to reading in bed, and has lost the habit of sleep. He has begun to take sleeping tablets, and now cannot do without them. Most of all he is afraid of not being able to sleep, and this fear prevents him from sleeping.

Early one Sunday morning my wife asked me to take the dog out. I did so, but I was protesting inwardly. My protest was the assertion of my right to sleep on a Sunday morning! There was also self-pity at having to get up. I went back to bed with these negative thoughts turning over in my mind. The result: I found it impossible to go back to sleep. And the fact that I could not get back to sleep again encouraged my negative thoughts and complaints. All at once I realized that what was stopping me sleeping was not my morning walk, but the complaining thoughts about it that I had allowed to develop in my mind. I saw that I should have got back to sleep long before if my inward complaints had not kept sleep at bay, that I was the victim of my own attitude, and not of circumstances. I went to sleep again at once.

This is the way hypersensitive states are set up. Let N be normal sensitivity, and N^x that of a nervous person. The latter, on comparing himself with others, is ashamed of his N^x sensitivity, and tries to mask its manifestations instead of discharging it by means of these emotional manifestations. Being thus unaccepted, it increases via the vicious circle to N^{xy}, and the patient is even more afraid of himself. If the neurotic feels he is understood and trusted, the vicious circle is broken, and the coefficient can return to N^x, but not to N. He must accept his sensitive nature on pain of having it made worse. It is a fact that all the hypersensitive people I have seen have had a negative attitude toward their sensitiveness, the source of so much suffering for them. They cannot accept it until they see it as a talent which God is commanding them to put to use, so that it may bring a return in the form of tact, kindness, understanding, sympathy, artistic creation, and intuition. One of my teachers used to say, "Nervous people have to put up with extra suffering in life, but they also get more out of life." As soon as a hypersensitive person becomes aware of the special vocation in the world of people such as he, he is enabled to accept his nerves. And even if he is not understood by those around him, he feels that he is understood by God.

This lack of understanding by others plays an important part in the pathogenesis of hypersensitive conditions. The neurotic symptoms of these patients, their flight into disease, are no more than defense mechanisms to protect them against the injuries which their sensitive natures cannot bear. Like electric fuses which melt when the system is overloaded, and so cut off the current, nervous reaction, even attacks of hysteria, are protective discharges aimed at warding off more serious accidents. Once this view is accepted, it is easier to understand such reactions, and one no longer dismisses them as "play-acting."

One of my patients obstinately refused, as nerve sufferers often do, to recognize that her functional disorders were "nervous." Sometimes she went further, asking me what hysteria was, if she suffered an attack. For a long time I took refuge in evasive replies which, without being false, were nevertheless not really honest. I would tell her that the ideas of such men as Charcot or Babinski about hysteria were now abandoned, and that modern psychoanalysis had reduced the conception of hysteria to something which was more or less present in every one of us. But there remained a feeling of unease. Untold harm has been done to psychological medicine by the idea of "imaginary disease," from Molière onward, and by the notions that the public—mistakenly—gleaned from the writings of Babinski. It is true to say that nowadays the expression "it's nerves" suggests to everybody's mind the idea that "it's hysterical—it's imagination—it's mere suggestion—it's playacting." There attaches to all these expressions a feeling of contempt, a mistaken idea that the sufferer could rid himself of his trouble if he really wanted to, an accusation of dishonesty —all of which is thoroughly unjust to the patient, who has no means of defending himself against the suspicions implicit in these remarks, other than to deny that his trouble is "nerves." And this prevents his liberation.

There came a day, however, when between my patient and myself there was established that spiritual atmosphere which made it possible for me to say to her, without provoking a hostile reaction: "Yes, your troubles are hysterical, and if I were to consult one of my colleagues about your case, that is the diagnostic term I should use."

There and then she told me what lay behind her fear of hysteria. It had been communicated to her by her mother, who when still a child had had the word "hysterical" thrown at her as a term of abuse.

This same diagnosis which, when hurled at the mother, had provoked only repression, I was now able to pronounce again—but this time to liberate the daughter.

What antagonizes a patient is not the truth, but the tone of scorn, pity, criticism, or reproof which so often colors the statement of the truth by those around him. It is that which sets up in him the fear of being cured. That same patient had once said to me in a letter: "I have to tell you that I am afraid of feeling myself becoming normal. I feel that everyone is going to be taking advantage of me, treating me unkindly. . . . I am defending myself in advance."

I could mention many other psychological vicious circles, such as that set up between parents and children—the more worried a mother is, the more troublesome her child; and the more troublesome the child is, the more worried the mother becomes.

André Thomas pointed out the importance of these vicious circles when he wrote:

Moral perturbation expresses itself in physical reactions and heightened emotivity; the physical reactions, falsely interpreted as the result of all kinds of suggestions (suggestions which are the more active in so far as the subject's emotivity is increased and his mental control diminished), maintain or even augment the emotivity. The latter in its turn tends to give rise to new emotions, which accentuate the physical disturbances, and so the process continues."[8]

To break all these vicious circles, to smash through the chains of cause and effect, what is needed is a confidence strong enough to transcend them, which springs from an experience of God's grace. In the presence of God, in an atmosphere of trust and sincere fellowship, two persons can all at once break free from all the bonds that have been determining their attitude to each other, and have the courage both to see clearly into their own souls and to allow themselves to be seen as clearly.

[8]Quoted by Fr. De Sinéty, *Psychopathologie et direction* (Paris: Beauchesne, 1934), p. 71.

The Field of Consciousness

The theory of the contraction of the field of consciousness, which we owe to Pierre Janet, and which has been developed by the psychoanalytical school, provides the best explanation of neurosis. These psychologists have shown that when a deep-seated tendency opposed to the moral ideal of the subject makes its presence felt within him, or shows itself through actions of which his conscience disapproves, the memory of these guilty feelings or acts is driven out of the field of consciousness. Later these repressed tendencies and memories reappear, disguised in the form of mental pictures, dreams, bungled actions, or else as neurotic symptoms, paralyses, functional disorders, obsessions, and so on.

This doctrine can be seen to be in full accord with Christian teaching on the human personality. The only difference is that Christianity calls these "deep-seated tendencies opposed to the moral ideal of the subject" simply sin. The Bible shows that man naturally tends to shut his eyes to his faults and to his sufferings. He tends to eliminate from the field of his consciousness any thoughts, memories, events, or temptations connected with sin. Christ, quoting the words of the prophet Isaiah, speaks of the eyes which do not see, the ears which do not hear, and the hearts which do not understand (Mark 8:17-18). The contraction of the field of consciousness could hardly be more clearly described. On the other hand, the Bible shows that the fundamental religious phenomenon is repentance—that is to say, the recovery of consciousness of a sin, the memory of which has been only too successfully eliminated.

To hear the applicants for sickness insurance policies, one would think that serious diseases such as syphilis, tuberculosis, cancer, or mental disease were extremely rare. Insurance companies are aware of this tendency, and on principle they suspect the good faith of applicants. One does not need to be an expert in analytical psychology to realize that this is an example of sincere "forgetfulness," that is to say the elimination from the field of consciousness of painful memories or serious faults.

This elimination is a sort of dishonesty toward oneself, an instinctive refusal to recognize one's unaccepted suffering and one's sin.

On the other hand, the better a man succeeds in becoming honest with himself once more, the more clearly he will see himself, and his field of consciousness will expand once more. When a man meditates in the presence of God, he learns once more how to look his faults in the face. There takes place within him an expansion of the field of consciousness comparable to that obtained by Janet using hypnosis, and by Freud using the analysis of dreams and bungled actions. In Christian soul-healing I always feel that I am accompanying my patient on a tour of his mind. He ventures into it as into a darkened room: At first nothing is visible, and then gradually one begins to make out shapeless masses—particular problems, one presumes. Slowly these masses loom up out of the darkness, take on more definite outlines, begin to show more and more detail, until, by the light of Jesus Christ, the mind is known. A patient has been able, after a great struggle, to confess some sin which he has never dared to admit before. He comes back the following day, not with his mind relaxed and at ease, as one might have expected, but looking gloomy and depressed: He has a new confession to make—usually more serious than the first. Sometimes in the early days, when I had as yet little experience of confession, I used to doubt the patient's sincerity, to doubt whether he was really being frank with me when after the first confession he would assure me that he had told all. Now I realize that this is in fact a case of the contraction of the field of consciousness. It is only when one sin has been brought back to the field of consciousness, only when it has been confessed, that the field can expand further, and the memory of other sins can be brought back in their turn.

So true is this that those who have learned how to look themselves in the face, how to examine themselves daily in meditation, acquire an eye for their own faults which others find it hard to understand. It often happens that when I talk of some sin of my own—a lie, for example—the person I am speaking to will interrupt me, and say, "Oh! But that's not what I call a lie, that's just a clever dodge. There's no harm in that!" So the practice of meditation leads to a progressive recession of the frontier between the conscious and the unconscious. For the unconscious is what we are hiding from ourselves.

Germaine was sent to me by her doctor. Her life was one long series of sufferings, the details of which I cannot go into here: an unhappy childhood, an irascible father, lack of understanding and jealousy on the part of the family, a conflict with her mother when she married, unjust suspicions, early widowhood, and the sickness of her child.

The telling of all this took up our first few interviews, and helped me to understand her. But I told her that if her visits were to be really fruitful she must prepare for them by meditation. In the silence, in God's presence, I told her, she would be able to throw light on the whole of her life, so that her confidences might not be mere narratives, but come to grips with the essential problems of her life. She promised she would do so.

When next she came, I could see that she was in the grip of a lively emotion. As soon as she had started her meditation, a childhood memory had come into her thoughts, one that she thought she would never be able to tell me. And yet she had realized that if she did not find the courage to do so, all her consultations with me would be in vain. It was a difficult interview. A tremendous struggle began in her. It was only after we had prayed together that she was able to tell me about an emotional shock she had suffered in early childhood at the hands of a vicious classmate. One day, when in hospital, she had read a book entitled *What Every Young Man Ought to Know,* which had horrified her. She had spent several sleepless nights. But she had been unable to bring herself to tell her doctor about this.

Thereafter our interviews progressed smoothly. At each consultation Germaine spoke more freely, appeared happier and more self-confident. Soon the road of meditation took her further: She reported to me no longer the sufferings of which she had been the victim, no longer the faults into which she had been naïvely led by others, but the faults she felt guilty of herself, the memory of which was now coming back into her field of consciousness.

So meditation in the sight of God, and letting oneself be inspired by him, leads to a progressive extension of the field of consciousness. The greatest service we can render to a patient, as to a healthy person, is to teach him by our own example how to meditate, so that he can learn how to become honest with himself.

So also, when the analysts help a person to see more clearly the mechanisms at work in his mind, the motives of impurity, selfishness, and dishonesty which lie behind his actions, they are really practicing soul-healing, for they are helping the person to become more honest with himself. There lies, I believe, the secret of their success, for to help someone to become more honest with himself is to bring him nearer God, even though neither the patient nor the analyst may be conscious of performing a religious action.

Freud would say that the Christians practice psychonalysis without realizing it. One may also say that Freud practiced soul-healing without realizing it.

But I must take the matter further. Christianity is never a matter of method, but of spirit. All the methods—Dubois' persuasion, Freud's psychoanalysis, the re-education of conscious control practiced by Vittoz, Dessoie's exploration of the unconscious by means of spontaneous drawing, Baudouin's autosuggestion, Janet's psychological comprehension—all give results. But these results are due not so much to the individual method itself as a specific technique, as to the Christian content of the attitude of the therapist who applies it. Insofar as he is honest with his patient, is interested in him, gives him his love, patience, and understanding, helps him to unburden himself and to see himself as he is, the therapist really helps him. And conversely, all the failures, whatever the method, are due not to the method itself but to some sin in the heart of the therapist: dishonesty, preoccupation with himself, lack of love, impatience, a spirit of criticism, or impurity. What I have just said implies once again the truth that a "Christian method" does not necessarily involve talking about Christ or the Bible, or even meditating oneself and teaching the patient to meditate. If we have no more love, understanding, trust, and patience to bring to our patients than other therapists have, then we are no more Christian than they. But I must point out, however, that though what characterizes Christian soul-healing is less its method than the state of mind of the therapist, it nevertheless goes much further than any non-Christian method. Of course it is true that the love that the psychoanalyst shows for his patient is a Christian virtue, which makes that psychoanalyst in some measure a Christian psychotherapist, even if he is an avowed atheist. But that love, however great it be, cannot lead to the decisive result which only comes of a personal encounter with Christ. The patient who has found Christ has found the source of power which will assure him of victory thereafter in every other circumstance of his life. A fundamental change has been operating in him.

I said just now that getting to know a man was like visiting an unknown room with him. It sometimes happens that some almost imperceptible hesitation gives me the feeling that concealed in the tapestry is a secret door which gives access to a hidden chamber, into which this man both wants and fears to take me. The slightest thing, and we pass by that door without opening it, and the consultation remains barren. Sometimes I have been aware that I was aiding and abetting this flight, for fear of the new problems which might loom up in the gloom, for fear I should not know what to say in answer to them. But if we pause together in silence for a moment in our journey of exploration, the man will open the hidden door and let the light shine into the dark crannies of his repressed memories.

This is the only way really to understand another person, and the only way really to understand ourselves. Science studies man from without. Meditation reveals him from within. We see then how often the conscious and the unconscious counterbalance each other; a conscious virtue hides an unconscious failing. We find that the true motives of our behavior are less flattering than we think, and we see that we are the brothers of all sinners and of all the sick. We discover that in ourselves there are repressed ideas, pretenses, deceit, and fears just like those of our patients, and we can help them then to free themselves from them. I strike my dog because he has been disobedient. But when I consider this during my meditation, I realize that in reality I was annoyed with my wife because of a remark she had made to me, and which at the time I pretended to accept, when in fact I had not accepted it. As soon as I make this discovery and write it down in my notebook, or tell my wife about it and ask her to forgive me, I perceive that I already knew of it, but did not dare to admit it clearly to myself. Meditation was needed before I could become aware of what I already knew. In certain kinds of blindness, the image is formed normally at the back of the eye, but the brain takes no cognizance of it. It is the same with our moral blindness. In reality, only that which is formulated is truly conscious, hence the necessity of writing it down or saying it aloud.

Those who find meditation hardest to practice are the intellectuals. They are assailed by doubts, and wonder if their thoughts are coming from God; whereas a manual laborer, for example, will set down right away on his paper everything that comes into his mind. Then he sees that it is so true, so concrete, and so forthright that he cannot doubt that it comes from God. A slip of the tongue is provoked by an association of ideas or a tonal association. But we do not make a slip of the tongue on every such occasion. It only happens when the slip touches an area in which there is an intrapsychic conflict. This is why the psychoanalyst sees such slips as betraying secret complexes. Similarly, in meditation, among the thousands of possible associations of ideas, God guides our minds toward certain associations which our complexes (that is to say, our sin) would have prevented us making in any other circumstances. There is therefore no contradiction between psychological determinism and guidance by God of the mind in meditation.

Meditation is neither the asyntactic recall that occurs in dreams, nor the free association of ideas, nor is it thought systematized through constellation. It is thought guided by God. Nothing is better for the mind than a few days spent in solitude and devoted entirely to meditation and to the pooling of thoughts discovered in this way. My wife and I have done this several times. It is the best kind of holiday, the most luminous days it is possible to live through. It is also the profoundest way for a married couple to get to know each other.

As well as a pathological contraction, there is also a pathological expansion of the field of consciousness. The first is the basic mechanism in neuroses, while the second seems to me to be characteristic of paranoid states. Every person is constantly taking up attitudes in regard to others, the underlying motives of which are in his unconscious. These hidden motives result from sins, such as jealousy, self-centeredness, or the desire to cover up faults. If, however, one of those other persons is endowed with an extraordinarily acute perceptive capacity, so that he can discern these secret motives, he will see wickedness, dishonesty, and hostility in even the most ordinary attitudes, and behave as if he were in fact being persecuted in this way. If one looks closely at these paranoid states, one sees that there is always a modicum of truth in their accusations. Those whose guilty feelings are thus denounced are unconscious of them, and so they protest their innocence and treat the accusations as the ravings of a sick mind. The paranoiac, faced with these denials, is driven to systematize his accusations and to accumulate evidence in support of them.

I will give a simple example. An elderly maiden lady, of modest origins, finds herself mixing with Christians of all social classes in the life of her parish church. Her sense of social inferiority sets going a well-known compensatory mechanism, which causes her to make a special point of cultivating the interest and esteem of those who bear aristocratic names. Thus, a pastor who comes from an aristocratic family cannot meet her without her finding some means of prolonging the conversation on some futile pretext, as if she needed to persuade herself that she is appreciated in spite of her modest social status. It happens that one day the pastor passes her by in the street without seeing her. She naturally feels a keen resentment at the failure of the pastor to greet her, and begins to spread all sorts of accusations against him. She claims that he is "too proud" to condescend to recognize her in the street. A very delirium of complaints bursts into life in her heart. In time it will take in other persons as well as the pastor she accuses.

The pastor comes to hear of the matter, and at once goes to see the injured lady, and assures her most cordially that he did not see her in the street, that on the contrary he esteems her far too highly ever to wish to avoid her, and so on. These protestations, however, do not fully convince her. And in fact, anyone who knows something of the psychology of the unconscious can see what happened: The pastor knows very well that he cannot greet the old lady without being detained for a long time talking to her. And so, since it happened that he was in a hurry that day, his unconscious protected him against the inopportune delay by preventing him from noticing her in the street. But the lady, made more sensitive by her sense of social inferiority, has intuitively discerned what was in the pastor's unconscious mind. She knows very well, despite all his protestations, that his failure to notice her signifies a desire to keep her at a distance. He will describe her accusations as pure imagination, seeing them as the complaints of an unbalanced mind, and yet there is some truth in them. If he practices meditation he recognizes that the maiden lady importunes him partly because she is always wanting him to show her some mark of esteem. He thinks he will calm her down by assuring her that he holds her in the highest consideration, and is surprised that she does not believe him. He would do more to disarm her if he frankly admitted that there is a grain of truth in her criticism, since a complainant complains all the more when the little bit of truth in his complaints is denied.

While the Christian answer to the contraction of the field of consciousness is prayerful meditation, the answer to its pathological expansion is forgiveness. Real forgiveness leads to the forgetting of the wrong that has been suffered. Instead of denying even the little truth there is in his complaints, one must help the complainant to forgive in others even what is unconscious in their feelings toward him.

Here is a case which illustrates this. Gilberte was brought to me by her husband, whom she was tormenting with accusations of infidelity. The husband assured me that he had tried to disillusion her by being completely open with her, giving her a detailed account of how he spent his time when his work took him away from home. He had admitted to having visited nightclubs of somewhat doubtful reputation, but absolutely denied having been unfaithful to her.

These explanations, far from bringing peace, only gave rise to more serious arguments. The wife persisted in her systematic accusations. The pathological nature of her criticisms was plain, for she placed a doubtful interpetation on the most harmless attitudes and words on the part of her husband. All argument with her on this point was fruitless. The more it was denied, the more convinced she was that her husband had been unfaithful to her. They were both miserable: she because of being, as she thought, deceived; and he because of being, as he thought, unjustly accused by her.

Naturally I asked Gilberte to tell me her life story in detail. It would take too long to give the whole story here, but with its factors of heredity, temperament, emotional shocks in childhood, paternal complex, instability of life, and disappointments, it was sufficient explanation for the formation of a psychopathic tendency on the basis of which this obsession had evolved. She told me she remembered having visual and auditory hallucinations in her childhood, which had been spent under the influence of a mother who suffered from a paranoid religious obsession.

A psychoanalyst also would not fail to note the fact that she had had a broken engagement, due to the infidelity of her fiancé. The memory of this awakened in her such a keen emotion that one sensed that the shock, and the resentment she felt, had never been liquidated. She was no doubt unconsciously identifying the two men in her life, and the accusations of infidelity which she addressed to her husband were probably aimed in her unconscious at the unfaithful fiancé.

That was all no doubt true. Moreover, she understood it quite well, but it brought no solution to the situation. She even declared that she longed passionately to be delivered from her obsessive ideas, and to forgive her husband for his alleged unfaithfulness. She had tried to do this with the help of some Christian friends. At one point she believed she had forgiven him, and then the obsession returned, and a thousand new arguments, drawn from the most ordinary everyday happenings, had pressed in upon her mind.

In any case, how could one forgive a person who not only did not ask to be forgiven, but even denied the facts of the accusation?

Then I explained to her the mechanism of the expansion of the field of consciousness. The sphere of marital unfaithfulness is particularly conducive to it. It will be recalled that in the Sermon on the Mount Christ declares that whoever merely looks at a woman lustfully has already committed adultery with her in his heart.

On that score there is no husband living who has not been unfaithful to his wife. But in the case of most men this kind of unfaithfulness is in a sense unconscious. A man needs to have acquired, through long experience of meditation, a certain perspicacity in regard to himself before he can spot the thousand and one daily infidelities of this kind, and recognize them as sinful.

If, however, instead of the husband himself, it is the wife who, through a pathological expansion of her field of consciousness, acquires this exceptional perspicacity in regard to the faults of the husband, a paranoid obsession is born. Witness those poor wretches who have derived from a course of psychoanalysis such an acute eye for the hidden motives of others, that they assail their relatives with a host of complaints, in a veritable frenzy of criticism, which the relatives are quite at a loss to understand.

Gilberte's intuitive and sensitive nature, overexcited by her unresolved complexes, had made her too quick to see the tiniest gradations in her husband's affective behavior. She had reached the point of being able to perceive infidelities hidden in his unconscious, of which he, being a simple, straightforward type, was unaware. And so she spoke of facts that were obvious to her, but which he denied simply because he could not see them. Argument only accentuated the two opposing attitudes. Faced with her husband's denials, she was always looking for further proofs, and became more and more adept at spotting the slightest signs of disaffection on his part (which, of course, her aggressive jealousy did nothing to diminish), until she got to such a pitch of mental confusion that she no longer made any distinction between unfaithfulness in the heart and unfaithfulness consummated in fact.

The Christian answer to this problem is forgiveness. What the wife must do is to learn at Christ's feet how to pardon her husband—to forgive even the unfaithfulness in his heart of which he is unaware himself.

The greater our insight into men's sins, the more we need to learn to forgive them.

My conversations with Gilberte took place just before Easter. Good Friday was marked by a more serious marital argument than ever. But on Easter Day Gilberte had an important religious experience. She suddenly had a vivid feeling of the presence of Christ, and an inward conviction that he alone could deliver her from the whole of her past and all her rancor and bitterness.

When she came back to see me we prayed together. When she got to her feet she told me that she felt as if all her bitterness was falling away from her like a chain. She felt free and lighthearted. She completely forgave, not only her husband, but also the fiancé who had been unfaithful to her in the past. She was ready to trust her husband unreservedly and love him without jealousy. Her face shone. Her husband, to whom I spoke about all this a few days later, confirmed that a radical change had taken place in his wife's attitude toward him since that day.

Constance was a little old woman of rather senile mentality, who was devoured by a fierce jealousy. She trembled all over and could think of nothing else, going over all the details in her heart.

It is well known how strong a hold systematic obsessions of this kind can get on an aged person's mind. The doctor generally takes a rather fatalistic view of these symptoms, and confines himself to proffering a few vague and affectionate words of encouragement.

I started quite simply talking to her about Jesus Christ, about forgiveness, and about the peace that comes of giving oneself to him. Her old eyes looked at me in increasing astonishment. Soon she began to weep, and then to pray, in order to bring her bitter feelings to God and ask him to set her free. When she left me her face was wreathed in smiles.

I was even more moved than she.

Forgiveness, then, can be seen to be the treatment for pathological expansion of the field of consciousness.

When this expansion does not relate to the unconscious of another person, but to that of the subject himself, the clinical picture presented is that of exaggerated self-analysis, overscrupulousness, and obsessional neurosis. This, moreover, is what happens to us doctors, when we have been concentrating so much on the study of psychological phenomena that we suddenly feel a little dizzy with it all. We need to go for a walk in the fresh air to work out of our systems the toxin of all this analysis! We feel the same anguish growing within us as is experienced by the obsessive neurotic. What distinguishes us from the neurotic is that with us it is no more than a slight feeling— we know how to stop ourselves in time. The fact remains that we have already become too aware of things that are normally unconscious.

An important part of our psychological mechanism must remain unconscious if it is to function normally. In the same way the mechanism of a watch is concealed behind the dial, so that the hands will stand out against it and show the time clearly. If the watch were transparent, so that all its works were left visible, it would be very difficult to tell the time from it.

But the striking thing about neurotics is that alongside the clouding of their field of consciousness on certain points, there is subtle clarity of vision on others. While they are capable of forgetting important events in their past, they can distinguish with morbid perspicacity some of the hidden motives at work in their own behavior, and that of those around them—including that of the doctor. This extraordinary intuitive lucidity, which forms such an odd contrast with their blindness on other points, is a source of suffering to them.

There are zones in them which ought to be clear, and which are plunged in obscurity; and others which ought to be unconscious, and which are in the full light of consciousness. In these cases there is pathological expansion and pathological contraction of the field of consciousness at the same time—in other words, displacement of the field.

Consciousness may be likened to energy: Its quantity remains constant, but its localization varies. In order to escape a temptation, or to thrust an unconfessed sin into oblivion, we turn aside our moral gaze toward other objects which are then brought to light. This is the mechanism of overscrupulousness, obsession, and the spirit of criticism.

I have frequently been asked whether it is not dangerous to encourage overscrupulous people to indulge in meditation. I think not, provided the meditation is done properly. What the overscrupulous person is doing is to exaggerate very minor problems in order to avoid having to face up to other much more important ones. As soon as he has the courage to face up to them, he is delivered from the perpetual and futile search for unimportant problems. There is no greater mistake than to confuse these escape mechanisms with Christianity. Such scruples have nothing in common with the true conviction of sin, which is the very thing that the mind is trying to escape from by means of these petty scruples. Intellectual objections to faith have nothing in common with a true religious anguish against which the mind defends itself by means of continual argument. Philanthropic do-goodery has nothing in common with the true charity which the mind tries to get out of by creating all sorts of duties that have to be performed.

The spirit of criticism also arises from a displacement of the field of consciousness. Christ spoke clearly about this when he said: "Why do you see the speck that is in your brother's eye, but do not notice the log that is in your own eye?" (Matt. 7:3.) In this passage he gave a lesson in the psychology of the unconscious. We are constantly observing that it is those who are most indulgent with themselves who are most critical of others. The searchlight which they do not use to light up their own consciousness is directed at those around them, revealing all sorts of failings, faults, and veiled or ridiculous motives. I have heard many people say: "How could I get rid of my spirit of criticism? I can't after all shut my eyes to other people's faults, when they are so obvious." The usual answer they get is that they should love other people more, and then they would not notice their failings. This reply seems to me to be vague and ineffective. We have often been exhorted to be more loving, but this does not help us to acquire more love. Further, it is not at all certain that love will make us blind. On the contrary, true love often makes us see in those we love failings we never noticed when we did not care about them. And so? . . . And so we must go back to what Jesus said. He does not deny that there is a speck in our brother's eye, nor that it may be a charitable act to try and get it out for him. He simply tells us to consider first the log in our own eye; that is to say, to direct the searchlight of our field of consciousness upon ourselves. The more clearly we learn to see our own faults, the freer shall we be from the spirit of criticism.

Thus through the repentance and forgiveness to which it leads, Christian soul-healing provides the answer to all the disorders of the field of consciousness: contraction, expansion in respect of other people, expansion in respect of oneself, and displacement.

But it brings furthermore a quite different kind of succor to the troubled mind, a succor whose effect is synthesis. I have mentioned the danger of overdoing self-analysis. The safeguard against this danger is the Christian vocation of which I shall be speaking in the next chapter. "Overcome evil with good," writes St. Paul (Rom. 12:21), and in doing so he invites those who are getting lost in the labyrinth of self-analysis to turn their eyes away toward the positive call of the gospel of Jesus Christ. Meditation is a way of analysis, but it is also a way of synthesis. The mind finds in it not only a conscious analysis of past faults, but also a vision of the task to which God is calling it. "Forgetting what lies behind, and straining forward to what lies ahead, I press on toward the goal," writes St. Paul again (Phil. (3:13-14). Conscious of God's forgiveness, the mind, without going analytically into all the remote factors in its difficulties, can resolve them all by making the leap of faith. It abandons the fruitless search into the past, and the empty analysis of the present, and can turn its thoughts toward action.

Having been shown by means of analysis the psychological mechanism which is at work within itself, the mind finds in meditation a new motive force which can set it going along new paths.

Micheline was a young woman studying music. She had real talent, but was handicapped by nervousness. She intellectualized all her problems, she analyzed herself to excess, and sought complicated explanations for everything. Her psychical development had been distorted by complexes arising out of tensions within her family.

A course of psychoanalysis had enlightened her on this subject. But in accordance with her natural tendency she took a certain pleasure in losing herself in the labyrinth of problems thus brought to light. Her behavior was affected by an attitude of rebellion against her lot, particularly in the emotional sphere.

The consequence was that she suffered from dysmenorrhea, the situation being made worse for her by the fact that her periods always made their appearance on the very day on which she had to give a perfomance.

But she had already been made alive to spiritual matters. Helped by a friend, she had begun to practice meditation in order to find a solution to her difficulties with the family. She was therefore accessible to the idea of accepting life and her sufferings by means of an act of faith.

Warned against having a solely analytical concept of meditation, she made a point of seeking in it the dynamic element of faith, courage, and action, which would help to rid her of her negative attitude.

She soon found assurance, joy, and liberation.

And when a few weeks later Micheline sat for her examination, the brilliance of her playing, and her lack of "nerves," so astonished her professor that he asked her: "What has happened to you, Mademoiselle? You are a different person!" She answered simply: "I have found faith."

Vocation

I have just shown that self-analysis is only one aspect of the inner life. If it fills the inner life entirely, distortion results. Analyzing ourselves, finding out what is wrong with our lives, is a means, and not an end. It is a negative phase of the inner life, which ought to prepare the way for a positive phase. There is also the risk that it may tempt us to make ourselves once more the center of our lives. We must put our lives in order day by day, but this is solely to enable us to use our lives and to make them bear fruit in action.

In the practice of spiritual meditation one becomes able to see clearly into one's own mind, but one also learns to see more clearly what it is that God is expecting one to do. A young man once told me of a conversation he had had the day before with a friend. As he was speaking to him about looking for God's will in meditation, his friend interrupted him with these words: "What you call God, I call my conscience."

"Our conscience tells us what we must not do," the young man replied, "but God tells us what we must do."

God has a plan for each one of us. He has prepared us for it by means of the particular gifts and temperament he has given to each of us. To discern this plan through seeking day by day to know his will is to find the purpose of our lives. Having an aim in life is a fundamental condition of physical, moral, and spiritual health. We constantly see sick people whose physical resistance is giving way because they have no longer any aim in life, nothing to do that interests them. We often see young people who are uncertain of their vocation, and as a result are full of self-doubt. They let themselves slip, become discouraged, and turn into physical and psychical weaklings.

It often happens that the doctor is consulted by a young man whose studies are not progressing satisfactorily because of a diversity of circumstances (such as a change of schools or a move from one district to another), or for psychological reasons (such as indiscipline, faulty methods, or inability to concentrate).

The student's lack of progress has upset him and given him a feeling of inferiority.

But it has also upset his parents and hurt their pride. Their disapproval, and their exhortations—the mildness of which scarcely conceals a certain irritation—only turn the son more in upon himself. He feels he has lost their confidence.

It is not long before they are saying to him: "You aren't going to be good at anything. If you don't pull yourself together you'll have to go and work on the land." And so when he is sent to a farm school, though his parents look upon it as a chance for him to make good in his life, he himself feels it as a mark of psychological and social failure.

The total effect of his negative feelings is to diminish his moral resistance, and he falls into misdemeanors which he hides from his parents for fear of turning them still more against him.

When he is asked what would give him real joy and satisfaction in life, he replies without hesitation, "To make the grade in my parents' eyes. But I don't think it's possible. I'd have to do something brilliant. They have lost confidence in me."

Then he dreams of brilliant deeds, and feels all the more miserable because of the contrast between his daydreams and the reality of his life.

The Christian answer in such a case is twofold.

On the one hand, the parents must be shown that if they want to win back their son's trust and help him to confide in them, they must not interrogate him, but themselves must confide in him. This is quite a simple matter, but one that is often forgotten: The key which opens our children's hearts is the opening of our own hearts to them.

I know many parents who would "give anything" to know what is really going on in their children's minds, but they are not in fact prepared to pay the price, which is to allow the children to see what is going on in their minds.

The other part of the answer is for the son to see that God has a plan for his life. And the finest life for all of us is to live in accordance with God's plan, whatever it may be. A person who is convinced of this fact is freed from all prejudice concerning the relative value of one job against another. If God has not fitted a man, through the talents with which he has endowed him, for an intellectual career, this is because he has some other purpose for him. It is only after this acceptance of himself as he is that a man can really start seeking with an open mind to know for what career God has prepared him in giving him the talents and disposition he has.

Then he can recover his confidence in himself and in his usefulness to society. He can take up a new career joyfully, and persevere in it, finding in successes and in victories over self fresh encouragement in the task of putting his life in order.

The following is a case involving vocational guidance. It concerns Leon, a young man of Jewish extraction. Having entered the business world, he wonders if he ought not to leave it and go back to the university, to prepare himself to undertake an academic career.

His entire childhood was dominated by feelings of inferiority, doubtless due in part to the fact that he was a Jew.

He was shut in upon himself, and avoided the society of other children and their games. Instead he would sit silently in a corner at home, listening to his parents' conversation. He has had no important conflict with the other members of his family, but neither has he ever really confided in them.

He took refuge in ambitious dreams. He had an overpowering desire to do some great act in his life, to prove his worth both to himself and to others. He threw himself into his work, and soon was at the head of his class. His desire to hold the first place was prompted by his need to compensate for his feelings of inferiority, which showed themselves in a certain disdain for his comrades.

He was afraid that classical studies would take too long to bring him success in life. His father had always given him the money he asked for, but his pride made him want to fend for himself as soon as he could.

He went, therefore, to the School of Commerce, and the moment he had his diploma he accepted the first job that came along. It was a post as buyer to a firm—a job completely unsuited to his withdrawn temperament. But his ambition to be financially independent, so as to demonstrate his personal worth, was such that it overcame his shyness.

So zealous was his work that it brought him success; soon he found himself head of a foreign branch, with a large number of employees and representatives under him. But his feelings of inferiority have still not been dissipated. He now has an exaggerated concern for the respect due to him as head of the office, and there are increasing conflicts with both his subordinates and his chief.

Following upon some unimportant incident he hands in his resignation, without weighing the consequences. He comes back to his own country, and wanders bitterly from one poorly paid employment to another. At the moment he is an insurance agent, in conditions which have little moral or material attraction, and which form a striking contrast wtih the situation he once occupied abroad.

And so he is toying with the idea of going back to his studies in order to take up an academic career.

Meanwhile, his brother has been converted to Christianity. Leon has been very impressed by this, because his brother asked him to forgive the wrongs he had done him, and made amends for them. Since then, Leon has been worried. He has a presentiment that the encounter with Jesus Christ would be the answer to his problems. He feels that there must be some cause in his own heart for the failure of all his zeal and his efforts to get him anywhere better than the lamentable position he now finds himself in. He has begun to read the New Testament. He has already made amends for several wrongs committed. But two things are holding him back.

First there is the question of baptism: Ought he to be baptized? Is it not the heart that Christ claims, rather than a sacrament? Would it not be a betrayal of his people, at the very moment when they are being persecuted? And why cannot he have himself baptized as a Christian, without having to choose among several different denominations?

The second point—and it is this which brought him to consult me—is that he has prayed to God to ask him what is his will for his life, whether he ought to stay in business or enter a university, and has had no answer.

We often meet cases like this, where people have asked God some question, and are disturbed at getting no answer. They begin to think that God has no plan for them. It is generally because the question has been put too superficially. Moreover, when we are face to face with God the important thing is the questions God asks of us, rather than those we put to him.

As a result of our conversations, we had a quiet time of meditation together, and Leon received his answer. He saw first of all that he must be baptized and give himself without reserve to Jesus Christ. Next he saw that it was his feelings of inferiority and his compensatory ambitiousness which had frustrated his life. He saw that the idea of changing his occupation was just one more illusion, since he would take with him his unchanged heart. He saw that it was still his compensatory ambitiousness which prompted the idea of becoming an intellectual, and that it would be a mere pretext for leaving the business world. He saw that he must be prepared to accept his life, whatever it might be.

A few days later he telephoned me. He told me of the deep sense of liberation which had filled his heart as soon as he had accepted that he must live his life as a businessman with conviction. He had scarcely made his decision when he received out of the blue an offer of a most interesting post abroad. He was preparing to leave, resolved to live now in the liberty and obedience of his new faith.

It is in this way that the two aspects of meditation of which I have spoken are bound up together: the ability to perceive clearly both our faults and our vocation.

Take the case of a woman social worker who was in conflict with the director under whom she worked. She had already tried to set matters right in a letter, but had not felt any sense of liberation. The mere thought of meeting the director again provoked such violent nervous reactions that I had to order her to bed. I began talking with her about her childhood, and the sources of her vocation. Someone had told her that her nervous troubles were evidence of a "vocational crisis." She could not get this expression out of her thoughts, and it was making her doubts and worries ten times worse.

After several days of meditation and conversations on subjects of secondary importance, she requested a decisive interview, for which she prepared herself thoroughly. She came and confessed a secret sin which had no direct connection with her employment. But as soon as she had unburdened herself of it, she saw that this was the real cause of her nervous reactions, and that they had nothing to do with a vocational crisis. We can picture our vocation as the road along which God has called us to travel. Sin is like stones lying on the road. It is easier to doubt the existence of the road under the stones that hide it than to set to work to clear the stones away.

Then and there, my patient realized that she must renew her dedication to God, and write a letter to her director admitting to him that it was only the unavowed sin in her own heart that had made her doubt her vocation.

This twofold action brought double liberation, and a few hours later she was able to say to me: "For the first time in years I have been able to say Yes to life."

The world desperately needs people who have a firm conviction of their vocation. When one asks people about what it was that determined their choice of career, one is surprised to find that very many have no clear idea. Others admit to having acted on lesser motives— the hope of earning a living more easily, obedience to a family prejudice, a more or less naïve admiration for an elder brother or sister. The man who receives his vocation from God (and of course this applies to a lay vocation as well as to an ecclesiastical one) brings a quite different conviction to it. God's purpose for society is realized by men who take up in it the positions that God has prepared for them, and for which he has fitted them through the talents with which he has endowed them. They are possibly more modest places than could have been secured for them by the intervention of their influential uncles. But the people will be happier and more useful in them.

A conviction of vocation—any vocation—is a real motive force in a person's life, ensuring full physical development, psychic equilibrium, and spiritual joy.

When an artist does not create, his vitals are gnawed by the fire within him, and illness results. The creative force which is in him, and which can give rise to so many psychological complexes, must be offered to God if it is to become fruitful.

Take the case of an impulsive, sensitive, artistic, imaginative, and undisciplined man whom we shall call Frederick.

His father, a hardworking and methodical man, found it very difficult to understand the son's whimsical nature. In order to teach him to stand on his own feet, the father boarded him out when he was still quite young. Frederick's injured sensitivity rebelled and reacted in all sorts of ways. He was continually being moved to new lodgings, and when he used to come home he was spoiled in compensation, which only made his weakness of character worse. On the spur of the moment he made a love match, which did not stand the test of time. He was not happy in his work, and soon found himself unemployed. He sought worldly consolations for the awful dissatisfaction he felt with his life, spending money recklessly, always a square peg in a round hole, giving way to every kind of passion. He was a talented musician, but had never been able to work with the conviction and perseverance necessary for a real career.

His moral and social decay soon became obvious, and this cut him off from his family and meant that the only friendships open to him were unsavory ones.

He went from clinic to clinic, quarreling with every doctor that tried to impose upon him a discipline which found no echo in his heart.

But in one of these clinics he came under the influence of a Christian doctor, a man with a radiant spiritual life, and Frederick met God. All at once he realized that putting God at the center of his life would be the only way out of the impasse to which he had come; that this would be the way to that fulfillment which always eluded him, and to the discipline which he longed for but against which his nature always rebelled when it was imposed on him from without.

It was to be a decisive turning point in his life. Everything had to be built up again, but the principle of reconstruction had been found. No longer would he be a sick man, disillusioned, quarrelsome, useless, and hopeless.

A friend who was visiting the clinic offered to receive him into his home. There Frederick served for several weeks his apprenticeship in the practice of the Christian life which he had decided to follow. He learned to meditate and to look for the source of all discipline in daily converse with God.

Soon Frederick decided to dedicate his musical talent to God. He took up his instrument again, and started to work methodically and perseveringly. His playing had an overwhelming effect on those who heard it. He was radiant with joy. He astonished his former comrades in loose living when he told them that his life had changed, and he resisted their dangerous solicitations.

It was not long before he obtained a place in a large orchestra. The leader of the orchestra encouraged and helped him. But he became the object of an attempt to oust him on the part of the union, which did not take kindly to a newcomer taking the place of former comrades who had lost their jobs. Then he spoke up before all his colleagues. He explained to them frankly the sort of mistakes he had made and how he had decided to rebuild his life. He asked them whether they wanted to help him or to reject him. All their jealousy disappeared, and every hand was held out to him in friendship.

The months went by. He stuck to his job, in spite of the exacting task that faced him as an artist who had never before played in an orchestra. Of course there were difficult times, backslidings in matters of discipline, slips in money matters. But he now had Christian friends whose help he could call on when he felt himself giving way.

What could never have been done for him by external constraint had been spontaneously brought about by an inner change.

A man who has decided to submit his life to God's authority does not look to him for guidance only when he has some great decision to make, such as the choice of a career or a wife. Day by day he finds in meditation fresh inspiration for his daily work, his personal behavior, and his attitude toward those about him. I have given a number of examples of this in the course of this book. My experience is that when God's guidance is sought in this way, those conditions of life which are most favorable to health are gradually established. We still make frequent mistakes over what God is expecting of us; we often take our own inclinations for a divine call; we still frequently disobey. And yet if we remain loyal we become more and more able to see our own errors, and more faithful in correcting them.

A diet governed by God, and not by gluttony or fashion; sleep, rest, and holidays dictated by God, and not by laziness or selfishness; a career, work, and physical recreation guided by God, and not by ambition or fear; a sex life, marriage, and family life directed by God, and not by the desire for personal gratification or by jealousy; personal discipline in the use of our time, in imagination and thoughts, imposed by God and not by caprice or the need to escape—these are the fundamental conditions of health both physical and psychical.

The Bible is mainly the story of men who believed in the will of God, who sought to know and to follow it even in the smallest details of their personal life. It shows us men who knew how to listen to God's voice and obey him, who sought to know what God wanted them to say, where he wanted them to go, and what he wanted them to do. All the books of the Prophets, and that of the Acts of the Apostles, are but pictures of men's lives guided by God. The Gospels recount the completely guided life of Jesus Christ. They show him meditating and fasting in the desert, fighting against the temptations of the Devil, and seeking God's inspiration for his ministry. They show him going away by himself in the early morning to meet God face to face and receive his orders for the day's work. They show him constantly escaping from the flattery of men and their worldly requests, to continue on his way from place to place, in accordance with God's plan. They show him, on the eve of the Passion, withdrawing with his disciples, at Caesarea Philippi, and hearing God's call to go up to Jerusalem to suffer and to die there, and telling his disciples of his decision. They show him in the Garden of Gethsemane, still seeking to follow God's will rather than his own.

And throughout the church's history, all the saints who have exerted a profound influence on humanity have been men and women who, breaking away from the conventions of society, and even from the customs of church people, have obeyed God's commands— commands which their contemporaries often failed to understand.

I believe then that one of the tasks of the doctor is to help his patients to see what is God's will for them, and to show them how to win the victories of obedience. But no one can lead others along this road without traveling along it himself. Medicine has made tremendous progress. It will go on doing so. We have at our disposal powerful means of diagnosis and treatment. The world does not need a new medicine: it needs doctors who know how to pray and obey God in their own lives. In such hands medicine, with all its modern resources, will bring forth its fruits in abundance.

There are countless doctors who look upon their vocation as a social priesthood, and who, in remote valleys or in the slums of our great cities, give themselves unstintingly in the fight against the sufferings of mankind. I am very far from disregarding all their noble zeal and all their disinterested charity. It is to them that I speak. Believers or not, they live in the shadow of Christ. But they occupy an observation post that is particularly well placed for seeing the sufferings that are heaped upon humanity by sin. And, like me, they know that sin creeps craftily into the most dedicated of lives, and the struggle is a hard one. Like me, they know that the materialism which has dominated medicine for a century has not helped us in this struggle against ourselves. Like me, they know that on their personal victory depend the moral victories of their patients, that on the quality of their personal lives depends the beneficent effect they will have on the lives of many a family. And they often feel lonely, discouraged, and overwhelmed.

They are saddened by some of the trends observable in the way our profession is developing, its moral decline, the ravages wrought by the lust for monetary gain which has been denounced in several excellent books.[1] They are well aware that there will be no real amendment of this situation apart from a spiritual renewal in the soul of the doctor. The artisans of this amendment will be doctors who accept the sovereignty of Jesus Christ over their lives, and his moral demands.

But let me hasten as I finish this chapter to denounce once again the old error of religious formalism to which affirmations of this sort can give rise. The Christian life does not consist in being perfect, much less in claiming to be so. On the contrary, it consists in being honest about one's shortcomings so as to be able to turn to Jesus Christ for forgiveness and liberation.

I shall not go at great length into the physical course of the illness of a patient whom I shall call Maurice. He had tuberculosis, and had once suffered from Pott's disease. Undernourishment in childhood probably played a decisive part in this. He came of a poor family, living on coffee and soup. He was also timid, his father being a very severe man.

Now the tuberculosis had become localized in a number of places —pulmonary, pleural, intestinal, and osteoarticular. It was one of those torpid tuberculoses which last throughout life, generally getting worse. He had seen many doctors. He was hopeless, bitter, and sometimes rebellious. His wife came and asked me to take him on, because she realized that he needed to be sustained as much morally as physically. There could be no doubt of the diagnosis. Moreover, from an articular puncture I drew a serous fluid containing several Koch's bacilli. His general conditon was becoming more and more precarious, despite a diet designed to build up his strength. There were signs of hepatic insufficiency, and chronic eczema. He reacted badly to every kind of treatment.

[1] Renè Dumesnil *L'Âme du médecin,* Collection "Présences" (Paris: Plon, 1938).

A stay in the mountains had scarcely any effect. Time and time again I was on the point of sending him into hospital, but I felt that his moral condition was such that even if he had the best physical attention he could get, he would go into a decline if he were deprived of the support of his wife and his work. I saw his employer and pressed that he should be retained despite his being unable to pull his full weight.

Maurice spoke to me more openly than he had ever done to anyone else, and on several occasions we experienced real spiritual communion. He told me how much it had helped him, though I still felt that I was not leading him toward any decisive experience. I had, too, a vague feeling of embarrassment when I was with him. I felt a sense of inadequacy in the face of physical and moral distress such as this.

He became suddenly worse. I began prescribing sedatives. On my last visit he told me of the profound impression made on him by Ebba Pauli's book, *The Hermit*.[2]

On Sunday morning his wife telephoned to say that he was worse. I said I would call during the day. At midnight I suddenly realized I had forgotten to do so. Without praying about it I told myself that I would go first thing on Monday morning. In the morning I learned that he had died during the night.

Psychoanalists have made a close study of forgetfulness. They have shown that it always has a deeper meaning. This is why when we forget something we are always very embarrassed about it, although on the face of it it seems that we could not help it. For the Christian the serious significance of forgetfulness is that it is a sign of sin. This is one of the ways in which psychological analysis helps us to see our sin more clearly.

As soon as I prayed about having forgotten to visit my patient, I saw what it really meant. Whereas on the conscious level I felt nothing but affectionate solicitude toward Maurice, coupled with real friendship, my unconscious was putting a brake on my feelings. And the true cause of this unconscious go-slow was my professional and my spiritual pride. As a doctor I was disappointed at my own impotence in the face of a physical disease that I had been unable to check. I was

---

[2]English trans. by Ingeborg Arvedsen (London: H. R. Allenson, 1931).

embarrassed at the thought of facing a dying man who had expected more effective succor from me. As a spiritual doctor also, I was discontented with myself, discontented at not having been able to bring, as I had wished, the full light of Christ into that poor life.

I realized also that I had to say all this to his widow, whatever it might cost me, and to seek with her in prayer Christ's forgiveness for my sin.

She received me generously and with understanding, but just when I wanted to pray, Maurice's mother arrived. I had to begin my confession all over again, and when I was about to pray a brother-in-law arrived. I saw then that I must be humbled utterly before I found forgiveness at the Cross.

We prayed all together.

A few days later I received from that young widow a letter that was a fine Christian testimony.

Realism

I cannot conclude a book in which I have shown the favorable consequences to health of a specifically Christian experience without touching upon a question which more than one reader, no doubt, would
like to put to me: "May there not be unfavorable consequences? Are
there not some mental disorders which are actually brought about by
a religious experience? Are not some patients who believe they have
had a spiritual experience of this kind simply the victims of mental
disorders?" Yes, of course; that is incontestable. I side unequivocally
with the Rev. Fr. De Sinéty, who maintains[1] that no greater disservice
can be done to the cause of Christianity than to deny that pathological disorders can simulate genuine religious experience. But he points
out that the fact that there are pseudo-mystics does not give us the
right to deny that there are real ones.

The same is true of miraculous cures, which I have intentionally by-
passed, because they are rather a special case among the subjects
that have a bearing on the relationship between medicine and religion. We have no right to deny that miraculous cures do sometimes
take place, simply because a large number that are claimed as miraculous can be shown to be merely the result of psychological suggestion.

Finally, it is only right for me to say that I could report several

[1] *Psychopathologie et Direction* (Paris: Beauchesne, 1934).

cases where I have been called upon to deal with serious mental disorders that have made their appearance following religious experiences, particularly meetings for witness. I have several times had to have such people sent to mental institutions. There are few subjects more disturbing for the Christian doctor. And even in many psychopathic cases, where mental disorders properly so-called can be ruled out, one cannot deny that there is an inextricable mixture of authentic religious experience and psychical reactions of a definitely pathological nature. At a religious retreat once I was discussing this with a colleague from abroad, when before our very eyes a person suffered a fit of insanity. I remarked to my colleague that if God appeals to the faith of doctors, he certainly entrusts them with a special reponsibility—that of being on the watch, for their patients' sakes, with the utmost vigilance, for the pathological reaction, so as to be able to distinguish it from the normal. It is for this reason that I have often intervened in order to keep people of unstable psychological equilibrium away from collective religious manifestations that might harm them.

Spiritual power is the greatest power in the world. Although, in order to shake a person out of his state of self-satisfaction, make him look at himself properly, and draw him out of the fortress of compromise in which he has taken refuge from an unquiet conscience, it is often necessary to subject him to the intense emotion of long spiritual retreats, this same power can in others spark serious mental accidents. Such accidents are in fact a proof of the power of the spiritual, just as medicinal intoxication is a proof of the pharmacodynamics of medicines. All around us there are people whose psychological equilibrium is so unstable that they are ready to burst out at any moment. Any emotional shock can spark off the conflagration: bereavement, being thwarted, even a physical disease. It is not surprising therefore that experiences touching on a subject as emotionally charged as religion should also be capable of provoking it.

Does this mean that neurotics ought to be kept away from the message of Christianity? What I said just now about the pharmacodynamics of medicines seems to me to provide the answer to this question. The same message which when delivered too abruptly and wholesale may provoke mental disorders, may also, when given in proper doses, be a healing agent. The unstable equilibrium of a person with neurotic tendencies is made up of countless compromises; nevertheless it is an equilibrium. A total decision for Christ is capable of producing a better equilibrium. But such a decision first reopens so many unresolved problems that there is a critical zone to cross.

Furthermore, the dissociation of fantasy and reality which is present to some extent in all of us, tends to be worse in the neurotic. The result is that he is more ready to make a bold spiritual decision to dedicate his life to God, and finds it more difficult to see the contrast between this decision to make a change in principle, and everything that remains unchanged in his real life. In other words it is harder for him to see the practical consequences of his decision, and harder to make them a reality when he does see them. This divorce between the will to accomplish and the actual accomplishment tears the personality and sparks off mental accidents.

To be religious one does not have to be simple-minded. It does not help neurotics if we are taken in by their facile spiritual enthusiasms. Charity demands that we be severe and realistic with them, that we should always be bringing them back to the concrete problems of their lives, that we should not be content with anything but a patient effort to solve these problems, denouncing every unconscious attempt to escape in the direction of some easy mystical mirage, and helping them to put into practice, little by little, each new glimpse of God's will for them. There are many people—both among believers and among those who use this as an argument against the Christian faith —who make the mistake of thinking that the Christian must necessarily be naïve. Jesus showed himself a true realist when he said that his disciples would be recognizable not by what they said but by the quality of their lives, like a tree by its fruit. We betray the spiritual cause if we allow ourselves to be deceived by people who think their lives have changed because their state of mind has changed, without any real fruit being borne in their daily lives. I could record here many sad cases of neuropaths, especially those of cycloid personality type, who, following upon a theological discussion with a believer—very frequently belonging to one of the Protestant sects—have thought they "understood everything," and have made much of a "conversion" which actually has been purely intellectual. What in fact has happened is that their humor has oscillated from pessimism to optimism, but it is as unreal as it was before. Of course, I do not question their sincerity, nor that of those who have communicated to them their theological thoughts. But with those who suffer from nervous disorders one cannot be too realistic, nor too severe in demanding that every new discovery in the realm of the spirit be accompanied by concrete acts of obedience. When one has oneself experienced conversion, one knows what inner battles are involved. One no longer underestimates sin's powers of resistance, and one stresses that the Christian answer is the most costly of all.

I am reminded of one of my patients whose life was a skein of problems of all kinds. In our very first interview she told me that she wanted to follow the way of the Christian life. I told her at once that such a decision was valueless and would only lead to disappointments unless she undertook at once courageously to measure the full consequences of it. And I sent her, that same day, to see a young woman who had the patience to devote her whole time to her for four days running, until my patient had written the letters of apology and put into effect the practical decisions necessary to create a new climate in her life.

Our concrete acts of obedience have no virtue in themselves. Their sole significance is that they are the sign of our faith. But without that sign the impulse of the heart is no more than a naïve illusion.

Many neurotics know themselves quite well, and are afraid of what they know—afraid of deluding themselves, of being carried away by enthusiasm, of slipping back into despair after bursts of sentimental feeling.

Nora was a girl of moody temperament, sentimental, introspective, and impulsive. She took after her father, who was artistic, imaginative, weak, and bohemian. She had therefore become too attached to him, at the expense of her relationship with her mother, who was intellectual, rational, and cold. It was a disunited home, and Nora suffered on this account more than a normal person would, since she needed the steadying influence of a real home to prevent her going from one excess to another. Then had come disappointments and moral shocks. She did things she ought not to have done, and was afraid of her own nature. She was tossed about uncertainly in life, not having the steadying support of her family. Her value lay in her simplicity, her spontaneity, and her sociability. But this was just what she was afraid of, because she could not exercise these qualities without being sentimental and impulsive, and this had led her to disaster in the past.

She had quite recently become converted, and she had felt that her new-found faith was the answer to the disquiet of her life. Real Christian friends, to whom she had been able to open her heart in complete trust, had been providing for her the thing she had always lacked.

She had felt wildly happy. And then she was suddenly afraid of this very happiness, afraid of religious sentimentalism, of an escape into mysticism, of pathological outbursts of religious enthusiasm. She was afraid of going mad.

Religion can increase Nora's tendency to escapism as well as answering her need for readaptation to reality. If, instead of using her faith as a means of escape from her unresolved difficulties, she employs it to resolve them, to re-establish real intimacy with her mother, to put some method and order into her everyday life, to undertake and persevere in a serious job of work, and to discipline herself, she will really find that her Christian life is a safeguard against the psychological dangers of her personality, and will be liberated from her fear of madness.

Faith is not a matter of feeling. For fear of seeming neurotic, many people refrain all their lives from making any affirmation of their faith, from taking part in any religious meeting or ceremony, or even from consciously facing the religious problem which nevertheless haunts them. They are afraid of religious psychosis. They are afraid of becoming enthusiastic only to be disillusioned later on.

They have not yet realized that true Christianity does not in fact consist of unreal flights of fancy, but of quite concrete experiences.

There are three roads in front of every man: reality without God, which is the dissociation of the materialists; God without reality, which is the dissociation of the pseudo-mystics; and, lastly, God with reality, which is the Christian faith.

This last is the hardest of the three. For it is far easier to live life as we find it, remaining deaf to God's call; or else to answer his call sentimentally, while closing one's eyes to reality. It is easier to be either a materialist or an idealist. What is difficult is to be a Christian.

I come back here to the point from which I started this book, that men's lives are full of concrete problems, material as well as psychological. A religious conversion which avoids these problems, leaving them unresolved, is what too often brings Christianity into disrepute. But a conversion which brings the solution of the problems in a person's life is a living proof of the power of Christ.

Here is another case, the painful history of which it would take too long to tell. It concerned a man—we shall call him Jerome—who was the victim of the upheavals, the revolutions, and the poverty which followed the first World War. He was also the victim of the divorce of his parents, of sexual shocks in childhood, and of his own hypersensitivity, which made the effect of all these things on him ten times worse. All this had made him antagonistic and hopeless.

Jerome began to have bouts of depression, and functional disorders made their appearance. He had been in one clinic after another, having had to give up work altogether and submit himself to the varying forms of treatment each clinic offered. Now he was no more than a piece of flotsam, always worrying, interested only in himself, at odds with his wife, and no longer on speaking terms with his mother-in-law.

I suggested to him that he should accept his life, make it up with his mother-in-law, and go back to his work despite his nervous disabilities, and that he should ask God to grant him the strength needed to win this triple victory.

At first he considered that I was being very hard on him; nevertheless he came back to see me again. By the time we had our fourth consultation he was able to tell me that he had just experienced the happiest days he had known for many a year.

Shortly afterward he took up normal work, and found that his home life was quite transformed.

The peoples of the world today are tired of an intellectualized culture which makes great discoveries, does fine things in theory, but has ceased to help them in leading their real lives. They are weary of scientists and scholars who become more and more learned, but shut themselves up in their studies and abdicate their responsibilities as the guides of mankind, because all their science does not help them to know where they themselves ought to be going.

The great task to which God is calling our generation is the reconciliation of the spiritual and the material, the breaking down of the wall of partition which separates them. We must stop thinking that the spiritual world has nothing to do with science, psychology, politics, commerce, or medicine.

Giving one's life to God means becoming disciplined materially as well as mentally. It means becoming real and concrete. The following case, that of Isaline, seems to me to confirm this point. She was a thin, restless woman, her face a narrow triangle with strong bony prominences. Her hands were twisted and knotty, long and trembling.

A few details of her history will help the reader to understand her anxious, unstable, and willful character. While still quite young she was already thin and lacked appetite, a creature of impulse and sentiment. She was frightened of her father, and attached herself closely to her mother, a gentle soul who remained the ideal of her life.

At the age of eight, Isaline suffered an emotional shock. At thirteen she lost her mother—a tragedy in her young heart which was to have incalculable consequences. From that time, deprived of the emotional stay of her childhood, her psychic life was impulsive, oscillating between grand enthusiasms for high ideals and rebellions and rancors in which she withdrew into herself and nursed her private secrets.

She had a succession of governesses. Some she hated, others she admired too much, but she won the confidence of none of them, and deceived them all. One of them believed that in order to grow spiritually it was necessary to mortify the flesh, and this idea had taken root in Isaline's mind and controlled most of her reactions and all her flights from concrete reality. She made a mental opposition between spirit and flesh. She began to eat as little as possible so as to kill the flesh, and to cultivate her imagination at the expense of her body. Under her pillows she would hide books which she spent the whole night reading. When she was fifteen she used to set her alarm for two o'clock in the morning, in order to study until it was time to get up. She wanted to be intellectual and literary; she became a voracious reader of novels, wrote poetry, and lived in an abstract world. She wanted to be a missionary, and then was filled with doubts; her Confirmation was the occasion of a terrific inner conflict. She felt she was taking a false oath, but had not the courage to break away from convention.

She became a sort of "anticoquette," dressing herself badly so that she would be appreciated only for her inward qualities. She took up a correspondence with a young man, in a romantic and unreal vein, and felt misunderstood when her father found out about it and scolded her for engaging an "affair of the heart" which was really an affair of the mind.

Her father married again. The stepmother was kind to her, but other people poisoned her against the new wife, and she enjoyed being pitied because she had a stepmother.

At the age of twenty she went abroad. She dazzled a young man in the boarding house where she stayed, with the learning and high-mindedness she displayed. She was most surprised when he asked her to marry him, for this was not the man of her dreams. She considered herself superior to him. But she was caught in her own game, and did not want to undeceive him. She would marry him, raise him up, instruct him. She dominated him with her intellectualism. He was only a clerk in a commercial office, which was a disappointment to her. She tried all the more to compensate for her disappointment by escape into a world of ideas.

All this time, of course, she was mortifying her flesh in order to demonstrate to herself her intellectual superiority. She was very thin, and also despised their sex life in order to prove to herself her detachment from the flesh.

She was becoming more and more nervous and agitated, always looking for absolute principles. She was not long in wearying her husband with her subtleties and her superior airs. This all led to a long and difficult period of ill health. One illness followed another, and her general condition was deplorable.

It was at this point that she met Christ and gave her life to him. A considerable easement took place. She became reconciled with her stepmother, and also with her father, and lost her fear of him. And so harmony was restored with her family.

But she still understood Christianity after her own fashion, as a great effort into which she must pour her enthusiasm. The opposition she had always made between the flesh and the spirit was transferred into her new-found faith. She wearied her husband with her Christian principles, insisting on them with something of her old domineering spirit. She was irritated because he would have nothing to do with her ideas. She lost interest in her work because it was "too material." She slept very little, read much, and refused to have anything to do with looking after the garden, as being no proper interest for an intellectual. She suffered from constipation as a result of undernourishment. There were signs of Basedow's disease and ptosis.

I explained to her that God had created earth as well as heaven, the body as well as the soul, and that his will is to be glorified in matter was well as in spirit. It was he who made the flowers in her garden grow, and she could commune with him by tending them as well as by reading religious books. It was he who made vegetables grow, and she could take an interest in cooking without being cut off from him. She saw then the deep ditch she had dug between herself and her husband. She could fill it up again if she asked him to forgive her for having thought herself superior to him, and by taking a real interest in him, in his life, and in his work. I prescribed physical exercises, gardening, rest, and particular attention to her diet.

She has written to me several times since, and several of her friends have spoken to me about the extraordinary change that has been wrought in her by this welding together in her life of the spiritual and the carnal. A physical transformation has taken place in her: She has put on weight, looks healthy and years younger. She sleeps well, has become tranquil, and is interested in her garden and her home. Her husband, surprised to find that her spiritual life makes her calmer now, instead of exciting her, has begun to take a much greater interest in religion. A quite new love and joy have entered their home. Her sex life has developed. Her faith itself has become more profound, stable, and radiant, and her church work is more fruitful and natural.

Finally, she has discovered that her husband is a much more interesting person that she thought, and that his work in commerce can be seen, in the sight of God, to have a meaning that is full of interest. She has made friends with the women who work in her husband's firm; she has brought several of them to faith, and communicated to them her vision of the Spirit of God permeating material life, the life of the body, the life of nature, the life of commerce.

Théophile was another of my patients, animated with a genuine faith. Everywhere in religious circles he was esteemed and valued. He was entrusted with spiritual tasks—perhaps more than he could in fact carry. He was admired. Something special was always expected of him. But precisely because he was always set up on a spiritual pedestal, no one gave a thought to helping him, to the difficulties with which he had to contend in secret, or to giving him a chance to talk about his hidden anxieties. He hid them for fear of shaking the faith of those who looked up to him as a leader. He was expected to give, to appear strong, and he himself was given little. In fact, despite the Christian ministry he exercised, he lived a life of isolation, enduring moments of terrible anguish in the secrecy of his own chamber.

I was called urgently to him one day: He had tried to kill himself.

I was struck by the contrast between this fine life of Christian service, through which so many others had been led to find in faith the answer to their distress, and that despairing act which betrayed the man's spiritual solitude, and his sense of defeat.

Such contrasts are more frequent than is generally believed. When a person seems strong he is left alone, without help, and is afraid to show his weaknesses. His isolation undermines his powers of resistance. His faith, which fortifies others, is insufficient for his solitary battle.

I entrusted this patient to a Christian colleague who was able to help him, through daily meditation, to build a bridge between his spiritual life and his real life, which were proceeding side by side, but without any real connection between them. In one sense his religious activity was a sort of compensation for the failures of his real life, which it failed to illuminate.

When I saw him again he was a new man. He had found inner harmony because his faith had been integrated into his real life. His life was no longer so full of zealous, but tense, religious activity. His new-found serenity was winning over to the faith some of his old unbelieving friends whom he had been unable to influence in the days when he was so much in demand in religious circles.

It is a far cry from this feverish activity, in which the church so often exhausts the strength of those who have faith, without helping them to follow out all its consequences in their personal life, and the quite natural, peaceful, and almost involuntary witness of the person who has found in contact with God the solution to his personal problems.

This case reminds me of one last patient, whom we shall call Virgile. He was an old philosopher, who knew all there was to know about biblical exegesis, religious psychology, and metaphysics. He knew seventeen ancient and modern languages, was a corresponding member of several philosophical societies, had himself made modern translations of the Gospels, and could quote to me from memory the many variants of the Greek text.

But there was in him a deep dichotomy between his intellectual life and his practical life. On the level of intellectual discussion, of philosophical, spiritual, and psychological erudition, he was a virtuoso, his conversation a veritable fireworks display. But on the level of real life he was a wretched creature, a prey to all kinds of naïve fears, lost in a medley of complicated diets which he used to invent in the vain hope of alleviating his digestive disorders. He was indecisive and undisciplined, tormented by all kinds of scruples, to which he was always adding but to which his great knowledge provided no answer at all.

At first I wondered what I could possibly have to give to a scholar who unfolded before me all his intellectual objections to faith with a superiority that left me dumb. I thought to myself that if ever I could get him to eat everything that was set before him, the battle would be won, and he would find a new faith. I told myself that we must get away from intellectual discussion and come to practical matters of everyday life. But it was not easy, for the tragedy of his life was this very psychological escape into intellectualism, by which he was trying to hide his own failures from himself. But I knew that the real reason for his coming to see me was that he had a vague sense of unease because of this inner divorce.

To cut his arguments short would be merely to raise a barrier between us. For a long time (and not without real pleasure) I followed him through the subtle byways of his thoughts. One day, seeing that I was getting nowhere, I asked him if he would not break into our discussions for a moment to make a practical trial of meditation. He answered that he did not believe that God could be revealed to order in this way, as I claimed, but still, out of friendship for me, he would honestly try the experiment.

We were silent.

I was writing down all the thoughts that came into my mind. He sat motionless, deep in meditation.

When I had finished, I asked him if he had thought of anything. He answered, "Nothing."

I read him what I had written.

Then he told me that he had in fact thought of something, but said it "had nothing to do with God."

After much hesitation, he at last brought himself to tell me what he had thought about. He had seen in his mind's eye his study table, which was in an indescribable state of disorder, heaped up, like the rest of his study, with all sorts of things, which his wife had been begging him to sort out for the last twenty years. When she had, now and again, tried to do something about it herself, she had been met with such violent protests from him that she had had to desist. And when in a burst of good will he had tried to undertake the task in order to please her, he had turned up so many old papers that caught his interest that the tidying up made little progress.

I asked him if he were quite sure that this thought "had nothing to do with God."

A week later he came back to see me, his eyes shining. "That's it!" he burst out.

"What is?" I asked him.

"Tidying up, of course! It's incredible! I don't know how it's happened. The one that's most astonished is my wife—she said it was a miracle."

Thus it was a concrete meditation that had led him to meet God. Our conversation that day followed a different course from the preceding ones. He no longer talked about religion, but about his real life, about all that his wife had had to put up with from the disorder and indiscipline of his life. He could see new steps that he must take along this new road in which he had begun to walk. He devoted some time to meditation every day, in order to see what God expected of him. He had found a deeper fellowship with his wife.

When I saw him some time afterward he was radiant, and looked ten years younger. He could eat anything, and his stomach was giving him no further trouble. He had a lively and contagious faith.

He became for me a real friend.

One day several years later he came to see me and asked me if I knew the story of Descartes' basket of apples.

On my replying in the negative, he explained. Descartes wrote somewhere, he said, that if we sniff a basket of apples and conclude from the smell that some of them are rotten, we empty the basket on to the table and pick up the apples one by one, putting the good ones back into the basket. "That is what I want to do together with you," he concluded. "I am no longer very sure of myself. My faith has weakened. All kinds of objections are worrying me. I should like to do a thorough sorting out."

I realized that to sort out a philosopher's basket of apples would be no small matter, and I suggested that we should go into the mountains for three days for the purpose.

I shall always remember those three days. Amid the splendors of nature we followed the footpaths from morning until night. He talked and talked. I listened. I followed him step by step, both physically and intellectually. I was learning a lot. One digression followed another, and still I could not see the bottom of the basket of apples.

The morning after the first night, I suggested that he should come and meditate with me. But he declined, saying that he thought it would not be honest.

The following morning he declared that he was ready to be there when I practiced my meditation, provided that I promised not to question him about the thoughts that came to him, for he still had serious objections to attributing them to God.

But on the third morning he came to me joyfully with his notebook. It was he who read a passage from the Bible, and then we meditated together for a long time. I was overcome with emotion when he read me all he had written. There was no longer any trace of his intellectual objections or his philosophical digressions. It was a detailed confession of tiny acts of disobedience which had blocked his spiritual life. And his last thought was that he would come home with me to thank my wife for having "lent" me for three days.

Two months later he died in the faith, carried off within a few days by a serious disease.

Perhaps I may be permitted to add a little note to this story.

A few days before our stay in the mountains, I was visiting a patient who lived a long way away, and had brought with me one of my sons, then aged eight, so as to have a chance to talk with him. While we were driving along a long straight road I suggested that we should be quiet for a moment, to meditate. Naturally I thought about my old philosopher friend and of the time I was going to spend with him. The thought came to me that I ought to follow him along all the diversions of his conversation, like a little dog following his master.

I spoke of this to my son, in order to let him share in my task, and so that he should understand why I was going away. Of course I told him about Descartes' excellent image of the basket of apples.

After a while my son said: "You know, daddy, if it's only to pick out rotten apples, I think it's not worth the trouble. I hope you'll find some nice fresh ones for him!"

I have often thought of this piece of childish wisdom when I have been tempted to fill my spiritual meditation with too much self-analysis, picking out only the rotten apples. And then I ask God for some fresh apples, some new inspiration to direct my thoughts once more toward action and reality.

Epilogue: "Field Ambulance III/10, on Active Service"

The various elements making up this book were already assembled when World War II began and general mobilization took me from my study.

At first I thought I would leave them there. Were not the tragic events which were engulfing Europe demanding too much of our attention to leave us any leisure to reflect on the course of modern medical thought and practice?

But I have brought my manuscript with me, and I have worked at it during the empty hours of military life.

For the real meaning of this book, the meaning I intend it to have, is that it should be a contribution, in the medical sphere, to the spiritual renewal which our world needs.

The awful crisis through which mankind is passing compels us to think again through our intellectual disciplines, and to go back to the sources of our vocation.

The fact that the crisis has brought us now to the war which we have felt threatening us for so long is only one further reason why we must build a new world in our hearts, our homes, and our professional lives.

The disappointments of these last "interwar" years have clearly shown us that peace is not to be ensured by means of a few fine legal phrases. Pacts and declarations will never build a world. Every man's life must be reformed.

A new world will not be built in the air, but stone by stone. It will result from the daily action of devoted people who have experienced in their own lives the power of Jesus Christ.

Glossary

acrocyanosis. A condition marked by coldness and blue discoloration of the hands and feet.

albugo. A white corneal opacity.

albuminuria. The presence of protein (albumin) in the urine.

amenorrhea. Absence or stoppage of menstruation.

anatomicopathological. Pertaining to the anatomy of diseased tissues.

anatomicophysiological. Pertaining to anatomy and physiology.

angina. Spasmodic, choking or suffocative pain; often used for the disease or condition producing such pain.

angina pectoris. A disease marked by paroxysmal chest pain.

arteriosclerosis. A condition marked by loss of elasticity, thickening, and hardening of the arteries.

asthenia. Loss of strength; weakness.

asystole. Incomplete contraction of the heart.

ataxia, locomotor. Degeneration of the dorsal columns of the spinal cord and of the sensory nerve trunk.

auscultation. The act of listening for sounds within the body, chiefly for ascertaining the condition of the lungs, heart, pleura, abdomen, and other organs.

autotoxic. Pertaining to poisoning by some uneliminated toxin generated within the body.

Basedow's disease. Exophthalmic goiter.

bradycardia. Abnormal slowness of the heart beat.

carbuncle. An infection of the skin.

cardiac neurosis. A condition characterized by breathlessness, giddiness, a sense of fatigue, pain in the chest, and palpitation.

catatonia. A form of schizophrenia characterized by negativistic reactions, phases of stupor or excitement, and impulsive or stereotyped behavior.

cecum. The dilated intestinal pouch into which open the ileum, the colon, and the appendix.

chirology. The study of the hand.

chlorosis. A form of anemia.

Dakin's solution. A buffered aqueous solution of sodium hypochlorite, used as a bactericide.

dermatosis. Any skin disease.

diastole. The stage of dilatation of the heart (cf. systole).

digitalis. A drug which stimulates heart action.

diiodotyrosine. An amino acid occurring in the thyroid gland.

dysmenorrhea. Painful menstruation.

dyspepsia. Impairment of digestion.

dyspnea. Difficult breathing.

endocrine. Pertaining to internal secretions.

enteritis. Inflammation of the small intestine.

enterocolitis. Inflammation of the small intestine and the colon.

erethism. Excessive irritability or sensitivity to stimulation.

exophthalmos. Abnormal protrusion of the eyeball.

extrasystole. A premature contraction of the heart which is independent of the normal heart rhythm.

fistula. A deep sinuous ulcer, often leading to an internal hollow organ.

furunculosis. A condition resulting from boils.

gastralgia. Pain in the stomach.

glucosuria. The presence of glucose in the urine.

Graefe's sign. Failure of the upper lid to move downward promptly and evenly with the eyeball in looking downward.

graphology. The study of handwriting.

hebephrenia. A form of schizophrenia characterized by unnatural actions and speech, smiling and laughing without cause, and distortions of the countenance.

hemoptysis. The spitting of blood or of blood-stained sputum.

hepatic. Pertaining to the liver.

hyperchlorhydria. Excessive secretion of hydrochloric acid by the stomach cells.

iodism. Ill health resulting from injudicious use of iodine or iodine compounds.

irrigation, continuous. Steady maintenance of a stream of fluid over an inflamed surface.

Koch's bacillus. The bacillus causing tuberculosis.

lesion. A pathologic change in body tissue, or the loss of function of a part.

lunule. The whitish crescent at the root of the nail.

metritis. Inflammation of the uterus.

nephritis. Inflammation of the kidney.

neuralgia. Paroxysmal pain that extends along the course of one or more nerves.

neuritis. Inflammation of a nerve.

neuropathic. Pertaining to nervous disorders.

neurovegetative. Pertaining to the involuntary nervous system.

nosology. The science of the classification of diseases.

organicism. The theory that all symptoms are due to organic disease.

organotherapy. The treatment of disease by the administration of animal organs or their extracts.

osteoarticular. Pertaining to bones and joints.

osteomuscular. Pertaining to bones and muscles.

paraplegia. Paralysis of the legs and lower part of the body.

Parkinson's disease. Shaking palsy.

pathogenesis. The development of disease.

pharmacodynamics. The study of the action of drugs on living organisms.

phlebitis. Inflammation of a vein.

phosphaturia. A high percentage of phosphates in the urine.

physiognomy. The determination of mental or moral qualities from the appearance of the face.

plethora. Overfullness of blood vessels or of the total quantity of blood or other fluid in the body.

pneumothorax. An accumulation of air in the pleural cavity. In the treatment of pulmonary tuberculosis, air is introduced into the pleural cavity to collapse and immobilize the lung.

Pott's disease. Inflammation of the bone, usually of tuberculous origin.

pruritus. Intense itching.

ptosis. Drooping of the upper eyelid.

puerperal fever. Infection of the genital tract following childbirth.

quinidine. A drug which depresses heart action.

sebaceous follicle. A gland of the skin which secretes an oily substance.
septicemia. A disease resulting from the presence of pathogenic bacteria in the blood.
sonority. Resonance.
systole. The stage of contraction of the heart (cf. diastole).

tachycardia. Excessive rapidity of heart action.
thenar eminence. The mound on the palm of the hand at the base of the thumb.
tonicity. The normal condition of tone or tension.

vegetative nervous system. The involuntary nervous system.

xiphoid appendage. The lowest portion of the sternum.

Index

Abauzit, Frank, 227
Acceptance, 16, 32, 59, 84, 97, 143-146, 154-55, 161, 173-75, 182, 185, 217, 220, 241-42; Christian response to life, 32, 143; fruitfulness, importance in healing, 146, 150, 156; of life, 12, 15, 25, 50, 91, *156-72;* strength for, 165
Activism, overactivity, 30-31, 109, 111-113, 116, 283
Acts of the Apostles, 268
Addiction, 104-107, 187
Aging, 143, 157-61, 240
Albugo, 208
Albuminuria, 35-36
Alcoholism, 26-27, 34, 42, 105-108, 176, 213; in parents, 11, 17, 105-106, 136
Allendy, 67
Ambition, 11, 102, 110, 113, 234, 268
Anemia, asthenia, debility, 98, 121
Anger, 30, 46, 116, 221, 234
Anxiety, 7, 27, 38, 41, 47, 108, 116, 121, 143, 236, 279; secret, 36-8, 282
Appendicitis, 14
Aquinas, St. Thomas, 134
Arteriosclerosis, 29
Artistic activity or sensitiveness, 48-51, 73, 75-78, 107-108, 111, 259, 266-67, 276

Arthritis, 26-28
Asthma, 6-8, 42-43, 128, 205-206

Babinski, 242
Barthez, 135, 212
Baudouin, Charles, 21, 248
Bereavement, 8, 15, 17, 27, 42-43, 47, 52, 57, 108, 143-150, 222, 236, 247, 274; in childhood, 12, 22, 44, 137, 279
Bergson, Henri, 214-15
Bernard, Claude, 9, 64
Bible, the, xiv, 117, 130, 141-42, 151, 174, 185, 197, 204, 208-209, 223, 245-46, 264, 268-69, 286; laws of life and answers in, 141-42, 204
Bichat, 212
Biot, R., 67, 72, 134
Bircher-Benner, Dr., 202-203
Bleuler, 135
Boils, 10, 36-37
Boinet, 134-35
Bon, Dr. Henri, 212
Bouchard, 203
Brock, Dr. Jack, 190
Bronchial diseases, 22, 205-206
Buchman, Dr. Frank, xiii-xiv
Buisson, 212

Cabanis, 134